Singing in the Spirit

Singing in the Spirit

African-American Sacred
Quartets in New York City

Ray Allen

upp

UNIVERSITY OF PENNSYLVANIA PRESS   Philadelphia

Publication of the American Folklore Society New Series

General Editor, Patrick Mullen

The author wishes to thank the following publishing companies for permission to reprint song lyrics:

"There'll Be Peace in the Valley," by Thomas Dorsey. (c) 1939 Unichappell Music Inc.; Renewed. All rights reserved. Used by permission.

"I'll Fly Away," by Albert Brumley. (c) 1932 Hartford Music Company, renewed 1960 Albert Brumley and Sons. All rights reserved. Used by permission.

"Can't Nobody Do Me Like Jesus," by Ruben Willingham. (c) Ani Music Publishing Group. All rights reserved. Used by permission.

"Memories of Mother's Teachings" (c) 1990 and "Pray a Prayer for Peace" (c) 1990 by Billy Walker. Used by permission of composer.

The author has made an exhaustive search to locate the copyright holders to song lyrics cited in this work. Any publishing companies not cited above who hold copyright to song lyrics should contact the University of Pennsylvania Press to arrange reprint permission in the case of a second printing.

Library of Congress Cataloging-in-Publication Data
Allen, Ray.
Singing in the spirit : African-American sacred quartets in New York City / Ray Allen.
p.   cm. — (Publications of the American Folklore Society. New series)
Includes bibliographical references and index.
ISBN 0-8122-3050-7 (cloth). — ISBN 0-8122-1331-9 (pbk.)
1. Gospel music—New York (N.Y.)—History and criticism. 2. Afro-Americans—New York (N.Y.)—Music—History and criticism. I. Title. II. Series: Publications of the American Folklore Society. New Series (Unnumbered)
ML3187.A44   1991
783.1'41825—dc20   91-16943   CIP

Frontispiece: The No Name Gospel Singers, 1988. Photo courtesy of Aaron Chestnut.

Cover: Wonder Boy and the Spiritual Voices, Brooklyn, 1988. Photo by Ray Allen

In Memory of Angeline Schilling,
My Great Aunt and First Teacher

Shout joyfully to the Lord, all the earth.
Serve the Lord with gladness;
Come before Him with joyful singing.

Psalm 100:1-2

There can be little doubt that shouting is a survival of the African "possession" by the gods. . . . it is a sign of special favor from the spirit that it chooses to drive out the individual consciousness temporarily and use the body for its express. . . . Shouting is a community thing. It thrives in concert. It is the first shout that is difficult for the preacher to arouse. After that one they are likely to sweep like fire over the church.

Zora Neale Hurston, *The Sanctified Church*

Contents

Preface:
Fried Chicken in Bed-Stuy

In a small furniture shop in the heart of Bedford Stuyvesant, Brooklyn, New York, five African-American men stand in a tight semi-circle, singing into a single microphone. Charlie Storey, the store proprietor and leader of the group, mops his brow and looks crossly at Billy Walker, who is struggling to find his baritone part. "You're not making that turn right," he chides Walker. "Listen, it's right here: Lord, Lord Jesus, can I just have this talk with you. Now hit it again, and don't run up on the tenor part!" Guitarist Jerome "Pee Wee" Ellis strums a chord and the group resumes the chorus. Four voices join in close harmony, and this time Walker holds his part on the final chord change. As the last notes fade, bass singer Sam "Brown" Copney jumps back from the mike and bellows "There you go, Bro, now we got the blend!" Storey nods his head in approval. Walker laughs sheepishly and turns an inquiring glance toward Storey. "Think we can do that one on Saturday night?" "God willing," responds Storey. "If the Spirit is moving, we just might try it."

The singers break for cold fried chicken and soft drinks. The air in the furniture shop is hot and close, and the group has been working on this new arrangement for well over an hour, hoping to have it ready for Saturday night's program. But Charlie Storey isn't worried. "I've been in the singing business a long time, and the Lord will guide me when we take the floor," he assures me in his thick Georgian drawl. Indeed, Storey has been in the "singing business" for some time. A native of Camake, Georgia, Storey migrated to Brooklyn in 1928 where his father, a Holiness preacher, set up a church in the family's small house at 711 Gates Avenue. Soon after their arrival Storey and his sisters formed a vocal "spiritual" group and began singing in neighborhood churches. His searing lead tenor brought him considerable attention, and when gospel quartet singing boomed in the early 1940s, he was recruited by a well-known Brooklyn group, the Jubilee Stars. During the early 1950s Storey briefly went on the road with a quartet named the Brooklyn All Stars, but eventually left the group and returned to New York. "There wasn't much money in the singing business back then, and there still isn't today. See, I liked my home, liked to spend time with the family, liked to eat regularly," he explains. "So I figured I'd do better helping my home town, getting singers together, teaching young groups how to sing—I got a lot of joy out of that!" Back in Brooklyn he established a small furniture and moving business and reared a family. But Charlie Storey never stopped singing. For the past forty years he has led a succession of local quartets who sing on weekends in African-American churches in and around New York City. At age seventy-five, Charlie Storey, affectionately known in the neighborhood as the "Mayor of Fulton Street," continues to epitomize the spirit of non-professional, community-based quartet singing. "We sing for God, not money," he concludes.

It's slightly after 8 p.m. on a warm June evening, and Fulton Street still teems with shoppers, making last minute preparations for their Saturday night festivities. At the corner of Fulton and Nostrand Avenue a street preacher vies for the crowd's attention, but is drowned out by calypso music blaring from a West Indian record shop two stores down. Street vendors hawk everything from incense and African kente cloth to telephones and VCRs. The traffic is impenetrable. I finally pull off Fulton and find a parking space on Macon Street in front of a vacant lot. Charlie Storey's Auditorium is just down the street at the corner of Macon and Nostrand, right above a Blimpie's sandwich shop.

Officially Storey's establishment is called an auditorium, but to most neighborhood residents it's simply another storefront church. An impressive sign above the entrance announces that Bishop N. A. McNeil of the Faith Temple Deliverance Church for All People holds services every Sunday at noon. The space, which has room for approximately 250 folding chairs, is also rented out for revival meetings, weddings, and church banquets. But this particular Saturday night it's a gospel program, a benefit for the Right Way Pentecostal Church. The heavy smell of fried chicken greets me as I climb the stairs to the auditorium's second floor entrance where Sister Marie Wright is taking tickets. Admission is seven dollars, but she waves me in. Since I book the All Stars and other local groups at festivals I am considered a promoter, and gospel promoters are always admitted free. She knows I'll return the courtesy.

I head for the back of the auditorium, where people are chatting and eating dinner. Charlie's wife, Mary Storey, is busy serving hot barbecue, fried chicken, cole slaw, corn bread, and sweet potato pie from a small kitchen. "Why not take a whole pie home?" she asks a hungry looking customer, "It's only two seventy-five." "Lord, I came here to shout, not to shop for groceries," the woman replies. "I'll just take a piece." I too indulge in some pie while reminiscing with Thurman Ruth, the leader of Brooklyn's legendary Selah Jubilee Singers, about quartet singing in the early 1940s. "The first gospel quartet I ever saw was the Kings of Harmony," he recalls. "They'd start singing and one would jump over here and one would jump over there. Folks were falling out like flies, getting happy!" We continue to gab as the singers gradually drift in. A group of teenagers laden with drums and guitar amplifiers arrive and are ushered to the small front stage where Billy Walker is testing the sound system. It's after nine and the crowd is growing restless.

I finally take a seat as an elderly deacon from the Right Way Pentecostal Church steps to the microphone to open the program. There are close to a hundred people in the audience as the deacon breaks into a familiar congregational song, "This Little Light of Mine." Halfway through the song a drummer and an organist pick up the beat and a chorus of voices joins in the singing. As the song comes to a close the deacon welcomes the audience and asks:

How many of y'all are here to have church tonight?
I don't know about you, but I didn't come for the crowd,
I came to have church!
And I believe the Lord is here tonight,
I believe we're going to have a good time!

He delivers a lengthy prayer, then reads from the One-Hundredth Psalm, emphasizing the verse about "joyful singing." Next comes a brief period of "testimony," when audience members take turns leading songs and telling dramatic narratives about the ways God has recently blessed their lives. As one woman recounts the story of her straying daughter's return to church her voice tenses with emotion, then soars in a chanted cadence that culminates with a joyful shout of "Thank you Jesus." Several more congregational songs complete the devotional segment of the program, and the microphone is turned over to Thurman Ruth, the emcee for the remaining song service.

Ruth greets the audience with an easygoing patter meant to welcome them to the program while reminding them they have gathered to "have church." Since none of the featured groups wants to be called first, Ruth brings up the youth choir from the sponsoring church. The eight youngsters are obviously nervous, but survive a shaky start and eventually have the entire audience singing along to "Yes, Jesus Loves Me." Ruth compliments the youngsters, then stalls for time by acknowledging distinguished audience members above the din of the next group's drums and buzzing electric guitars. Finally he asks for a warm welcome for Brooklyn's own Deacon Jones and the Pilgrim Sounds.

A band consisting of electric guitar, bass, and trap drums jumps into a driving R&B progression, as four middle-aged men dressed in matching silver-grey suits rise from the back row and stride forward toward the stage. Deacon Jones picks up the lead mike, turns to face the audience, and sings:

Lord, you know that I'm your child,
   and I'm doing the best that I can.
And I've been praying oh so hard,
   my friends just don't understand.
Oh Lord,
   I need you to hold my hand.

The background singers chime in, the audience begins to clap. Obviously everyone is ready to have church. The Pilgrim Sounds run through several numbers, leaving the members of the audience on the edge of their chairs with a slow, heart-wrenching version of a favorite gospel song, "The Lord Is Blessing Me Right Now."

Next Ruth calls the House Wrecking Bibleways, a teenage quartet from the neighboring New Testament Church of God in Christ. The group is greeted with enthusiastic applause, particularly from New Testament church members who have come to cheer them on. After a smooth contemporary song showcasing their sweet high harmony, the House Wrecking Bibleways kick into a sanctified rocker appropriately entitled "I Feel the Spirit." The group, too, lives up to its name. As the lead singer prances up and down the aisle, audience members rise to their feet, clapping and shouting encouragement. Several women break into euphoric holy dance and must be restrained. Ten minutes later, as the singers process off the stage, the hall is rocking.

Ruth calmly restores order, but before the energy can dissipate he calls on Charlie Storey and the All Stars. More spirited applause. Storey thanks the crowd and comments on the Bibleways' moving performance, noting how encouraging it is to see "kids getting high on Christ instead of crack and dope." He reminds his audience that he sings "the old time way" because he has the "old-time religion," and moves right into the song "Lord Jesus, Can I Just Have This Talk With You." Walker carries his baritone part and the background voices blend tightly. The audience responds approvingly as bass singer Brown Copney takes the mike and booms out "Meeting Tonight," a blues-inflected account of a southern revival meeting complete with "singing, shouting, and praying in the old-time way." Next Billy Walker croons a Sam Cooke-influenced arrangement of the hymn "Pass Me Not, Oh Gentle Savior." The lead mike is passed back to Storey, and the audience shouts enthusiastically as he declares "Right now we've had our time. We hope you have enjoyed it, and our way of singing. Now here's a song about all those dark clouds." Dramatically he breaks into chant:

Now one of these days,
    when storms will pass over,
Ah ha, and dark clouds,
      will pass by.
And I look around tonight and think,
    when we get in glory,
      everything's gonna be all right—

Storey's voice shifts easily from the tense preacher's chant to the relaxed melodic flow of song. Pee Wee Ellis joins in on guitar, and the song takes off.

Jesus bore his cross alone,
    so all the world could go free,
Jesus bore the cross,
    for everyone,
There is hope, for you and me.

Now everything's gonna be all right,
Everything's gonna be all right,
You know that storms will pass over,
    clouds will pass by.
Everything's gonna be all right.

Another verse and chorus and the song moves into what singers call the "drive" section. The background singers repeat the phrase, "everything" while Storey improvises on top.

No more trouble,	(Everything)
No more trials,	(Everything)
Nothing but joy,	(Everything)
Joy in the morning,	(Everything)
Joy in the evening,	(Everything)
Nothing but joy,	(Everything)
Over there,	(Everything)
When I get in glory,	(Everything)
I'll see my mother there,	(Everything)
I'll see my father there,	(Everything)
I'll see Jesus,	(Everything)

At this point Storey sets his microphone aside and struts into the crowd, waving his right hand high and continuing to chant in short, clipped phrases. The entire audience is standing, the hall reverberates to the beat of clapping hands and stamping feet. Caught up in the moment I too jump to my feet and chime in "Go ahead, sing your song, sing!" Now the three background singers abandon their microphones and join Storey in a final processional down the center aisle, singing and clapping to the beat maintained by guitarist Ellis, who remains alone on stage. As the processional nears the last row of seats, an elderly woman begins to hop up and down frantically, then whirls about shouting, "Praise Him, praise Him!" Her chair crashes over, prompting several bystanders to surround her quickly to prevent injury. Off to the side a neatly dressed gentleman who offered a fiery testimony during the devotional period is kicking his feet in a series of low hops that resemble an old-time buck dance. The singers are slowly wending their way through the ecstatic crowd, chugging like a powerful freight train. Finally they reach the rear of the hall and turn back to face their audience. Storey tosses his handkerchief in the air, a signal to bring the performance to a close. As the singers' voices come to rest on the final tonic chord, several women up front, on the verge of tears, arms stretched high, are wailing, "Thank you Jesus, thank you Jesus."

The applause and shouting continue as Ruth picks up the microphone and demands another round of thanks for Charlie Storey and the All Stars. And so the evening rolls on, as the Heavenly Tones, the Singingaires, the Gospel Wings, and the Angelettes are called, in turn, to the stage. There are no out-of-town "featured" acts tonight, just the locals. As the hour grows late Ruth asks the groups to limit their time to two selections, a standard emcee's request that is commonly ignored if singers catch the Spirit.

"You've got to look out around here." Brother Brown cautions as he walks me to my car. "Lots of crazy people out here at night, lots of crack heads." It's just after midnight as the Angelettes' sweet harmonies flow from the open auditorium windows and follow us down Macon Street. "Yes sir, same on my street," I affirm grimly, acknowledging that the upsurge in drug-related crime has turned many of central Brooklyn's streets into violent battlegrounds. But now I'm safe in my Honda, crawling down Nostrand Avenue toward Eastern Parkway and home. The sidewalk overflows with people, the street is jammed with traffic. The smells of fried chicken and barbecue, along with the choking stench of bus exhaust fumes, permeate the humid June night. Reggae, soca, funk and rap music pour from the clubs, from the cars, and from passing beat boxes—engulfing the street in the infectious spirit of the good-time Saturday night. The gospel singers weren't kidding, I surmise; the Devil's music is certainly alive and well on Nostrand Avenue!

Gridlock at St. John Street: the traffic stands still and the van next to me is throbbing to the thunderous rap beat of Public Enemy. Since my own car radio was unceremoniously "removed" last fall, I am grateful for this brief interlude of entertainment. Slowly my mind drifts back to the gospel program and I confront a recurring question: why am I so attracted to black gospel quartet singing, and why am I so intrigued by the African-American church? After all, I am, strictly speaking, a cultural outsider—a white man in a black world, a sinner among the sanctified. Can I ever fathom what really just happened during the past three hours of gospel ritual? Yes and no, I tell myself. While many of the experiences of an urban African-American gospel quartet singer seem far removed from my white suburban upbringing, I cannot deny there are genuine points of cultural contact.

The music, I suppose, is the most obvious link between these two worlds. Having come of age in the 1960s, I was reared on a diet of rock, soul, and rhythm and blues—styles of popular music that could never have assumed their present shape had it not been for the immeasurable contribution of black church and gospel quartet singing. I was stunned the first time I heard a live gospel quartet ten years ago in Memphis, Tennessee, while working for the Center for Southern Folklore. The chords, the harmonies, and the dazzling vocal styles were overwhelmingly familiar. How ironic, I think, that as a teenager in Glen Cove, Long Island, I chorded away on my Farvisa "Combo Compact" organ at the local YMCA rock dance, while unbeknownst to me, in the nearby inner city, black quartets were "shouting churches," probably using the same chords and keyboard.

I have seen how the power of African-American gospel quartet singing can move many audiences—black or white—and yet music is only one component of the performance. Indeed, I have come to learn in recent years that what their performances are really about is ritual and religion—"lifting up God's word through song," as they put it. So how do I deal with this? After all, I can hardly be described as a religious person; I never have been, and probably never will be, "saved, sanctified, and filled with the Holy Ghost." Yet I was reared a Presbyterian, and years of Sunday school training and regular church attendance left me well-acquainted with and appreciative of biblical doctrine and the Protestant hymn tradition. Of course, coming from a northern Presbyterian background that frowns on demonstrative worship, I had never experienced the intense emotionalism that characterizes southern (black and white) Protestantism. "Getting happy" in church was not in my early realm of experience. I chuckle as I imagine my great aunt Angie, pillar of the First Presbyterian Church of Glen Cove and for years my Sunday school teacher, listening to exhilarating gospel renditions of her favorite hymns like "Jacob's Ladder," "Rock of Ages," or "I Come to the Garden." Would she find a genuine "spirit" amidst all that clapping and shouting? Would she approve? Yes, I believe she would, and if we ever meet again, "over yonder," I intend to ask her.

But there must be more to all this than some semi-conscious desire to connect my earlier musical and religious experiences with the vitality of the black folk church. A genuine fascination with African-American music and ritual may have accounted for my initial attraction, but it was the people I met, and the relationships I established within the gospel community that sustained me through four years of research. Research—is that all I've been doing? Fulfilling dissertation requirements for a Ph.D.? Gathering ethnographic grist for the publication mill? I think back on my early field experience. My initial meeting with Charlie Storey was on a sweltering Sunday afternoon in August of 1985. I found him outside his auditorium, overseeing an annual neighborhood sidewalk gospel singing. "See, once a year we bring the singing out on the street," he told me, "and we give free ice cream to the kids—it's a community thing." I explained to Storey and Thurman Ruth (whom I had previously spoken to on the phone) that I was interested in learning about gospel quartet singing for a college research project. Immediately they introduced me to Reverend Floyd King, a smartly dressed, elderly gentleman who proudly straddled an ancient bicycle and carried a huge, space-age looking audio cassette recorder. Reverend King is a "real old-timer," Storey quipped, "And he still teaches young fellahs how to sing a cappella." And so within an hour I had met three singers who would become key informants and close friends. During the next few years we would work together on various performance and recording projects, and I would accompany Reverend King and his group, The No Name Gospel Singers, on a singing tour of France. "The Lord works in beautiful but mysterious ways," Reverend King would later point out as our plane prepared to land in Paris.

That fall, following my initial contact with Storey, Ruth, and King, I began to attend local gospel programs in Brooklyn, Jamaica (Queens), and Harlem. When introduced to singers I was often asked if I were a talent scout or record producer—a natural role, I only later came to realize, for a young white man at a black gospel program. I was quick to deny such status, and presented myself as a graduate student who was writing a paper on the history of sacred quartets in New York. This explanation seemed to suffice, and I was accepted (or at least tolerated) at such events because I was polite, sincere, and demonstrated a genuine interest (and some knowledge) of gospel quartet singing. Of course I was a curiosity, because white folks rarely attended gospel programs in African-American urban neighborhoods. But, as I was often reminded, God's Kingdom is open to all, and I was made welcome.

The problems arose in the second phase of work, when I attempted to attend rehearsals and conduct a number of in-depth interviews with selected singers. Friendly individuals who were happy to chat at programs were more reluctant to invite me to their homes to record rehearsals and lengthy interviews. Here my outsider's status—that of a non-churchgoer and a non-African-American—undoubtedly worked against me. Tight personal schedules also came into play, as many young and middle-aged singers worked six days a week, with family and church obligations gobbling up their remaining time. After being stood up for several interviews I came to the painful realization that most busy, urban, working class black churchgoers had little time to spare for a white graduate student writing a research paper.

Fortunately during this time two folklore colleagues, Steve Zeitlin and Amanda Dargan, approached me about coordinating a series of gospel concerts for the Queens Council on the Arts. At first I was reluctant, fearing that such a project might interfere with my "objective" role as a field researcher. But I eventually acquiesced, in part because of the modest coordinator's salary that helped finance some of my field work and writing (dissertation support was scarce in the 1980s). We were able to secure funds from the New York State Council on the Arts, and in the spring of 1986 produced four successful gospel concerts featuring a dozen groups I had heard the previous fall. Within months other community arts agencies were contacting me about gospel groups. Citylore, a non-profit public folklore organization that Zeitlin directed, agreed to sponsor a project to record several of the older groups. The following year, upon completing my dissertation, I took a job with the World Music Institute, where I continued to book gospel singers in "cultural" settings outside the black church community. Carnegie Recital Hall, Central Park's Summer Stage, Prospect Park's Celebrate Brooklyn Series, Queens Day Festival, Lincoln Center's Out of Doors Festival, the Statue of Liberty Centennial Celebration, and numerous colleges showcased the groups I recommended.

With these developments my status in the local church community changed dramatically. For better or worse I was now identified as a promoter. The role I first denied and later resisted now permitted me to work closely with a select number of groups. We eventually reached a tacit agreement—the groups allowed me to record their concerts, rehearsals, and personal histories, and in return I provided them with pictures, well paying engagements, and in a few cases, the opportunity to record professional quality cassettes. In short, I was now welcome to hang out with the groups, who saw me as a liaison to a world of performing opportunities that had not previously been open to them. Of course my role as gospel promoter was not without mishaps. I was not always comfortable wearing the hat of talent scout, especially when it demanded choosing certain groups rather than others for prestigious engagements. Gospel quartet singers are very competitive, and many do not hesitate to voice feelings of discontent and jealousy. Some groups were reluctant to sing on programs that included certain rivals, and on more than one occasion I was admonished for showing favoritism toward certain groups. A number of younger groups were disappointed, perhaps angered, at my inability to obtain funds to record them. In spite of these frustrations, the overall experience was invaluable to me. Only through involvement with the conflicts and tensions of daily life does a cultural outsider start to move inside and catch glimpses of what a community is really about.

I finally break through the traffic and turn right down Eastern Parkway, zooming toward the Brooklyn Museum and home. Now familiar feelings of self-doubt begin rumbling inside my head: you don't really know *them*, you can't begin to approach the sense of community or the depth of spiritual experience *they* share. No, four years is not enough time to overcome the barriers of race and class that divide Americans, nor to penetrate the depths of a sacred world view I do not personally share. But I console myself by thinking about those times when my roles as researcher, arts coordinator, and friend converged. At those moments my insights into art, religion, and black urban life were the sharpest, and my appreciation for the singers as friends, artists, and colleagues was most profound. And those moments, I realize, I came closest to grasping what it must be like to "sing in the Spirit."

The contributions of many have made this book possible. First I wish to thank my professors at the University of Pennsylvania's Department of Folklore and Folklife, Roger Abrahams, Kenneth Goldstein, John Roberts, Morton Marks, and Steve Feld, as well as my fellow student, Stephen Stuempfle, for their advice and insights that shaped the early research and dissertation stages of my work. I am further grateful to my friends and colleagues who reviewed and critiqued more recent portions of this manuscript: Gerald Davis, David Evans, William Ferris, Ray Funk, Archie Green, Barbara Kirshenblatt-Gimblett, Kip Lornell, Jay Mechling, Patrick Mullen, Doug Seroff, Robert Taylor, Jeff Titon, and David Wilson. Thanks also to Linda Franz Brown, Michael Gross, and Beth Blackman for their editorial assistance.

Very special thanks to Robert Browning of the World Music Institute, Steve Zeitlin and Roberta Singer of Citylore, Amanda Dargan of the Queens Council on the Arts, Robert Baron of the New York State Council on the Arts, Nancy Groce of the New York State Council for the Humanities, and Michael Schlesinger of Global Village Music for their assistance with the gospel programming and audio documentation projects that became part of my research. I am most grateful to the National Endowment for the Arts and the New York State Council on the Arts for making funds available for concert production and recording. Thanks also to Jack Vartoogian for use of his splendid photographs, and to Cathy Glasson for her ongoing efforts to document and promote the local New York groups.

My greatest debt of gratitude goes to the many singers and members of New York's African-American church community whose cooperation and support made this study possible. I am especially indebted to Thurman Ruth, Mamie Taylor, Charlie Storey, and Aaron Chestnut for their assistance in introducing me to numerous singers during the early stages of my field research. As for the groups, special thanks to The No Name Gospel Singers of Brooklyn, the Heavenly Tones of Brooklyn, the Faithful Harmonizers of St. Albans, the Sunset Jubilees of New York, the Golden Jubilees of Jamaica, the Wearyland Singers of Corona, the Brooklyn Skyways of Brooklyn, the Biblettes of Jersey City, the Spiritual Voices of Brooklyn, the Mighty Gospel Giants of Brooklyn, Charlie Storey and the All Stars of Brooklyn, the Golden Sons of Brooklyn, and the Ecstatistics of the Bronx.

And finally, my deepest appreciation to Laurie Russell, editor, critic, friend, and lover. Her constant support has seen me through the best and worst of times.

1. The All Stars in rehearsal, Brooklyn, 1989. (left to right: Billy Walker, Samuel "Brown" Copney, Jerome "Pee Wee" Ellis, Charlie Storey). Photo by Ray Allen.

2. Charlie Storey in the Spirit, Brooklyn, 1988. Photo by Jack Vartoogian.

Introduction: Studying the Local Scene

The joyful sounds of sacred quartet harmony have resonated through the homes and churches of African-American communities for over a century.* Yet the full story of this magnificent tradition has only recently begun to be told. In spite of its impact on American popular music, from rhythm and blues to rap, sacred quartet singing and its close cousin, gospel music, have received surprisingly little attention from scholarly and popular authors, the commercial media, or the major cultural institutions. Today millions of African-Americans experience quartet singing at live gospel programs and through radio, recordings, and television, but relatively few individuals outside the black church community recognize or appreciate its significance.

The scope of African-American sacred quartet singing is nothing short of stunning, as thousands of groups have been active in the United States since the late nineteenth century. But only a scant number have received national exposure or commercial success. At the turn of the century, quartets from black educational institutions such as Fisk University pleased black and white audiences across the United States and abroad with polished arrangements of traditional spirituals. Jubilee quartets like the Golden Gate Quartet and the Southernaires achieved wide recognition during the 1930s and 1940s through their nationally syndicated radio broadcasts. And more recently, the Dixie Hummingbirds' performance on Paul Simon's

* When used in reference to African-American vernacular music, the term "quartet" refers to small, one-on-a-part vocal harmony groups. As the name implies, most early quartets consisted of four voices—bass, baritone, lead, and tenor. In later years this number was expanded to include additional lead and high tenor singers. Today quartets may vary in size from four to six voices and usually include several instrumental accompanists.

mid-1970s pop hit "Loves Me Like a Rock," and the stellar role of the Five Blind Boys of Alabama and the Soul Stirrers in the dramatic 1983 production *Gospel at Colonus*, brought brief national attention to the gospel quartet tradition. These glamorous examples aside, the handful of professional quartets who still eke out a full-time living through their music are supported almost exclusively by the black church community, remaining virtually invisible to the larger public.

The few scholars and popular journalists who write about gospel music and sacred quartet singing have emphasized a select group of big-name stars. The contribution of the non-professional local singers—those masses of community-based performers who form the backbone of the quartet singing tradition—is usually ignored. As a result, when quartet singing is written about at all, it is discussed as commercial entertainment, while the role of the music in the social and religious lives of working class black people is underplayed. Reviewing the historical treatment of African-American sacred quartet singing brings this problem into clear focus and points to the need for a broader approach that includes local, non-commercial singers.

African-American sacred quartet singing is usually categorized as one style of twentieth century gospel music, but the roots of this venerable harmony tradition stretch back to the mid-nineteenth century.[1] Harmony singing was popularized on the post-Emancipation minstrel stage by groups of black artists whose repertoire included spirituals, jubilee songs, and popular plantation numbers.[2] Towards the end of the nineteenth century, jubilee choirs and quartets from southern black institutions such as Fisk University, Hampton University, Tuskegee Institute, and Utica Institute traversed the country, raising money for their schools. Trained in European aspects of harmony and intonation, these college jubilee groups sang formal arrangements of traditional "Negro" spirituals and folk songs.[3]

While minstrel and college-trained jubilee groups popularized sacred harmony singing for commercial gain, accounts by early documenters of slave songs suggest that non-professional, untrained African-American singers were engaging in quartet singing as early as the 1850s.[4] During Reconstruction, shape-note singing—a form of musical notation where pitch is delineated by the shape of the written note rather than its position on the music staff—introduced many southern African-Americans to the concept of four-part harmony.[5] By the 1890s, informal quartet harmony singing had become so popular among southern African-Americans that black scholar James Weldon Johnson remarked, "Pick up four colored boys or young men anywhere and the chances are ninety out of a hundred that you have a quartet. Let one of them sing the melody and the others will naturally find their parts. Indeed it may be said that all male Negro youth in the United States is divided into quartets."[6] Increased urbanization during the early decades of the twentieth century spurred the formation of community quartets in southern cities such as Birmingham, Norfolk, Atlanta, New Orleans, and Jacksonville. Such urban centers provided an environment where working class African-Americans could easily organize quartets in churches, schools, and places of work.[7] The Great Migration of African-Americans to northern and mid-western cities after the first world war carried the quartet tradition to Chicago, Detroit, Cleveland, New York, and Philadelphia. By the 1920s, quartet singing was an established pastime for black men and women throughout the South and in certain northern urban communities.

We can only speculate how the first nineteenth-century African-American quartets might have sounded, as none were recorded until 1895. Turn of the century sound recordings of such institutional groups as the Dinwiddie Colored Quartet (from the John A. Dix Industrial School in Dinwiddie, Virginia) and the Fisk Jubilee Quartet reveal the influence of European choral singing. These groups stressed precise, a cappella four-part harmony, clear diction, and straightforward rhythms, while employing minimal vocal ornamentation and only an occasional hint of syncopation.[8] Commercial recordings made during the 1920s, however, suggest that the singing of untrained, community-based quartets was characterized by more traditional African-American stylistic techniques—"blue" notes (slightly flatted sevenths and thirds on the western scale), melisma, falsetto swoops, moans, vocal improvisation, and strong rhythmic syncopation.[9] Many of the South's finest sacred quartets, both institutionally trained and community-based, were recorded during this period on "race" records issued by companies like Columbia, Victor, and OKeh, while live radio broadcasts brought quartet singing to larger audiences. Known as "jubilee," "spiritual," or "harmonizing" quartets, a few of the more commercially successful groups such as the Norfolk Jubilee Singers recorded secular jazz numbers as well as traditional religious material.[10]

By the early 1930s, African-American religious music was undergoing a radical transformation that would leave an indelible imprint on quartet singing. The Holiness/Pentecostal movement that swept the South during the early decades of the twentieth century had become firmly entrenched in southern and northern urban black communities. The worship practices of such churches featured ecstatic preaching, driving music, religious dance, and possession by the Holy Spirit. Their music, commonly referred to as "sanctified" music, was characterized by repetitive lyrics, powerful rhythms, and the use of drums, tambourines, and guitars, as well as the piano. And sanctified church performers freely incorporated elements of popular secular styles such as blues, ragtime, and jazz into their music.[11]

The rise of sanctified music was critical to the evolution of twentieth century African-American gospel song. There is no concise agreement on the exact origin or meaning of the term gospel, and many African-American church people use the term generically in reference to all their sacred music. One scholar, David Evans, suggests that early sacred quartet singing and sanctified music might be considered the first bona-fide black gospel music.[12] Most music historians, however, attribute the evolution of black gospel song to a number of urban composers who were active during the early decades of this century. While C. A. Tindly of Philadelphia was perhaps the first African-American to compose a gospel-like song, Chicago-based Thomas Dorsey was the leading exponent and catalyst of gospel music. Dorsey, who is credited with first applying the term "gospel song" to black religious music in the mid-1920s, composed more than four hundred songs, including his renowned "Precious Lord" and "Peace in the Valley." He also founded the National Convention of Gospel Singers, and inspired hundreds of soloists, groups, and quartets to tour the country.[13]

The gospel music that Tindly and Dorsey helped shape was characterized by flowery, often sentimental lyrics that centered on Jesus as well as human dependence on God. The tone became highly evangelical. Musically, early black gospel borrowed the verse/chorus structure and elementary harmonies of the older folk hymns and white gospel (revival) songs.[14] But the style was distinctly African-American, as the music incorporated the driving rhythms and instrumentation of sanctified music along with the melismatic moans of the older spirituals and Dr. Watts hymns, the syncopated licks and "bent" notes of jazz and blues, and the ecstatic emotionalism of southern preaching. Songs were ordered around a basic call-and-response structure: a highly ornamented, improvised solo voice led, while background singers and/or instruments responded in a repetitive manner. Gospel music's emphasis on antiphonal response, dynamic rhythms, variable vocal timbre, improvisation, and body movement, all combined in the context of demonstrative worship, led Pearl Williams-Jones to conclude that gospel "retains the most noticeable African-derived aesthetic features" of any form of black American culture.[15] Gospel song, together with its immediate antecedent, sanctified music, revitalized urban black religious music with older African-American and African stylistic sensibilities.[16]

Dorsey and his cadre of Chicago-based female singers, who included Sallie Martin, Mahalia Jackson, Roberta Martin, and Willie Mae Ford Smith, were largely responsible for the spread of gospel music during the 1930s. At first the music's strong rhythms, heavy instrumentation, and emphasis on emotionalism were met with resistance by many middle class, conservative black churchgoers. Eventually, however, through the persistent efforts of these early singers, gospel music gained acceptance in most Baptist and Methodist churches in the northern and mid-western cities. And, for the growing numbers of southern rural migrants who moved into the northern urban centers during this period, the new gospel sound satisfied a desire for down-home musical and spiritual expression. Further, Dorsey and his singers helped found the professional field of gospel music, with thousands of composers and performers following in their footsteps, seeking fame and commercial success. Unlike the earlier folk hymns and spirituals of the rural South, a significant amount of post-1930 urban black gospel music was composed, copyrighted, recorded, sold, and performed by professionals.

The increasing popularity of sanctified music and early gospel song among urban African-American churchgoers did not go unnoticed by innovative quartet singers. Although community-based jubilee and spiritual quartets undoubtedly had been employing traditional African-American vernacular vocal techniques for years, in terms of performance style they tended to stand relatively still, or "flat-footed," while concentrating on close harmony and precise timing. By the 1930s, however, they began adopting the driving rhythms and emotional fervor associated with sanctified and gospel music. While it is impossible to credit one group with pioneering the emerging gospel quartet sound, researchers working with early commercial recordings argue that the deep South, most notably Alabama and Texas, was the earliest breeding ground for this style.[17] Two groups from Birmingham, the Famous Blue Jay Singers and the Kings of Harmony, along with the Soul Stirrers of Houston, were among the first to record the more powerful, "hard" gospel singing style. The Soul Stirrers were particularly innovative, and may have been the first quartet to employ double lead singers for dramatic effect.[18] Lead vocalists began to move out in front of their groups, run up and down the aisles of churches, and sing in an explosive fashion that resembled the ecstatic shouts of sanctified preachers.

On the East Coast in the 1930s, quartet singing took a slightly different twist. The Golden Gate Quartet of Norfolk, Virginia, is credited with introducing a pulsing syncopation into quartet singing, a feature that group leader Willie Johnson readily admits was inspired by the rhythms of local Holiness churches.[19] The "rhythmic spiritual" style of jubilee singing they pioneered featured smooth, sophisticated harmonies, polyphonic, interlocking vocal parts, and a swinging beat. They adapted a number of Dorsey's gospel songs to this style, but their singing lacked the emotional fervor and evangelical tone that characterized the deep South's early gospel quartets. Although the Golden Gates inspired many imitators up and down the East Coast, by the 1940s the gospel sound was also catching on among quartet singers. Hard gospel shouters like Ira Tucker of the Dixie Hummingbirds and Julius Cheeks of the Sensational Nightingales, both natives of Spartanburg, South Carolina, were early architects of the East Coast gospel quartet singing.[20]

After the second world war, gospel music in general, and gospel quartet singing in particular, rose to new commercial heights. Its popularity was fueled by an expanding radio and recording industry, a well established touring circuit, and a growing black urban population that could afford to support professional singers. In fact there were now so many professional singers that a number of authors dubbed the fifteen year period following the War as the "golden age" of gospel music.[21] Female soloists like Mahalia Jackson, Willie Mae Ford Smith, Rosetta Tharpe, and Sallie and Roberta Martin carved out lucrative careers as recording and touring artists, while female groups like the Ward Sisters, the Davis Sisters, and the Gospel Harmonettes popularized three- and four-part harmony arrangements of gospel songs. But it was the male gospel quartets that dominated the field. Following the lead of the pioneering professional groups like the Golden Gate Quartet, the Soul Stirrers, and the Kings of Harmony, hundreds of community-based quartets recorded for independent record companies, broadcast on radio, and took to the road to try their luck as professionals. In describing the rise of professional quartet singing in the 1940s, Doug Seroff comments: "A scattered network of community-based folk artists emerged as a powerful force in the national entertainment world. Vast armies of black quartets traversed the country, singing in churches and public auditoriums."[22]

By the early 1950s influential touring groups including the Soul Stirrers, the Dixie Hummingbirds, the Swan Silvertones, the Sensational Nightingales, the Spirit of Memphis, the Five Blind Boys of Mississippi, the Fairfield Four, and the Harmonizing Four were setting the highest standards for post-war quartet singing. Some groups featured two lead singers, one to render the smoother jubilee numbers, the other to excite their audiences with an impassioned hard gospel delivery. The hard gospel style eventually took precedence as

most professional groups incorporated the demonstrative characteristics of sanctified worship—fervid preaching, shouting, holy dance—
into their stage presentations in order to invoke the Holy Spirit and
to "shout the church."

The popularity of professional gospel quartet singing reached its
zenith in the mid-1950s, and decline set in toward the end of the
decade. In fact, by the early 1960s, the entire commercial gospel industry appeared to be in a retreat. It was at this time that some of the
freshest young gospel talents left the church to seek fame and for-
tune as secular pop singers. Sam Cooke, Aretha Franklin, Lou Rawls,
Wilson Pickett, and Dionne Warwick departed from the ranks of the
faithful and went on to shape the burgeoning soul music movement.
The gradual secularization of black urban populations during this
period, coupled with the growing numbers of young white listeners
who avidly embraced black styles, created a huge pool of consumers
who demanded black pop music but showed little interest in gospel.
Further discouraged by the music industry's failure to help them
reach a broader, non-black audience, many professional quartet singers came off the road and returned to the home communities and
churches where they had started. There they performed again with
countless lesser-known singers who had never left the local churches
and who had remained relatively unaffected by the changing tastes
of the commercial music world.

As the popularity of professional quartets declined throughout the
1960s, soloists like James Cleveland and Shirley Caeser, often backed
by choirs, came to dominate the commercial gospel field. Cleveland
and Caesar maintained a traditional southern tone to their singing,
complete with spirited testimonies and hard-edged, shouting style vocals. As might be expected, their audience was almost exclusively
African-American churchgoers.

The unprecedented success of Edwin Hawkins and the Northern
California State Youth Choir's 1969 smash hit, "Oh Happy Day,"
shocked the music industry and won substantial worldwide exposure
for contemporary gospel music. Perhaps sensing the potential to
reach a wider market, a number of younger singers in the 1970s
broke ranks with the down-home style and adopted a more polished
approach in their music. Modernists like Andrae Crouch and Al
Green began to use sophisticated musical arrangements, advanced
studio techniques, stylistic elements borrowed from contemporary
black pop music, and less evangelical lyrics. Combining high, sweet
vocalizations with richly textured, synthesizer-tinged accompaniments, they fashioned a smoother version of inspirational music that
had at least some appeal beyond the black church community.[23] A

few vocal groups, most notably Detroit's Winans and Nashville's Take Six, successfully adapted contemporary songs and stylizing to the quartet format.

Gospel music and sacred quartet singing continued to prosper throughout the 1980s and into the 1990s. In the commerical arena there exists a multi-million-dollar recording industry whose main supporters are members of the black church community. While hundreds of gospel soloists, groups, and choirs record each year, most are on small, independent labels and receive little attention outside their home towns. A fraction of these recordings receive national distribution or broadcast time on the larger commercial radio stations. Most major cities with sizable black populations boast at least one radio station that is partially or entirely devoted to gospel or inspirational music. Their playlists are dominated by mass choirs, by choir-backed traditional soloists like James Cleveland, Shirley Caesar, and Timothy Wright, by contemporary, smooth sounding artists like Al Green, Andrae Crouch, the Winans, and the Hawkins Family, and by a handful of male quartets and female groups like the Mighty Clouds of Joy, the Jackson Southernaires, and the Clark Sisters. Today there are only a small number of professional gospel artists who make a full-time living through record sales and touring appearances. A few superstars—Caesar, Green, the Winans—can command high concert fees and collect handsome recording royalties. A small number of professional quartets, including reincarnations of the older Dixie Hummingbirds, the Soul Stirrers, and the Five Blind Boys of Alabama, as well as younger exponents of the post-war style like the Mighty Clouds of Joy, the Jackson Southernaires, and the Gospel Keynotes, continue to tour professionally. Most however, find the going rough, and often full-time recording and touring careers are cut back and supplemented with other employment.

In the local churches, non-professional choirs and soloists continue to perform every Sunday morning during regular worship services, and sometimes for weekday evening services as well. Many of the talented ones move beyond the confines of their home churches, appearing regularly at special gospel programs and anniversaries held in neighboring churches, schools, or other community centers—usually on Saturday evenings or Sunday afternoons. Often they sing for free, and what little money they do bring in is donated back to their home church or used for travel, uniforms, and other expenses.

While performances by soloists and choirs are not unusual at local gospel programs, such events tend to feature quartets and small vocal ensembles. Most of these groups use some form of instrumentation (electric guitar, bass, drums, sometimes keyboards), although a few still sing in the older a cappella fashion. A wide variety of musical styles are represented, ranging from traditional harmonizing and ju-bilee to contemporary message songs. Most, however, continue to perform in a post-war hard gospel style. Like the aforementioned choirs and soloists, most local quartets sing for little compensation, often accepting whatever is brought in from a free will offering or a small portion of the proceeds from a larger ticket program. Much of the money raised at these programs goes back to the sponsoring church to support maintenance costs, building funds, and other char-itable programs.

Finally, there are a significant number of quartets that occupy the middle ground between the full-time professionals and the local am-ateurs. These semi-professional artists perform at small local churches as well as larger programs, where they usually open up for visiting big-name acts. They often travel on weekends, but rarely far-ther than a day's drive from their home town. While they are some-times paid to sing, their compensation is minimal, and so they must depend on non-singing day jobs to earn a living.

While sacred quartet singing is no longer a dominant force in the contemporary commercial gospel industry, the tradition of small group harmony singing is in no danger of extinction. The notion that gospel quartets have declined from a "golden age" of the 1950s is somewhat misleading. Certainly fewer groups are touring today than were thirty years ago, but those few who do make a full-time career of singing are probably better off financially than their predecessors. More importantly, quartet singing continues to thrive in the com-munity sphere, as African-American church people throughout the United States persist in their enthusiastic support for local quartets.

Most of the scholarly and popular literature devoted to African-American sacred music has overlooked the fact that for nearly a cen-tury quartet singing has flourished simultaneously as commercial, mass-produced popular entertainment, and as community-based folk music. Full-length works such as Anthony Heilbut's *The Gospel Sound* and Viv Broughton's *Black Gospel* focus almost exclusively on the big names of the commercial gospel industry. While a number of other scholars have been more attentive to the social and religious dimen-sions of gospel music, their analysis has been based primarily on com-mercial recordings and performances by professional gospel singers rather than community-based singers or quartets.[24] Those who focus exclusively on quartet singing tend to work from a historical/disco-graphical orientation, reconstructing histories and analyzing the styles of the best known early recorded groups.[25]

There are at least three areas in which sacred quartet research has fallen short. First and foremost, the local, non-commercial scene has been sorely neglected, with the implication that community-based quartets are simply poor imitations of their commercial counterparts and therefore unworthy of serious consideration. Second, by emphasizing the commercial and stylistic aspects of quartet singing, researchers have downplayed the spiritual dimensions of the tradition. While no one denies that jubilee and gospel quartets sing religious material, there is little ethnographic information about the ritualistic nature of community quartet performance. And finally, most investigators have focused on the pre-war jubilee and the early post-war gospel quartets, leaving the contemporary scene relatively unexplored.

Recently, some of these issues have gained scholarly attention, thanks to a handful of publications that focus, at least in part, on non-commercial, African-American gospel singing in various southern communities.[26] The most thorough is Kip Lornell's social history of black gospel quartet singing in Memphis, *"Happy in the Service of the Lord"*. Lornell not only documents professional groups like the Spirit of Memphis, but also gives ample consideration to the lesser known community quartets. He aptly concludes that while the folk and popular quartet traditions are closely intertwined, the contributions of the latter remain generally unheralded:

Perhaps the most pressing concern is the decided lack of research on community quartets, which are the backbone of the gospel quartet tradition. Such groups are the least glamorous to research—most of them did not make commercial recordings, never traveled extensively, nor had a nationwide following. However, community quartets have had a strong local and regional impact, tend to reflect regional styles of singing, and are the wellspring for nearly all of the commercially successful groups.[27]

This book is, in part, a response to Lornell's call. It examines the production and consumption of non-commercial and semi-commercial sacred quartet singing within a particular local context, New York City's African-American church community. When viewed from an ethnographic perspective, the local quartet tradition emerges not simply as popular entertainment, but also as sacred ritual that shapes and reflects the religious world view and communal values of southern African-American migrants in their new urban environment. In performance, sacred and aesthetic concerns merge into what singer David Steward identifies as "spiritual entertainment":

Gospel music is spiritual entertainment, and it's something that was given to black people by God. And the Bible tells you, make a joyful noise. So you see it really is entertainment for spiritual people. You feel good, you have a good time in the name of the Lord, no matter where you are—in church, a school, a theater, no matter where![28]

Theories and methods from folklore, anthropology, ethnomusicology, communications, and oral history inform this inquiry. As ethnography my work aims at "thick description" and interpretation of religious and musical practices.[29] As a study in folklore performance and communication it seeks to contextualize traditional expressive behavior occurring within specially designated "events." Roger Abrahams defines an event as "a focused interaction that has been anticipated and prepared for. We recognize an event not only because of the intensity of involvement in common carried by the participants into the encounter but by their special rule-regulated behaviors."[30] Performance-centered folklorists seek to describe the setting and overall structure of such events, as well as the individual performances that unfold within them. The formation of a taxonomy of artistic forms, the manner in which cultural actors assume responsibility for performance, the ways in which competence is demonstrated and evaluated during actual presentations, and the role relationships formed between performers and their audiences are all major concerns.[31]

The analysis of performance must finally move beyond the description of formal structures and behavioral patterns to interpretation. Stylized events—rituals, ceremonies, celebrations, as well as various forms of modern commercial entertainment—offer excellent opportunities for observing the process by which social order and values are constantly being renegotiated and revalidated, as Roger Abrahams notes:

In placing intensive and stylized events at the center of ethnographic descriptions, we can observe extraordinary, if ideal, order being negotiated and achieved plainly and openly. Moreover, describing such expressive phenomena allows us to approach the areas of meaning and value as well as order.[32]

During such highly marked performances individuals collectively give patterned expression to their inner experiences, displaying the profound beliefs, core values, and vexing anxieties that shape their sense of the world. Deep-seated cultural tensions often surface in the form of symbolic expressions, which, in Victor Turner's words, "portray its [a community's] characteristic conflicts and suggest remedies for them, and generally take stock of its current situation in the known 'world'."[33] The interpretation of such symbolic expressions, argues Clifford Geertz, cuts to the heart of what a given culture is really about by illuminating values, attitudes and overall world view.[34]

The works of anthropologically oriented ethnomusicologists offer additional insight into the application of folklore performance and communications theory to musical systems. Since the 1964 publication of Alan Merriam's classic work, *The Anthropology of Music*, many ethnomusicologists have shifted their interests toward the social and cultural dimensions of musical experience. The term "music culture" is now used to refer to "a group of people's total involvement with music"; this includes the way they think about, organize, perform, and evaluate their music.[35] An increasing number of ethnomusicology field studies have focused on the process of learning and composition, occasions for performance, musical terminology, ethnoaesthetics, and the symbolic meanings that musical systems hold for their tradition bearers.[36] Several investigations of African and African-American music cultures have correlated changing patterns of aesthetic choice and performance style with changing social/economic conditions.[37] These latter works proved particularly useful in my own efforts to analyze critical stylistic transitions in black sacred quartet singing, for as Amiri Baraka suggests in his classic study, *Blues People*, the various social "transmutations" that African-Americans have gone through in the past three-and-a-half centuries are mirrored in their constantly evolving musical creations.[38]

Those students of musicology whose interests lie in comparative sound structure based on western music theory and notation will undoubtedly be disappointed that this study includes no musical transcriptions. In dealing with sound structure I chose to speak in the more general language of style, and whenever possible to use ingroup terminology.[39] I found this approach superior to one that imposes western musical concepts on a music culture whose aesthetic sensibilities owe more to the aural traditions of West Africa than to the written ones of Europe. Readers who are interested in western musicological analysis of jubilee and gospel quartet singing should consult the works of George Ricks and William Tallmadge.[40]

Lastly, my field research and interpretations were guided by David Hufford's "experience-centered" approach to the study of supernatural phenomena.[41] This method assumes that supernatural belief has some foundation in rational experiences and observations. Spiritual experiences should not be reduced to mere physiological, psychological, or social/functional behaviors, as past anthropological studies of religion have tended to do. Rather an experience-centered ethnography of belief seeks to elicit descriptions and explanations of spiritual experience from the actual participants, to understand better that experience from an insider's perspective. Obviously this process demands moving beyond the simple reporting of religious behavior

and organization into the realm of interpreting the personal and sub-
jective dimensions of human feelings, expectations, and meanings.[42]
Following Hufford's lead I have not attempted to draw conclusions
about the ultimate ontological nature of quartet singers' spiritual experiences, but their descriptions of falling under the anointment of
the Holy Ghost, or as they say, "getting happy," are thoroughly examined. And most importantly, their own words are offered, whenever possible, to interpret this phenomenon.

Sacred African-American quartet singing in local community settings lends itself to such ethnographic performance and experience-
centered analysis. Quartets appear at special singing programs which
are highly patterned, repeatable, ritualized events. These public performance occasions lie at the heart of the local quartet singing enter-
prise; singing at programs, is in fact, the quartets' *raison d'être*. The
singing program therefore provides the logical point of entry into the
music culture of the quartet singer, and the logical point of departure
for examining larger cultural issues of sacred world view, group identity, and acculturation to modern urban life.

Working from this ethnographic performance perspective I approach sacred quartet singing as a living, evolving tradition rather
than an antiquated relic from some bygone golden era. My emphasis
is on active gospel quartets and contemporary performance settings.
The historical component, which includes considerable information
on the older jubilee and the early gospel quartets, provides the necessary context for understanding the present-day scene. New York
City, which boasts a thriving but unexplored quartet tradition, is the
site of local study. Since the beginning of the twentieth century, New
York has been a prominent center of African-American culture. Bolstered by the rapid influx of southern migrants during World War I,
New York's African-American population quickly grew to the largest
of any city in the United States. Not surprisingly, the city's rapidly
expanding black church community nurtured a nascent quartet scene
that blossomed in the 1930s. By 1940 New York had established its
reputation as the jubilee quartet capital of the country. In the post-
war years the city produced a number of outstanding gospel quartets,
and today the tradition of small group harmony singing continues to
flourish in local churches. New York, then, offers the perfect setting
for tracing the development and understanding the significance of
southern quartet singing in the urban North.

In terms of organization, Chapter 1 presents historical background
on New York City's African-American church community and sacred
quartet tradition. The evolution of harmonizing and jubilee quartets

in the early decades of this century, and the emergence of hard gospel quartets in the post-war years are recounted.

The middle chapters describe various facets of New York's present-day gospel quartet scene. Chapter 2 investigates how singers acquire musical skills and develop their performance repertoires, and explores the critical role of rehearsal sessions. Chapter 3 focuses on the social setting and structural organization of community-based gospel programs. The various "performance strategies" used by local quartet singers are outlined in Chapter 4. The marriage of expressive song, narrative, and movement to achieve spiritual and aesthetic goals is considered. Chapter 5 examines community-based systems of aesthetics and strives to reveal the parameters by which New York singers evaluate "good" sacred quartet performance. The importance for non-professional singers to strike a balance between aesthetic and spiritual concerns is discussed. The spiritual dimensions of quartet singing are taken up in further detail in Chapter 6. Here the phenomenon of "getting happy" with the Holy Spirit is considered from the singers' perspective, and the ritualistic nature of community-based quartet performance is reviewed.

The final chapters consider the local quartet phenomenon in terms of the larger issues of southern migration, urbanization, and the evolution of African-American popular culture. Chapter 7 explores how gospel quartet performance serves as a symbolic vehicle for maintaining elements of rural southern religion and social values in a northern urban environment. Chapter 8 analyzes various transformations in quartet performance style in relation to the changing socio-economic conditions of African-American urban life and attitudes toward acculturation and identity maintenance. The complex, symbiotic relationship between community-based quartets and their professional counterparts are reconsidered in Chapter 9. Here the "folk" and "popular" dimensions of quartet singing are assessed in terms of the previous discussions of aesthetics, spiritual beliefs, and southern identity. And finally the future of sacred quartet singing and its continued study are considered in Chapter 10.

The ethnographic information that follows was gathered through observation at gospel programs and rehearsals similar to those described in the Preface. Between 1985 and 1989 I attended scores of gospel programs in black neighborhoods of Brooklyn, Queens, and Manhattan. These events varied in size from small programs in storefront churches, featuring several local groups, to larger ticket and anniversary programs, with a dozen or more groups, often including professional acts. Here I recorded the general organization of performance, the relationship between the artists and their audiences, and various facets of expressive and religious behavior through written notes and audio taping. I gathered additional data about the learning and song arranging process by attending numerous informal, private rehearsal sessions. These rehearsals were held in singers' homes, churches, or storefronts and usually lasted for several hours. They also offered excellent occasions for recording spontaneous commentary about music. Interviews with retired and active quartet singers filled out the historical picture and provided contexts for discussing the acquisition of performance skills, the organization of repertoires, the evaluation of performance, and how quartet singing fit into participants' larger social and religious philosophies. And finally, I absorbed vast amounts of information from hundreds of informal conversations with singers during programs, rehearsals, recording sessions, tours, and while socializing in our homes. The insights they shared inform every facet of the description and interpretations that follow.

Notes

1. The most comprehensive history of African-American sacred quartet singing is found in Kip Lornell, *"Happy in the Service of the Lord":Afro-American Gospel Quartets in Memphis* (Urbana: University of Illinois Press, 1988), pp. 11–35. See also Doug Seroff, "On the Battlefield: Gospel Quartets in Jefferson County, Alabama," in *Repercussions: A Celebration of African-American Music*, Geoffery Haydon and Dennis Marks, eds. (London: Century Publishing, 1985), pp. 30–53; and Kerill Rubman, "From 'Jubilee' to 'Gospel' in Black Male Quartet Singing," M.A. thesis, University of North Carolina, 1980.

2. For more on minstrelsy see Robert Toll, *Blacking Up: The Minstrel Show in Nineteenth-Century America* (New York: Oxford University Press, 1974).

3. J. B. T. Marsh, *The Story of the Jubilee Singers* (Boston: Houghton, Osgood, and Co., 1880).

4. Examples of slaves singing in harmony parts foreshadowing quartet harmony are found in Lornell, *"Happy in the Service of the Lord"*, p. 16.

5. The most comprehensive history of African-American shape-note singing is found in Doris Dyen, "The Role of Shape-Note Singing in the Musical Culture of Black Communities in Southeastern Alabama," Ph.D. dissertation, University of Illinois, 1977.

6. James Weldon Johnson, *The Book of American of Negro Spirituals* (New York: Viking, 1925), p. 35.

7. Seroff, "On the Battlefield," pp. 34–36.

8. Lornell, *"Happy in the Service of the Lord"*, p. 15.

9. Two reissued LP albums offer excellent examples of early African-American quartet singing. See William Tallmadge, "Jubilee to Gospel: A Selection of Commercially Recorded Black Religious Music, 1921–1953," John Edwards Memorial Foundation JEMF-108, LP record, 1981; and Doug Seroff, "Birmingham Quartet Anthology: Jefferson County, Alabama (1926–1953)" (Clanka Lanka CL-144.001, LP record, 1980).

10. See Ray Funk's liner notes to "Norfolk Jubilee Quartet, 1927–1938," Heritage HT 310, LP record, 1985.

11. Further information on sanctified music and its role in the development of modern gospel music is found in Lawrence Levine, *Black Culture and Black Consciousness* (New York: Oxford University Press, 1977), pp. 174–189; Anthony Heilbut, *The Gospel Sound* (2nd ed.; New York: Anchor, 1985), pp. 173–186; and Paul Oliver, *Songsters and Saints* (London: Cambridge University Press, 1984), pp. 169–189. See also Jon Michael Spencer, *Protest and Praise: Sacred Music of Black Religion* (Minneapolis: Fortress Press, 1990), pp. 153–197; and Zora Neale Hurston, *The Sanctified Church* (Berkeley, CA: Turtle Island Press, 1981), pp. 79–107.

12. David Evans, "The Roots of Afro-American Gospel Music," *Jazzforschung* 8 (1976): 119–135.

13. For further information on Thomas Dorsey and his contribution to the gospel field see Heilbut, *Gospel Sound*, pp. 21–36; Viv Broughton, *Black Gospel* (Dorset, England: Blanford, 1985), pp. 45–59; Levine, *Black Culture, Black Consciousness*, pp. 181–185; and Eileen Southern, *The Music of Black Americans: A History* (2nd ed.; New York: Norton, 1983), pp. 451–453.

14. White gospel songs, or revival hymns, became popular during the Third Great Awakening of the latter half of the nineteenth century. Its best known composers—Dwight Moody, Ira Sankey, and P. P. Bliss—wrote songs characterized by sentimental lyrics and a simple verse/chorus structure. For more on the influence of these early white gospel songs on the African-American tradition see Richard Raichelson, "Black Religious Folk Song: A Study in Generic and Social Change," Ph.D. dissertation, University of Pennsylvania, 1974, pp. 242–243, and pp. 315–317.

15. Pearl Williams-Jones, "Afro-American Gospel Music: A Crystallization of the Black Aesthetic," *Ethnomusicology* 19 (1975): 373.

16. For more on this revitalization process, see Levine, *Black Culture and Black Consciousness*, pp. 174–189.

17. Doug Seroff notes that the Famous Blue Jay Singers, the Kings of Harmony, and the Soul Stirrers were the first to experiment with "hard" gospel vocal techniques and theatrical devices during the 1930s. See Seroff, "On the Battlefield," pp. 42–43.

18. Anthony Heilbut claims that the Soul Stirrers revolutionized black sacred quartet singing by introducing the practice of double-lead singers. By the time the group reached Chicago in the late 1930s they were switching lead singers and practicing other demonstrative techniques. See Heilbut, *Gospel Sound*, pp. 78–79.

19. Johnson makes this statement during an interview with Doug Seroff. See Seroff, "On the Battlefield," p. 44.

20. For more on the contributions of Ira Tucker and Julius Cheeks see Heilbut, *Gospel Sound*, pp. 37–56, and pp. 121–130.

21. Heilbut, *Gospel Sound*, p. xxx, designates 1945 to 1960 as gospel music's "golden period." Broughton, *Black Gospel*, p. 61, identifies the period between 1945 and 1965 as the "golden age" of gospel music. Seroff, "On the Battlefield," pp. 43–45 specifies the years 1938/9 through 1960 as "the golden age of gospel quartet."

22. Seroff, "On the Battlefield," p. 44.

23. The best reviews of contemporary gospel and inspirational music are found in Heilbut, *Gospel Sound*, pp. 205–251; Broughton, *Black Gospel*, pp.

109–131; and Horace Boyer, "A Comparative Analysis of Traditional and Contemporary Gospel Music," in *More Than Dancing: Essays on Afro-American Music and Musicians*, Irene Jackson, ed. (Westport, CT: Greenwood, 1985), pp. 127–145.

24. Lawrence Levine, *Black Culture and Black Consciousness*, pp. 174–189; Southern, *Music of Black Americans*, pp. 444–454, 464–474; Pearl Williams-Jones, "Afro-American Gospel Music"; and Morton Marks, "You Can't Sing Unless You're Saved: Reliving the Call in Gospel Music," in Simon Ottenberg, ed.,*African Religious Groups and Beliefs* (Cupertino, CA: Folklore Institute, 1982), pp. 305–331.

25. See liner notes to the afore cited recordings: Doug Seroff, "Birmingham Quartet Anthology"; William Tallmadge, "Jubilee to Gospel"; and Ray Funk, "Norfolk Jubilee Quartet."

26. See Lornell, *"Happy in the Service of the Lord"*; Seroff, "On the Battlefield"; Evans, "Roots of Afro-American Gospel Music"; Burt Feintuch, "A Non-Commerical Black Gospel Group in Context: We Live the Life We Sing About," *Black Music Research Journal* 1 (1980): 37–49; Lyn Abbott, *The Soproco Singers: A New Orleans Quartet Family Tree* (New Orleans: National Park Service, 1983); and Daniel Patterson, " 'Going Up to Meet Him': Songs and Ceremonies of a Black Family's Ascent," in Ruel Tyson, Jr., James Peacock, and Daniel Patterson, eds., *Diversities of Gifts: Field Studies in Southern Religion* (Urbana: University of Illinois Press, 1988), pp. 91–102.

27. Lornell, *"Happy in the Service of the Lord"*, p. 129.

28. Personal interview with David Steward, March 16, 1986.

29. I refer to the term "thick description" as used by Clifford Geertz in reference to ethnographic description detailed enough to make the subtle cultural differentiation between a "twitch" (simple rapid eyelid movement) and a "wink" (a culture-specific kinesic signal). See Geertz, *The Interpretation of Culture* (New York: Basic Books, 1973), pp. 3–32.

30. Roger Abrahams, "The Structure of Nonsense on St. Vincent," in *The Man-of-Words in the West Indies: Performance and the Emergence of Creole Culture* (Baltimore: Johns Hopkins University Press, 1983), pp. 159–160.

31. A concise outline of this "performance centered" approach to folklore and related verbal arts is found in Richard Bauman, *Verbal Art as Performance* (Prospect Heights, IL: Waveland Press, 1977), particularly chaps. 1–5. Barre Toelken's *The Dynamics of Folklore* (Boston: Houghton Mifflin, 1979) provides an engaging introduction to the field of folklore and performance.

Performance centered folkloristics owes much to the ethnography of speaking and communication models developed by Dell Hymes. See Dell Hymes, "The Ethnography of Speaking" in T. Gladwin and W. Sturtevant, eds., *Anthropology and Human Behaviors* (Washington, DC: Anthropological Society of Washington, 1962), pp. 15–53; Dell Hymes, *Foundations in Sociolinguistics* (Philadelphia: University of Pennsylvania Press, 1974). For further applications of the ethnography of speaking model to folklore related materials, see Richard Bauman and Joel Sherzer, eds., *Explorations in the Ethnography of Speaking* (New York: Cambridge University Press, 1974).

32. Abrahams, *Man-of-Words*, p. xxiv.

33. Victor Turner, *From Ritual to Theatre* (New York: Performing Arts Journal Publications, 1982), p. 11.

34. Geertz, *Interpretation of Culture*, pp. 89–94.

35. Jeff Titon, general ed., *Worlds of Music* (New York: Schrimer, 1984), pp. 1–11.

36. See for example John Blacking, *How Musical Is Man?* (Seattle: University of Washington Press, 1973); Steven Feld, *Sound and Sentiment* (Philadelphia: University of Pennsylvania Press, 1982; 2nd ed. 1990); Charles Keil, *Tiv Song* (Chicago: University of Chicago Press, 1979); John Chernoff, *African Rhythm and African Sensibility* (Chicago: University of Chicago Press, 1979); and David Evans, *Big Road Blues* (Berkeley: University of California Press, 1982).

37. See Amiri Baraka (LeRoi Jones) *Blues People* (New York: Morrow, 1963); Charles Keil, *Urban Blues* (Chicago: University of Chicago Press, 1966); and David Coplan, *In Township Tonight!: South Africa's Black City Music and Theatre* (New York: Longman, 1985).

38. Baraka, *Blues People*, p. x.

39. My concept of music "style" has been shaped by Alan Lomax's cantometric approach to the description of oral folk music performance. While I selectively borrowed his general stylistic parameters—social organization of performers, complexity of rhythm and melody, variation in tempo and volume, degree and type of vocal ornamentation, and so on—I did not engage in the kind of analytical stylistic coding that Lomax outlines in *Folk Song Style and Culture* (New Brunswick: Transaction, 1968). The terminology used by quartet singers in describing sound structure and music style is outlined in Chapter 5.

40. George Ricks, *Some Aspects of Religious Music of the United States Negro* (New York: Arno, 1977), pp. 207–399; Tallmadge, booklet for "Jubilee to Gospel: A Selection of Commercially Recorded Black Religious Music, 1921–1953." Booklet accompanying JEMF-108 LP Record, 1980.

41. David Hufford, *The Terror That Comes in the Night* (Philadelphia: University of Pennsylvania Press, 1982), pp. ix–xxiv.

42. Hufford's method is part of a larger trend in anthropology, most recently advanced under the banner of "the anthropology of experience." For more on this approach to interpreting cultural experience, see the essays in Victor Turner and Edward Bruner, eds., *The Anthropology of Experience* (Urbana: University of Illinois Press, 1986). Bruner's introductory essay, "Experience and Its Expressions," provides a useful overview of the subject (pp. 3–32).

Chapter 1
Community and History
The African-American Church and Sacred
Quartet Singing in New York City

For the folklorist, the ethnographic study of any vernacular music begins in a community. While social scientists show little agreement as to the precise meaning of the term, "community" is used here to refer to broad human networks bound together by common social relationships, interactions, values, experiences, interests, and sense of identity. The term further implies the existence of a shared history, culture, and locality.[1] Like many forms of human social organization, communities are dynamic, fluctuating entities, and any individual usually belongs, simultaneously, to several communities.

New York's African-American sacred quartet singers readily identify themselves as members of the city's black church community. This social network consists of the working and lower middle class, African-American churchgoers of New York City whose family roots are in the rural South. Such individuals unquestionably share a common history, religion, and overall cultural experience. Racial segregation and economic disparity force most of them to live in one of several crowded black neighborhoods, thus intensifying social contact and interaction. Although the African-American church community is neither totally homogeneous nor always harmonious, its members refer to themselves as "church people," or as "southern church people." In terms of artistic achievement, gospel is unquestionably the central form of musical expression to emerge from this community in the past fifty years. Gospel music and quartet performances have in turn become focal points for the social interaction and shared values that help solidify the church community.

What percentage of New York's 1.7 million African-Americans belong to the black church community is uncertain. Many English and French speaking Afro-Caribbean people are lumped into the "black" census category, although their heritage and religious experiences differ from those of American-born black Protestants.[2] Moreover, a substantial group of middle and upper middle class African-Americans have established themselves in New York. Many of these individuals have turned away from the church or belong to larger Episcopal, Presbyterian, Methodist, or Catholic churches where worship may not include such demonstrative expressions as gospel music. And of course, there are also many working class African-Americans who simply reject the Christian church in preference for a secular world view and life style. These factors notwithstanding, the church still exerts a strong influence over the lives of many black New Yorkers.

New York City's present-day African-American population has its strongest roots in the southern migrations of the early twentieth century. But substantial numbers of African people have lived in the metropolitan area since the seventeenth century. During the colonial period most African-American residents were slaves who worked on Dutch and English farms or as domestics. Their original concentration was in Manhattan, but by the latter part of the eighteenth century both Queens and Brooklyn possessed sizable slave populations. On the eve of American independence, the 6,500 African-Americans living in these three areas constituted approximately 22 percent of the total population.[3]

After the Revolutionary War, a growing free black community slowly emerged in Manhattan, and by 1827 slavery was completely abolished in New York State. The population of the metropolitan area expanded rapidly during the nineteenth century, spurred on early by a huge influx of German and Irish immigrants, and later by the arrival of Italians and various Eastern European peoples. The black populace remained fairly small throughout this period, numbering only 60,666 (1.8%) by the turn of the twentieth century.[4] While a handful achieved success as teachers, clergy, or skilled craftspersons, most worked as laborers or domestics, living in the city's poorest and most rundown neighborhoods.[5]

New York, along with other large northern urban centers, saw its African-American population increase dramatically during the years just before the first world war, as large numbers of rural southern blacks came north for economic opportunity and escape from the oppression of southern racism. The move north was, according to critic Amiri Baraka, "an attempt to reassess the worth of the black man within the society as a whole, an attempt to make the American dream work, if it were going to. . . . the North now represented for Negroes a place where they could begin again, this time, perhaps, on more human footing."[6] Fueled by increased industrialization, the war industries, and declining economic conditions in the South, these "Great Migrations" continued almost without interruption up through the 1960s.[7]

Most of the earliest migrants came to Manhattan, eventually settling in Harlem (above 125th Street), which by the 1920s was destined to become the city's first exclusively black ghetto.[8] As Harlem began overflowing in the 1930s, and improved subway transportation facilitated travel, the city's black population began dispersing to other boroughs. The Bedford-Stuyvesant area of central Brooklyn became the center of New York's second major black ghetto, expanding rapidly during and after World War II.[9] During the 1950s the black populace continued to grow, establishing large centers in the Jamaica section of Queens and in the South Bronx.

According to the 1980 U.S. Census New York's 1.7 million African-Americans make up the largest black urban population in the United States. They are concentrated primarily in half a dozen areas of four boroughs. The central Brooklyn neighborhoods of Bedford-Stuyvesant, Crown Heights, Brownsville, and East New York are currently home to the city's largest black population. The southeast corner of Queens, including the neighborhoods of South Jamaica, Jamaica, and St. Albans, forms a second large concentration. Corona and East Elmhurst, in northern Queens, are slightly smaller, predominantly black sections. African-Americans share most of the South Bronx with the city's largest Hispanic population, and also claim much of Williamsbridge in the North Bronx. In Manhattan, Harlem remains the major black enclave.[10]

Based purely on geography and intensity of daily interaction, one might argue that there are in fact five or six African-American communities within New York City. But the southern churchgoing crowd is quite mobile, and a great deal of social interchange among neighboring boroughs seems to be the norm. This interchange is especially strong between the Harlem and South Bronx neighborhoods (which are adjacent, separated only by the Harlem River), and between the central Brooklyn and south Queens areas, which are approximately half an hour apart by car. On a typical Sunday afternoon or evening, it is quite common for people to travel extensively between the borough neighborhoods to visit family and friends, or to attend church and gospel programs. The social/geographic network is often expanded further to include black church communities in nearby Newark and northern New Jersey, Long Island, Westchester County, and Connecticut.

Turning to church history, we know that New York's eighteenth-century African-American Christians shared worship places with whites, usually sitting in special pews or galleries. Dissatisfied with the treatment of black parishioners in white churches, ex-slave Peter Williams broke ties with the John Street Methodist Church in lower Manhattan and established New York's first independent black church in 1796, the African Methodist Episcopal Church (Mother Zion). During the first half of the nineteenth century, many other African-Americans in Manhattan and Brooklyn left their white congregations to establish their own Methodist, Episcopal, Presbyterian, and Baptist churches.[11]

While little information is available about the ritual practices and musical traditions of New York's nineteenth-century black congregations, it can be assumed that their style of worship generally lacked the emotional quality of their rural southern counterparts. Arthur Paris suggests that, since northern black urban congregations were less affected by the Protestant revivals of the late eighteenth and early nineteenth centuries than were their counterparts in the southern states, the northerners were less apt to practice shouting and other ecstatic forms of behavior during their worship.[12] Franklin Frazier, also generalizing about northern urban churches, notes the emergence of an upper middle class elite who gravitated toward the Presbyterian, Episcopal, and Congregational denominations, whose services were "ritualistic and deliberate."[13] Moreover, since literacy rates were higher in the North, members of the older black urban churches probably relied more heavily on hymn books and European-style singing than did southern, rural worshipers.[14] Paris characterizes the tone of the larger, established northern churches as follows:

Thus, one sees the emergence of higher status Black congregations, especially in the North—the rise of Methodist, Presbyterian, and even Episcopal congregations among the elites as opposed to the enthusiastic Baptist practice of the rural populace—thus the gradual shift, in line with the higher-status denominational adherence, toward more decorous worship; the rejection of "gospel music" in favor of sober European hymns, and so on.[15]

Paris and Frazier argue that, as the established middle and upper middle class black churches made accommodations to the changing urban environment, they, like their white counterparts, took on a more secular tone.[16] The large, restrained congregations of the northern churches shared little with the waves of southern migrants who were accustomed to small, intimate churches that stressed fundamentalism and more emotional, demonstrative worship. This was most certainly the case in New York. The Reverend R. C. Lawson, who founded Harlem's Church of Christ, Apostolic Faith in 1919, is described by historian Gilbert Osofsky as a preacher who "decried the lack of emotionalism in the more established urban churches—copying the 'white man's style' he said—and offered recent migrants a touch of fire and brimstone and personal Christianity characteristic of religion in the rural South."[17] Bayard Rustin, a civil rights activist who lived in Harlem during the 1930s, told writer Jervis Anderson:

The big churches were too calm. Here were these people coming from the South. They were used to screaming and yelling at services, rolling in the aisles, and speaking in tongues. But the middle classes which supported the big churches were now beyond all these things.[18]

To meet this need for more emotional, "down-home" religion, many southern migrants turned away from the established urban churches and founded their own. The proliferation of small, so-called "storefront" churches in northern urban areas during the 1920s and 1930s was a direct response to southern migration as well as to the rise of the Holiness and Pentecostal denominations.[19] In these smaller, independent churches, southern African-Americans found the traditional style of worship, the fundamentalist interpretation of the Bible, and the more intimate sense of community they had become accustomed to in the rural South. The mushrooming of storefront churches in New York during the 1920s led W. E. B. Du Bois to suggest that perhaps Harlem was "overchurched."[20] Osofsky claims that during this period a full two-thirds of Harlem's 150 black churches were housed in small storefronts.[21] Reporting for the Federal Writers Project in the late 1930s, Wilfred Bain listed 150 storefront churches in Harlem and claimed that many more operated in private homes and lofts, where "the opportunity for emotional worship is comparatively unrestricted."[22] A survey of Brooklyn churches compiled in the 1930s found sixty-one storefront churches in the Bedford Stuyvesant area alone.[23]

The musical and worship practices of these urban storefront churches unquestionably grew out of southern traditions; emotionalism and full congregational participation were the norm. An early Baptist storefront in the San Juan Hill district of Manhattan, established by Virginia-born George Simms, was described as a "shouting" church where there was "much noisy getting of religion."[24] Of Harlem's storefront churches, Osofsky notes:

Services were fervent, loud and boisterous as members felt the spirit of the Lord and shouted and begged for His forgiveness. Tambourines sometimes kept up a rhythmic beat in the background and heightened the emotionalism to a state of frenzy. Neighbors of one storefront church sued the congregation for "conducting a public nuisance." The "weird sounds" which emanated from the building, they complained, seemed like a "jazz orchestra."[25]

This highly emotive style of worship, complete with rhythmic music and Spirit-induced shouting, was undoubtedly strongest among the various Holiness and Pentecostal groups, although the smaller urban Baptist congregations were gradually adopting a more demonstrative tone. The "weird sounds" and "jazz" music emanating from these storefronts was most certainly the sanctified music described in the previous chapter. Characterized by syncopated rhythms, heavy instrumental accompaniment, improvised vocals, and generous use of blues and jazz elements, this music became the mainstay of the smaller Holiness and Pentecostal churches. As the migrants swelled in numbers, some of the storefront congregations were able to move into larger, more conventional church dwellings, where members continued to practice their traditional southern-derived music and worship. These new urban churches provided a receptive environment for the gospel music that emerged during the 1930s and the gospel quartets of the 1940s.

Decades before the term "gospel" was used to describe African-American religious music, tight harmony singing in small ensembles known as quartets was popular in New York City and in other urban areas with sizeable black populations. In commenting on New York's black musical scene at the turn of the twentieth century, Mary White Ovington notes "men form male quartets that for five or ten dollars furnish an evening's entertainment."[26] Although such entertainers probably concentrated on secular love songs and minstrel pieces, their repertoires undoubtedly included spirituals and sacred jubilee songs.

By the late nineteenth century New York had become a center for commercial entertainment and was attracting many of the country's best minstrel and vaudeville acts. These shows often featured tight harmony singing groups, known as quartets, whose repertoires included secular novelty pieces, humorous songs, popular ballads, and parlor songs, as well as sacred spirituals and jubilee songs.[27] In 1894, an outdoor extravaganza in New York entitled "Black America" featured no fewer than sixty-three quartets, the best of whom were noted for their exquisite harmonizing on plantation numbers and operatic selections.[28] The Old Standard Quartette of Richmond, Virginia, was one of the most popular of these early minstrel/vaudeville quartets to record and entertain in New York's vaudeville theatres and exclusive social clubs.[29] The Four Harmony Kings, another popular New York-based vaudeville quartet, won considerable acclaim for their tight harmony singing in the early 1920s Broadway productions of *Shuffle Along* and *Chocolate Dandies*.[30] By the late 1920s, tight harmony quartets specializing in minstrel and vaudeville material were heard regularly on New York radio stations.

As early as the 1870s, jubilee groups from the southern black colleges such as Fisk University and the Hampton Institute were appearing in New York City.[31] Because these choirs and quartets rendered African-American spirituals and folk songs in a style that owed much to the Western European choral tradition, their audiences tended to be upper middle class concert-goers, both black and white. While many college-trained quartets visited New York to perform and record, at least one, the Utica Jubilee Quartet, actually relocated to the city in 1926. The group had been formed at the Utica Normal and Industrial Institute of Utica, Mississippi. Once in New York the singers took engagements in large churches, concert halls, and schools, performing mostly for white audiences. But on occasion they did sing in the larger middle class black Manhattan churches, including St. Mark's Methodist, Abyssinian Baptist, and Salem Methodist. In 1927 they began broadcasting over WJZ of the National Broadcasting Company, becoming the first African-American quartet to be featured on a nationally syndicated radio program.[32] Marshall Cole, an original member, recalls that the Utica Jubilee Singers presented a variety of traditonal spirituals, jubilee songs, and hymns, as well as secular plantation songs, work songs, and occasional blues or minstrel-derived numbers. The singing, he reflects, was "close harmony, concert style," delivered in a "formal" manner with no hand clapping and minimal body movement.[33] The recordings the group made during the late 1920s and early 1930s are characterized by sweet barbershop harmony with occasional hints of rhythmic syncopation. Surprisingly, the Utica Jubilee Singers were consciously excluded from Godrich and Dixon's standard discography of blues and gospel recordings. Evidently the group was too European-sounding for these authors' tastes; they dismissed the Uticas' recordings for exhibiting too "little distinctive Negroid content."[34] But this judgment is unwarranted. Although the group stressed precise harmony and clean vocal diction, songs like their classic 1928 recording of "Oh Mary Don't You Weep" unquestionably swung with a light rhythmic pulse typical of African-American jazz of the era. The Utica Jubilee Singers toured Europe several times and traveled extensively in America, singing mostly at white universities and middle class black and white churches.[35] In 1929, writing for New York's foremost black newspaper of the period, *New York Age*, critic Lucien White reviewed their "recital of Spirituals and Negro folk songs." While impressed with the quartet's well-honed vocal harmony, White was offended by the singers' stage antics, which included the dramatic enactment of song texts:

Without qualifying this opinion, which concerns the musical quality of their renditions, I must take exception to the tendency in several instances to give to their interpretations an atmosphere of buffoonery that is uncalled for, and as out of place as it is unnecessary. For instance, in singing "Little David," it was not necessary for Mr. Cole to simulate the flopping of buzzard wings, nor for the first tenor to ape a dice shooter. As to the latter, it is a distinct perversion, for when the Negro spirituals were created, in the travail and bitterness of ..?.. attendant upon slavery, there were no dice shooters.[36]

Given these biases, it is not surprising that the rougher, folk-style community quartets of this era were ignored by New York's black newspapers.[37]

Another influential quartet to emerge from the black university tradition was the Southernaires. Formed in New York, the group was led by tenor singer Homer Smith, a veteran of the Utica Institute and Wilberforce College quartets. The Southernaires made their first public appearance at the Williams International C.M.E. Church in Harlem in 1929, and the following year began broadcasting on radio stations WMCA and WRNY. The group was scouted by NBC, and in 1933 debuted "The Little Weather-Beaten Whitewashed Church," their legendary weekly radio show that was broadcast nationally on the NBC Blue Network for more than ten years. The show featured traditional spirituals and secular southern folk songs, as well as ser-monettes, recitations, and guest speakers who emphasized the achievements of African-Americans. In addition to their radio work, the Southernaires recorded a number of outstanding sides for the Decca label in 1939 and 1941 and performed frequently at churches and theaters throughout the New York area. The Southernaires' smooth, barbershop harmonizing and rhythmic arrangements of spirituals undoubtedly influenced many black vocal groups of the 1930s and early 1940s, and introduced white radio audiences to the magnificent black university style of quartet singing.[38] Their wide-spread appeal is attested to by reporter Alvin Goldstein, who noted in the *Detroit Tribune* in 1939:

Among the admirers of the Southernaires are the deeply devout and those who have strayed from the path of religious observance, the saint and the sinner, and every loyal member and sympathizer of the Barbershop Quartet Singing Society of America, who could no more resist the soft, close harmony of the four Negro singers than a swing addict could close his ears to Benny Goodman's clarinet.[39]

Two years later these sentiments were echoed by a review in the *New York Amsterdam News*:

Originally their [the Southernaires] audiences were almost exclusively colored because of the nature of their work, but the good word spread and the caliber of their performances made them the ambassadors of the spiritual to all races. Their appearances have been given in theaters, churches, concert halls, and in public organization meetings of all sorts. Their work is nationally loved because it is so essentially American.[40]

Closely related to the black university quartet and choir groups were the professional choruses. These were large choral groups of formally trained singers whose repertoires included substantial numbers of African-American spirituals and folk songs. Two of the country's most influential choruses, the Hall Johnson Choir and the Eva Jessye Choir (formerly the Original Dixie Jubilee Singers) were founded in Harlem in the mid-1920s. Both became extremely popular and were in constant demand for concert, theater, and radio appearances. Like the university choirs and quartets, these choruses helped popularize smooth, semi-classical arrangements of spirituals, and undoubtedly reached a large black audience through their regular radio braodcasts.[41]

During the 1920s and 1930s, New York's status as a media center also attracted many groups who were not formally trained in European singing, including some of the South's finest church-based quartets. Many of the major record companies who recorded early jubilee and gospel quartets on separate "race" series maintained studios in New York. These included Columbia, Okeh, Victor, Gennett, Paramount, Decca, and the American Record Company.[42] Three of Virginia's finest groups, the Norfolk Jubilee Singers, the Peerless Four, and the Silver Leaf Quartet, visited the city regularly during the 1920s to record, broadcast, and perform in large churches.

The Norfolk Jubilee Singers, led by bass singer Len Williams, actually relocated in New York in 1937 after a successful recording session for Decca. These splendid records led critic Ray Funk to characterize the Norfolks as "one of the tightest vocal groups in the country." The voices merge perfectly in a smooth, precise harmonic blend, then bounce, weave and swoop before coming to final rest in a chord of stunning blues intonations. The sound is light and clean, pulsing with an infectious rhythmic swing that explains why the group sometimes released secular recordings under the name of the

Norfolk Jazz Quartet. The group's ability to sing blues and jazz as well as spiritual material helped them find steady radio work on New York's WGL and WMCA stations. They also performed at churches and secular night spots, changing their name to the Four Alphabets for club dates, which included stints at the Famous Door on Broadway and at Jones Beach, Long Island. As the Norfolk Jubilee Singers they sang regularly at church functions alongside local quartets like Thurman Ruth's Selah Jubilee Singers and Alton Griffin's Golden Crown. Tenor singer Raymond Smith recalls that in 1938 the Selahs and Norfolks packed a church so full that the fire department had to be called out. Ruth claims that Len Williams actually suffered a fatal heart attack during a song battle with the Selahs at a local New York church.[43]

The popularity of the Norfolk Jubilee Singers and the Southernaires was eclipsed only by another group from Norfolk, the legendary Golden Gate Quartet. Unquestionably the most influential and commercially successful jubilee quartet of the pre-war era, the Golden Gates also made New York their home during the late 1930s and the 1940s. The group was formed in 1930 by Willie Johnson and Henry Owens, two graduates of Norfolk's Booker T. Washington High School Glee Club. The quartet embarked on a number of southern tours and in 1936 began broadcasting over WIS in Columbia, South Carolina. The following year the Gates recorded for the Bluebird label, and in 1938 moved to New York where they were contracted by CBS to do a weekly radio show. In addition to their radio work they sang at a number of New York's most prestigious black night spots, including the Cafe Society, where they performed mostly popular and jazz material.[44] Their radio broadcasts and early recordings on the Bluebird and RCA labels were instrumental in shaping the rhythmic style of spiritual singing that became popular among quartets in the 1930s. Indeed, Johnson and the Golden Gates are credited with injecting East Coast quartet singing with a renewed rhythmic intensity through a technique Johnson referred to as "vocal percussion."[45] The Gates attacked their words in a short, clipped, staccatto fashion resulting in a highly percussive effect; they literally aimed to "play" their voices like percussion instruments. The four vocal parts interlocked to produce a swinging pulse, owing much to the syncopated rhythms of the sanctifed church and jazz bands of the era. Listen, for example, to the group's classic 1937 recording of the spiritual "Jonah." The voices explode in a chorus of tightly meshed polyrhythms, then recede to a throbbing hum while Johnson narrates the tale of Jonah and the whale in a lilting, syncopated style not un-

like that of a jazz soloist.[46] Further, the Gates were masters of highly
refined harmonies and smooth vocal diction; their sound reflected an
urbane sophistication rarely heard among non-university trained
quartets of the time. Although the group rarely performed in black
churches, their recordings and radio broadcasts reached a broad national audience. This led the Golden Gate Quartet to become, according to Doug Seroff, "the most widely imitated and most commercially
successful of all twentieth-century religious quartets."[47] A number of
local New York groups, including Thurman Ruth's Selah Jubilee
Singers, cite the Golden Gates as an important influence on their own
style.

By 1940, due primarily to the pervasive influence of resident
groups like the Southernaires, the Golden Gate Quartet, and the
Norfolk Jubilee Singers, New York emerged as the leading north-
eastern center of jubilee quartet singing. The best-known groups enjoyed not only the support of black church audiences but also that of
select white listeners, who purchased their records, followed their radio broadcasts, and occasionally attended their performances at clubs
and concert halls.

While the professional groups who relocated in New York for commercial purposes have been well documented, little is known about
the city's community-based quartets during the pre-war era. Although written references are scarce, a review of the Radio Feature
section of the *Amsterdam News* during the late 1920s and early 1930s
reveals that "quartets" and "jubilee singers" received a good deal of
air time. For example, radio listings during this period include not
only programs by the nationally known Fisk Jubilee Singers and the
Southernaires but also performances by the Wandering Boys Spiritual Quartet, the Slow River Negro Quartet, the Metropolitan Four,
the Eveready Jubilee Singers, the Excell Jubilee Singers, the Eastern
Star Quartet, and the Grand Central Red Caps Quartet. It is pre-
sumed that these latter groups consisted of local New York singers.
In a 1932 review, members of the Grand Central Red Caps Quartet
were praised for their outstanding musical ability and original arrangements of "spirituals, old southern melodies and folk songs, and
occasionally popular tunes."[48] Two years later another review mentions that the YMCA Quartet performed selections including "Lul-
laby," "Hope I'll Join the Band," "Ezekiel Saw the Wheel," and "You'd
Better Mind" at a Musical and Tea held at the Baptist Education Center on West 129th Street in Harlem.[49] Some of these groups were
probably formally trained singers, and some obviously sang both religious and secular material.

While sketchy written reports suggest that sacred quartet singing was indeed popular in New York by the early 1930s, it is the recollections of older quartet singers that provide the strongest historical evidence. Thurman Ruth, founder of Brooklyn's most celebrated jubilee quartet, the Selah Jubilee Singers, migrated to New York from Pomaria, South Carolina, in 1924. Although he had been reared a Methodist, soon after his arrival Ruth joined St. Mark Holiness Church, a Pentecostal church located at 1980 Fulton Street in Brooklyn. Sometime in 1927 or 1928 he organized several other young members of the church's choir into a vocal group called the Selah Jubilee Singers. The group sang every Sunday evening, under the watchful eye of the church's pastor, Mother Lambert, who quickly realized their potential for attracting a large crowd. Black religious programming was just beginning to become popular on the radio at this time, and soon she had her Sunday night services, including musical selections by the Selahs, broadcast on several Brooklyn radio stations. Due to Mother Lambert's protective nature, the Selahs performed almost exclusively in their home church for nearly ten years. The group eventually recorded for Decca, and in the early 1940s began touring as full-time professionals, reaching their peak of popularity through their daily broadcasts on WPTF, a 50,000 watt radio station out of Raleigh, North Carolina.[50]

Thurman Ruth's memories of New York's early quartet scene are vivid. He recalls that on the Selahs' first anniversary—in 1928 or 1929—they invited some of the city's best non-professional quartets to St. Mark Holiness. One of these was a group known as Eastern Star, a Brooklyn-based quartet who were all members of the Cornerstone Baptist Church. The Eastern Star was evidently Brooklyn's top quartet prior to the Selahs, and Ruth recalls that the group broadcast regularly on Brooklyn radio stations. Deacon Brent, the Eastern Star's leader, was married to a woman who sang lead for another well known Brooklyn group, the Excelsior Four,[51] whose bass singer and leader, James Johnson, was known throughout New York's church community as a quartet voice trainer. Neither of these groups recorded, but according to Ruth both were admired for their intricate harmony style and often fared well in song contests. The Grand Central Red Caps—who evidently worked as porters in Manhattan's Grand Central Station—were another group on the program. Ruth recalls them as being "real high class," a quartet that read from musical arrangements and sang both spirituals and pop songs. The three sides the group recorded for Columbia in 1931 are characterized by complex harmonies and smooth diction, suggesting formal vocal training.[52] Ten years later the group would win a song competition

sponsored by the New York Chapter of the Society for the Preserva-
tion and Encouragement of Barber Shop Quartet Singing in America, only to be denied the chance to compete in the national finals
because of racial discrimination.[53] Also performing on the Selahs'
first anniversary concert were Harlem's Sunset Jubilees and Golden
Leaf Quartet, the Peerless Four from Norfolk, Virginia, and the Orange Jubilee Singers from East Orange, New Jersey.[54]

Another singer who was active in New York's early quartet scene is
Charlie Storey. Born in Camake, Georgia, and reared in Zebelon,
North Carolina, Storey moved north with his family in 1928. His father, a Pentecostal minister, eventually founded the Mt. Zion Pentecostal Church in Brooklyn. As a teenager, Storey began singing in his
father's church, both as a soloist and in a small ensemble that included his three brothers and two sisters. By the early 1930s this
group, known as the Storey Family, was often invited to sing at other
Brooklyn churches on Sunday afternoon and evening programs. Storey recalls that the most popular quartets in the 1930s were the Selah
Jubilee Singers, the Eastern Star, the Harmonizers of Brooklyn, and
the Rolling Stone Jubilee Singers. The older groups, like the Eastern
Star, tended to sing slow, reserved, harmonizing songs, while Ruth's
Selahs were known for their snappy jubilee style. Storey left his family group in the early 1940s to join the Jubilee Stars, a popular Brooklyn quartet that recruited him after their lead singer was drafted into
military service. Several years later he joined the Brooklyn All Stars,
and eventually started his own group, Charlie Storey and the All
Stars, which he still heads today.

One of Harlem's earliest and most noteworthy quartets was the
Golden Crown, led by The Reverend Alton Griffin.[55] A native of Eliz-
abeth City, North Carolina, Griffin migrated to New York in 1931.
Soon after his arrival he joined a local group known as the Galilee
Four that he heard performing at a Baptist church near his home.
Several months later, he was asked to fill in for an evening with the
Golden Crown, whose members, according to Griffin, were so im-
pressed with his lead singing skills that they "stole" him from the
Galilee Four. The Selah Jubilee Singers and the Sunset Jubilees were,
Griffin recollects, the top local quartets in the 1930s. Harlem also
boasted some excellent female quartets in those days, including the
White Rose, the Galilee Sisters, and the Nazareth Singers. Other local
quartets Griffin remembers singing with included the Excelsiors, the
Evening Star, the Starlights, and the Alphabetical Four. Little is
known about this last group, other than that they were organized in
New York sometime in the mid-1930s by the Reverend Emory Johnson and Curtis Brown. They did, however, make a series of exquisite

recordings for Decca between 1938 and 1942.[56] Unfortunately Griffin's Golden Crown never recorded, although they did broadcast on several radio stations, including a weekly program live from the 1939 World's Fair. While most of their performing was in churches in Harlem and Brooklyn, they did some out-of-town touring during the 1930s.

William Kelly, a native of Mt. Holly, North Carolina, arrived in Harlem in 1939. He went to work in a fur factory on Seventh Avenue, where he and several co-workers organized a quartet known as the Harmonaires. The group's first anniversary, Kelly recalls, was celebrated at the Golden Gate Auditorium in 1941. According to Kelly, the most popular quartets at that time were the Selah Jubilee Singers, the Golden Crown, the Sunset Jubilees, and Clara "Georgia Peach" Hudmon and Her Gospel Singers. Hudmon was obviously impressed by the Harmonaires, because she eventually recruited them as her back-up group and recorded several exciting sides with them for the Apollo label in 1946. The Harmonaires toured briefly with her, but soon disbanded. Kelly eventaully become the bass vocalist for the Sunset Jubilees, a group he sang with until his death in 1989.

A picture of New York City's pre-war quartet scene emerges from the reminiscences of these older singers. Clearly, by the early-1930s, there were a number of community-based quartets singing spiritual music in Baptist, A.M.E., and various Holiness and Pentecostal churches in the black neighborhoods of Harlem and Bedford-Stuyvesant. Quartets did most of their performing at Sunday afternoon and evening church services that were relatively small affairs meant to benefit host churches. Song contests, where two or more quartets would compete, were also becoming popular at this time. The best local groups broadcast on radio, and occasionally traveled out of town for a weekend engagement.

Precisely what these early spiritual and jubilee groups sounded like can only be surmised, although a handful of commercial recordings and a few lucid memories offer important hints. Ruth recalls that the first New York quartets he heard—the Eastern Star and the Excelsiors—sang mostly "harmony songs," which he describes as being slow, sweet, and "full of chords." Most of the early Selah Jubilee Singers songs were in this slower style, although at some point in the 1930s they adopted the quicker-paced, syncopated jubilee singing that the Golden Gate Quartet was beginning to popularize. Charlie Storey recalls that most of the quartets in the early 1930s sang slower songs, emphasizing tight harmony, and it was not until the late 1930s that the faster jubilee style became widespread. Reverend Griffin describes the early singing of his Galilee Four as follows:

They did more what I call barbershop. Barbershop chords in those days—the common name was harmonizing. They didn't do a lot of slapping and jumping and hollering. They did a little of it, but it wasn't their thing. Their thing was to see how close they could sing a song [how close the harmony parts could get], songs like "Lead Kindly Light." And they could sing those songs—in those days it sounded like organs, when they got together with the voices. You know, barbershop chords.[57]

With the Golden Crown, Griffin sang these slower, harmonizing songs, as well as faster jubilee numbers that he describes as "chopped-up stuff" with "punch." It appears that by the mid-1930s sacred quartets in New York were singing two types of songs: slower, harmonizing pieces, which were particularly popular in song contests, and faster, syncopated jubilee numbers. While some groups such as the Selah Jubilee Singers used a piano accompaniment, most groups sang a cappella.

It was the jubilee style that dominated the first substantial group of commercial recordings made by New York based quartets—those by the Alphabetical Four in 1938 and the Selah Jubilee Singers in 1939. The Alphabetical Four's renditions of "Get on Board Little Children" (1938) and "Do Not Pass Me By" (1940), along with the Selah Jubilee Singers' "Traveling Shoes" (1939) and "What More Can Jesus Do?" (1939) make use of the syncopated rhythms, the percussive vocal attack, the spoken/sung narration, and the well-developed, moving bass line that characterize the jubilee quartet style. The strong influence of the Golden Gate Quartet and the Norfolk Jubilee Singers is obvious on these early recordings, suggesting that the light, lilting style of the early New York quartets owed much to the Virginia tidewater quartet tradition. It is unclear why more of the barbershop style, harmonizing songs were not included in these early recordings. Perhaps the style was no longer in vogue by the late 1930s, or the tastes of the white-controlled record companies fell toward the snappier jubilee songs. Hints of this longer-phrased, harmony style are heard on the Selah Jubilee Singers' recordings of "I Will Guide Thee" (1941) and "My Lord's Gonna Move This Wicked Race" (1942).

The performance styles of these early harmonizing and jubilee quartets were markedly different from those of the post-war gospel groups. Songs were kept short, rarely exceeding three minutes. Groups simply introduced the title of their piece and sang, without the lengthy narrations and emotional testimonies popularized by the later gospel quartets. Ruth and Griffin recall that their groups would stand in a semi-circle, with the lead on one end and the bass on the other. While the lead singer might occasionally walk out into the congregation, in general the singers stood straight in their places. "In those days they sang flat-footed," recalls Charlie Storey, "there wasn't much moving, they never got excited." Griffin adamantly claims that the older groups did not stamp, clap, slap their thighs, jump around, holler, preach, or run around the way they do today. Reflecting back on the older groups he saw in North Carolina and those he heard when he first arrived in New York City in the early 1930s, Griffin states:

Back in those days, when the master of ceremonies called a group to sing, if you watched them, when they got up, most of them got up like there was a board nailed across them. When the first one made a move, everyone of them would get up, just like soldiers. Most of them would stand with their hands behind their back. They stood straight. Now you didn't see much moving. You might see the one that was singing lead, he might turn his head a little bit. Other than that they just stood there. They weren't emotional what-so-ever.[58] .

Griffin admits that his Golden Crown was not quite so strictly regimented; there was some movement during faster jubilee songs, and as the lead singer, he might walk—but never run—through the audience. However, at song contests where they were performing slower harmony songs, they always stood straight and still.

Audience behavior at these early quartet programs is difficult to assess. Older singers agree that congregations often responded to their singing with emotional clapping and shouting, but not with the level of intensity that characterized post-war quartet performances. Reverend Griffin recalls that women used to throw their pocketbooks when they "got happy." He recollects that once a woman became so joyful in the Spirit that she actually tackled him in the middle of a song. The degree of audience response tended to vary according to church denomination. Charlie Storey recalls that when he first began singing in Brooklyn, Baptist and Methodist congregations seldom reacted with strong emotion, while the Pentecostal and Holiness people were more apt to succumb to the Spirit and shout and even holy dance during a performance. The marked differences between Baptists and Pentecostals eventually diminished, as Storey notes:

Baptists used to be like more dignified people. They go there [to church] with rouge and powder on their face, and they didn't have to wipe their face until they got back home. But the Pentecostal people, they were washed down with perspiration. With the Spirit, they would shout, and they would really give God thanks. . . . Now, it used to be, when you walked into a Baptist church, you wouldn't see no shouting. If you saw somebody shouting in their church it was like a strange thing. But then the Pentecostals got to having such a good time, feeling the Spirit and all—and some of the Pentecostals joined the Baptists, they might have a husband there, maybe a mother there. And the Pentecostals got the Baptist people to moving too. Sometimes you can't tell which is which.[59]

It seems, then, that whether competing with another group in a song contest or singing at a small church benefit the primary goal of New York's pre-war quartets was to render impeccable harmony. They stood flat-footed and sang only sacred songs—usually older spirituals, folk hymns, and jubilee songs—although their presentations occasionally included humorous numbers where lyrics were acted out. While they appreciated demonstrative audience reaction, first and foremost the singers were concerned with showing off their vocal virtuosity. It should be noted that these early sacred quartets did not refer to themselves nor their music as "gospel." Rather, they called themselves "spiritual" or "jubilee" singers. The term "gospel," according to Ruth, did not come into fashion until the early 1940s.

As the second world war drew to a close, the popularity of African-American sacred quartet singing in New York increased significantly, and the music began to undergo dramatic stylistic changes. The jubilee and spiritual quartets gradually evolved into gospel quartets, and became, at the same time, more commercially oriented and more evangelical in tone. By the mid-1940s singers recall a marked upsurge in quartet activity in Harlem and Bedford Stuyvesant, as James Baldwin's description of post-war Harlem would suggest:

Harlem is filled with churches and on Sundays it gives the impression of being filled with music. Quartets such as my brothers' travel from church to church in the fashion of circuit preachers, singing as much for the love of singing and the need for practice as for the rather indifferent sums collected for them which are then divided. These quartets have "battles of song," the winning team adding, of course, immensely to its prestige, the most consistent winners being the giants in the field.[60]

With post-war prosperity came the rise of small independent record companies and all-black radio stations, offering African-American musicians exciting new commercial opportunities. In New York, Joe Bostic's "Gospel Train"—broadcast every Sunday morning on radio station WLIB—became the city's most popular gospel program. With the Golden Gate Quartet's recording and broadcasting career serving as a model for success, many New York black church singers formed quartets with dreams of becoming professional singers. Few, of course, attained such lofty goals, and most performed only in churches and auditoriums in the New York metropolitan area.

Meanwhile, quartet singing programs became larger and more commercial, often featuring out-of-town acts along with local performers. By the early 1940s Thurman Ruth was booking groups like the Dixie Hummingbirds and the Pilgrim Travelers into Harlem's Golden Gate Auditorium. More and more programs were held in auditoriums and larger churches. Revenues increased as ticket sales replaced free will offerings. By the 1950s, national promoters were booking "Gospel Extravaganzas" in New York's larger venues, featuring up to half a dozen professional soloists and quartets.

During the 1940s New York's older jubilee and spiritual quartets began to absorb elements of sanctified music and Dorsey's new Chicago-based gospel sound. Modern gospel compositions were added to the groups' repertoires. Lead vocalists took on more prominent roles, as they became masters of stunning vocal acrobatics and extended improvisation. And there were other changes: the evolution of a basic antiphonal call and response structure between the lead singer and the background vocalists; a movement of the background harmony into a higher register through the inclusion of a high tenor part and the eventual replacement of the bass vocal by an electric bass guitar; an increase in rhythmic intensity (often emphasized by the use of electric guitar and drum accompaniment); and the adaptation of a more evangelical tone to the overall performance, including the injection of emotional testimonies, snatches of preaching, and Spirit-induced movement and dance. The highly impassioned, shouting-style practices of post-war gospel quartets stood in marked contrast to those of the more sedate jubilee and spiritual quartets who emphasized close harmony. The difference is made clear by writer and singer James McGowan, who was active in a young Brooklyn quartet, the Starlight Toppers, in the mid-1940s:

We made an important distinction in the way the spirituals (sacred songs) were sung. One way was called Gospel, and the other was called Jubilee. To us, Gospel was a particular style of singing, and not necessarily the music itself. And the same with Jubilee. The groups that sang Gospel style depended, for the most part, on a single lead voice. Sometimes the arrangement would call for two lead voices—usually alternating. During the often emotional presentation of the song, the two lead singers would have a singing duel—"battling it out.". . . The background voices in these Gospel groups supported and accompanied the lead singer in such an individualistic manner that they could very well be considered another voice in themselves. In their supportive roles they could be subdued and sweet. Yet, in their accompaniment roles they could sing a phrase or hum a tune with such an emotional drive that they could move a congregation to a frenzy. . . . In Jubilee singing, on the other hand, the emphasis is on producing a total group sound; not dependent on a lead singer. Thus, the Jubilee groups concentrated more on harmony, using musical dynamics and striving for a sweetness of blend. The famous Golden Gate Quartet exemplify this style.[61]

It is essential to note that New York was not the only, nor by any means the first, major urban area to see its jubilee/harmonizing quartet singers embrace the more emotional, hard gospel style. Sacred quartet singing in other cities, both north and south, underwent similar changes in the late 1930s and early 1940s. Moreover, New York apparently lagged behind Chicago, Birmingham, Dallas, and Houston, where the hard gospel sound was catching on by the late 1930s. Undoubtedly the popularity of influential jubilee groups such as the Southernaires, the Golden Gates, and the Norfolk Jubilee Singers, who performed and broadcast from New York during the 1930s and into the 1940s, contributed to the tenacity of the jubilee style among the local New York quartets.

The complex web of social and historical forces that led to the eventual transition to gospel quartet singing in New York will be explored more fully in Chapter 8. At this point it will suffice to note that stepped-up southern migration during and immediately following World War II, the increasing economic independence of the rapidly expanding black urban working class, and the continued influence of the urban Holiness movement spurred on the proliferation of sacred quartets and catalyzed the emergence of the hard gospel style.

The rise of hard gospel quartet singing and the subsequent decline of the jubilee/harmonizing style in New York City was a gradual process. Members of the Golden Gate Quartet continued to record and broadcast their magnificent jubilee style singing throughout the 1940s, before eventually expatriating to Europe, where they are based today. Ruth's Selah Jubilee Singers also maintained a basic jubilee style, although they did add some gospel compositions to their repertoire, and their repetitive background phrasing on slower songs certainly suggests some gospel influence. The group continued to record and tour during the 1940s, eventually resurfacing in New York in the 1950s to cut several rhythm and blues tunes under the name the Larks.

The military draft split up some of New York's older groups, including Alton Griffin's Golden Crown. Others, such as the Eastern Star and the Excelsiors, continued to sing in the local churches, presumably maintaining their older jubilee/harmonizing style. The Jubilee Stars of Brooklyn recorded several jubilee sides on the Haven label in 1947 before disbanding. The Sunset Jubilees made a number of jubilee-style recordings in the late 1940s, before gravitating toward the more gospel-inflected sound they have today. The Sunsets, like many sacred quartets of this period, maintained both jubilee and gospel style songs in their active repertoires. Eventually, however, most groups either adopted elements of the newer gospel style or faded from the scene, replaced by younger exponents of the hard gospel quartet style that would dominate the post-war years.

By the 1950s gospel-style quartet singing was firmly entrenched in New York City. Although New York never produced gospel quartets as distinguished as the Chicago-based Soul Stirrers or the Philadelphia-based Dixie Hummingbirds, a number of noteworthy groups emerged. The Brooklyn All Stars, the group Charlie Storey sang with in the early 1950s, began touring professionally shortly after recording for the Peacock label in 1958. Led by bass singer Thomas Spann, the group eventually made Greensboro, North Carolina, its home base, and continued to tour and record into the 1970s. Equally successful were the Harlem-based Skylight Singers. The group's 1946 recordings for the Bibletone label were straight jubilee, but by the time they recorded for Lamp and Vee Jay in the mid-1950s they were singing in an exuberant hard gospel style. For example, their 1957 arrangement of "What Shall We Call Him?" opens with the Reverend James Williams feverishly chanting a sermonette over a dense background of organ and guitar improvisations, and finally swells to a crescendo of fiery sanctified rhythms. Sam Abrahams, who also sang lead, recalls that the group toured well into the 1960s before coming off the road and cutting back to local engagements and weekend travel.[62]

Another popular Brooklyn-based quartet was the Mighty Gospel Giants. Formed in 1949 under the tutelege of the Reverend Haywood Ellison, this group of young singers established themselves as one of the city's stellar exponents of the new gospel quartet style. In 1956 and 1957 they recorded a series of hard gospel classics for the Tuxedo and Savoy labels respectively. Their 1957 rendition of "Jesus Will Meet Me" showcases Eugene Tune, a hard-edged tenor who soars above a frenetic vocal bass line, relentless chorus, and churning organ accompaniment. The Giants began touring for extended weekends, but family commitments kept group members from pursuing full-time singing careers.[63] Two other highly regarded semi-professional quartets, the Brooklyn Skyways and the Singingaires, were organized in the late 1950s and remain active today. Hundreds of other quartets and small groups were formed at this time, most of whom sang locally and never recorded.

It would be difficult to fix the exact point in time when community gospel quartet singing reached its height of popularity in New York. Some local singers note a gradual decline in the tradition since the 1970s, citing increased competition from choirs and changing trends in the commercial gospel industry. However, small singing ensembles, identifying themselves as quartets or gospel groups, continue to flourish in the 1990s. These groups maintain a strong following among the older churchgoing crowd who grew up when quartet singing dominated the commercial gospel world. While many younger singers join choirs, a fair number of quartets featuring singers in their teens and twenties continue to appear, suggesting that the tradition is in no danger of disappearing. The number of quartets active today is difficult to estimate, as new groups are constantly forming while older ones disappear.

At present, on any given Saturday evening or Sunday afternoon, numerous quartet-dominated gospel programs are held throughout black neighborhoods in Brooklyn, Queens, Manhattan, and the Bronx. At such programs an array of quartet styles are represented. Most groups consisting of middle-aged, southern-born singers perform in a post-war, hard gospel fashion with electric guitar, bass, keyboard, and drum accompaniment. A growing number of the younger, New York-born singers, have become drawn to the contemporary gospel sound popularized by commercial stars like Al Green, Andrae Crouch, and the Winans. Some younger quartets have adopted this smoother approach to vocal and instrumental shadings that lacks the fiery testimonies and evangelical tone of their hard gospel predecessors. But most of the city's more popular young quartets take pride in their ability to sing both the hard and contemporary gospel styles, a versatility that lets them reach congregations of all ages. And finally, a diminishing number of older quartets continue to sing in the more traditional, pre-war jubilee/harmonizing styles that are rarely heard on commercial recordings or radio.

This historical sketch serves as a prelude for further examination of New York's present-day gospel quartet scene. The information and interpretations in the chapters that follow are based on my observations and conversations with numerous singers whose groups represent a broad spectrum of quartet styles. While I will draw freely from the performances of many groups, my understanding of quartet singing is shaped most deeply through contact with a dozen groups. *The No Name Gospel Singers* of Brooklyn reflect the strongest ties to the older jubilee/harmonizing tradition. Although the group has only been singing together since the early 1980s, their eighty-year-old leader, the Reverend Floyd King, has rigorously trained the four younger singers in very traditional, tight harmony, a cappella singing. *The Faithful Harmonizers* of St. Albans, Queens, formed by the Reverend Vernella Kelly in the 1940s, also maintain an older-sounding a cappella style, although Kelly's shouting vocals and steamy preaching reflect the influence of more modern, hard gospel singing. *The Golden Jubilees* of Jamaica, Queens, organized in the early 1940s by Clifton Johnson, use a strong moving bass vocal and syncopated singing slightly reminiscent of the older jubilee style. *The Heavenly Tones* of Brooklyn, organized in the late 1950s by Jordan Evans, continue to sing a cappella, but feature emotive lead vocals and a dominant call and response song structure characteristic of post-war gospel music. Charlie Storey's latest group, *The All Stars* of Brooklyn, along with the new *Sunset Jubilee Singers* of New York, perform in a straightforward hard gospel style. Both groups, however, continue to use a bass vocalist, depend on minimal instrumentation (guitar), and favor the older church hymns and gospel songs. While all six of these groups fall toward the traditional end of the spectrum in terms of current gospel styles, they enjoy strong support in the city's local churches, where they regularly perform gratis or for a nominal fee. Members of these groups tend to be older, ranging in age from early fifties to mid-seventies.

The shouting, hard gospel style with full band accompaniment is represented by *The Mighty Gospel Giants*, organized by the Reverend Haywood Ellison in 1949, *The Brooklyn Skyways*, formed by Willie Johnson in 1958, and *The Wearlyand Singers* of Corona, Queens, organized by David Steward in the early 1960s. These groups, whose members vary in age from mid-thirties to late fifties, depend on guitar, bass, and drums to back their vocalists. They are known for impassioned performances that include a great deal of preaching, testifying, holy dance, and other spirit induced movement. Three younger groups, *The Ecstatistics* of the Bronx (formed in 1972), *Little Wonder Boy and the Spiritual Voices* of Brooklyn (formed in 1961, with current young lead singers added in the early 1980s), and *The Golden Sons* of Brooklyn (formed in 1981) perform hard gospel songs, but also specialize in smoother contemporary pieces. All six of these groups fall into the semi-professional category, since they do approximately half their singing in local New York churches, and half out-of-town on weekend trips. While these groups are paid for most appearances, no members depend on performing for their entire livelihood.

Collectively these groups represent a microcosm of New York's present-day sacred quartet scene, one encompassing a variety of styles from the traditional to the contemporary. The musical experiences of these men and women are typical of those countless African-American church singers who, for generations, have chosen to make small group harmony singing a vital part of their social and spiritual lives. The fascinating story of how and why they sing inevitably leads us "back home" to the rural South, where, as youngsters, they learned musical skills and a repertoire of songs that formed the foundation of their later singing careers.

Notes

1. For an informative review of the subject, see Colin Bell and H. Newby, *Community Studies: An Introduction to the Study of the Local Community* (London: G. Allen and Unwin, 1971). Also see Judith Gardner and Richard McMann, *Culture, Community, and Identity* (Detroit: Wayne State University Press, 1976).

2. Some estimates suggest there are up to a million English and French speaking Afro-Caribbean people in New York City. This number, however, includes many illegal immigrants, who were not counted in the 1980 census which placed the city's entire "black" (southern and Afro-Caribbean) population at 1.7 million. See Constance Sutton and Elsa Chaney, eds., *Caribbean Life in New York City* (New York: Center for Migration Studies in New York, 1987), p. 15.

3. Edgar McManus, *A History of Negro Slavery in New York State* (Syracuse, NY: University of Syracuse Press, 1966), p. 199.

4. Mary White Ovington, *Half a Man* (New York, Hill and Wang, 1911, 1969), p. 5.

5. For more on New York City's postbellum African-American community see Gilbert Osofsky, *Harlem: the Making of a Ghetto* (New York: Harper and Row, 1971), pp. 3–16; Harold Connolly, *A Ghetto Grows in Brooklyn* (New York: New York University Press, 1977), pp. 3–44; and Ovington, *Half a Man*.

6. Baraka, *Blues People*, p. 96.

7. For further history of southern African-American migration, see George Davis and Fred Donald, *Blacks in the United States: A Geographic Perspective* (Boston: Houghton, Mifflin, and Company, 1975), pp. 29–93.

8. See Osofsky, *Harlem*, for an informative history of New York's oldest and most notable African-American neighborhood.

9. See Connolly, *A Ghetto Grows in Brooklyn*, for further details of the African-American settlement in Bedford-Stuyvesant.

10. The following population statistics for African-Americans in New York City are found in *Demographic Profile: A Portrait of New York City From the 1980 Census* (New York: City of New York Department of Planning, 1983):
Brooklyn, 689,626 (30.9% of borough population)
Bronx, 348,744 (29.8% of borough)
Queens, 341,059 (18% of borough)
Manhattan, 290,218 (20.3% of borough)
Staten Island, 24,480 (7% of borough)
total city, 1,694,127 (24% of city)

11. See Osofsky, *Harlem*, pp. 9–16; and Ruth Ann Stewart, *Black Churches in Brooklyn* (New York: Long Island Historical Society, 1984) for further background on early African-American churches in New York City.

12. Arthur Paris, *Black Pentecostalism: Southern Religion in an Urban World* (Amherst: University of Massachusetts Press, 1982), p. 9.

13. Franklin Frazier, *The Negro Church in America* (New York: Schocken, 1964), pp. 55–57.

14. Lawrence Levine reports that most upper middle class blacks favored congregational or choral arrangements of standard hymns or selected spirituals or "anthems." See Levine, *Black Culture and Black Consciousness*, p. 188. This is not to suggest that there was no emotionalism or traditional African-American singing in any northern urban churches. Frazier points out that the lower middle class Baptist congregations tended to exhibit more "emotional participation" in their worship. Frazier, *The Negro Church in America*, p. 57. One suspects that these congregations would have sung spirituals and folk hymns, probably using stylistic devices common to the rural black tradition such as call and response, heterophony, improvisation, vocal ornamentations, and body percussion.

15. Paris, *Black Pentecostalism*, p. 11.

16. See Frazier, *The Negro Church in America*, pp. 54–57; and Paris, *Black Pentecostalism*, pp. 7–30.

17. Osofsky, *Harlem*, p. 145.

18. Jervis Anderson, *This Was Harlem: A Cultural Portrait, 1900–1950* (New York: Farrar, Straus and Giroux, 1982), p. 248.

19. Most of the small storefront churches were Baptist, Methodist, or some form of Holiness/Pentecostal. See Paris, *Black Pentecostalism*, pp. 25–30; Benjamin Mays and Joseph Nicholson, *The Negro's Church* (New York: Institute of Social and Religious Research, 1933), pp. 94–113; and Arthur Fauset, *Black Gods of the Metropolis* (Philadelphia: University of Pennsylvania Press, 1944), pp. 1–13.

20. Quoted from Osofsky, *Harlem*, p. 144.

21. Ibid., p. 144.

22. Wilfred Bain, "Store Front Churches," in Federal Writers' Project, 1936–1941 Manuscripts, Schomburg Collection, New York.

23. George H. Hobart, *Survey, Bedford Stuyvesant Area, Brooklyn, New York, Spring, 1938, for the Bedford Stuyvesant Ministers Association and the Brooklyn Church and Mission Federation* (Brooklyn, 1938).

24. Quoted in Anderson, *This Was Harlem*, p. 24.

25. Osofsky, *Harlem*, p. 145.

26. Ovington, *Half a Man*, p. 69.

27. Writing in the early 1890s, black comedian and minstrel entertainer Ike Simond lists a dozen quartets that were active in the minstrel field at that time. Ike Simond, *Old Slack's Reminiscences and Pocket History of the Colored Profession from 1865–1891* (Chicago, 1891), p. 26.

28. Tom Fletcher, *One Hundred Years of the Negro in Show Business* (New York: Burdge, 1954), p. 97.

29. Doug Seroff, "Polk Miller and the Old South Quartette," *John Edwards Memorial Foundation Quarterly* 18 (1982): 147.

30. Johnson, *American Negro Spirituals*, p. 36.

31. For a brief history of the Fisk Jubilee Singers see J.B.T. Marsh, *Story*

of the Jubilee Singers. The Fisk Jubilee Singers' trips to New York City during the early 1870s are recounted on pp. 24–39. See also Southern, *Music of Black Americans*, pp. 225–228.

32. Ray Funk and Peter Grendysa, "The Southernaires," *Goldmine* (June 1985): 16, 24.

33. Personal interview with Marshall Cole, January 4, 1989.

34. John Godrich and Robert Dixon. *Blues and Gospel Records, 1902–1942* (Essex, England: Storyville Publications, 1982), p. 790.

35. Samuel Buchanan, "A Critical Analysis of Style in Four Black Jubilee Quartets in the United States," Ph.D. dissertation, New York University, 1987, pp. 54–55.

36. Lucien White, "Utica Singers and Davis Sisters in Concert at New Rochelle High School Before Large Assemblance," *New York Age*, March 9, 1929, p. 7.

37. A review of the music sections of the *Amsterdam News* and *New York Age* from the early 1920s through 1940 shows that a great deal of attention was paid to recitals of classical and symphonic music and choral group presentations by trained African-American artists. By the 1930s more space was given over to reviews of jazz and Broadway musicals. The few sacred quartets that received notice were those who sang in a more formally trained, European style or who had achieved substantial commercial success such as the Golden Gate Quartet and the Southernaires. The community-based quartets were generally ignored.

38. Funk and Grendysa, "Southernaires."

39. Quoted in Kerill Rubman, "From 'Jubilee' to 'Gospel,' " p. 40.

40. "Southernaires Got Started Eleven Years Ago in Church," *Amsterdam News*, January 25, 1941, p. 21.

41. For more on these professional choruses see Southern, *Music of Black Americans*, pp. 411–415.

42. For a discussion of these early quartet recordings see Godrich and Dixon, *Blues and Gospel Records, 1902–1942*, pp. 15–27.

43. Quotes and summary from Funk, liner notes to "Norfolk Jubilee Singers."

44. See Doug Seroff, "Biographical Notes on Some Performers." In Tallmadge, booklet for "Jubilee to Gospel," pp. 13–14.

45. Seroff, "On the Battlefield," p. 44.

46. The Golden Gates 1937 recording of "Jonah" has been reissued on "Jubilee to Gospel," JEMF-108, 1981.

47. Seroff, "On the Battlefield," p. 44.

48. *Amsterdam News* (July 6, 1932), p. 8.

49. *Amsterdam News* (April 21, 1934), p. 7.

50. See Doug Seroff, "The Whole Truth About T. Ruth," *Whiskey, Women, And—* 9 (July 1982). For listings of the Selah's early recordings see Godrich and Dixon, *Blues and Gospel Records, 1902–1942*, pp. 642–643.

51. This group should not be confused with the Excelsior Quartet from Norfolk, who recorded for Okeh in the early 1920s. Ruth claims they were two different groups.

52. The Grand Central Red Cap Quartet was perhaps the first New York based quartet to record. The three sides they recorded for Columbia in 1931 were "My Little Dixie Home," "They Kicked the Devil Out of Heaven," and

"Oh Sinner, Whatcha Gonna Do?" The university quartet and vaudeville influences are evident. See Godrich and Dixon, *Blues and Gospel Records 1902–1942*, p. 279

53. *Amsterdam News*, July 12, 1941, p. 11.

54. The Sunset Jubilees are evidently the same New York group that eventually recorded for Duke, Hub, Haven, and Okeh in the late 1940s. Ruth claims that the Golden Leaf Quartet was a New York based group led by a man named Bullit—not to be confused with the Alabama's Golden Leaf, who recorded for Brunswick in the late 1920s. Ruth suggests that local quartets often took their names from better known groups who had already recorded.

55. Griffin's Golden Crown should not be confused with the Norfolk group by the same name who recorded for Okeh in the late 1920s. Evidently these were two different groups.

56. See Godrich and Dixon, *Blues and Gospel Records*, pp. 38–39.

57. Personal interview with the Reverend Alton Griffin, April 24, 1986.

58. Personal interview with the Reverend Alton Griffin, May 1, 1986.

59. Personal interview with Charlie Storey, April 18, 1986.

60. James Baldwin, *Notes of a Native Son* (Boston: Beacon, 1955), p. 77.

61. James McGowan, *Hear Today! Here to Stay! A Personal History of Rhythm and Blues* (St. Petersburg, FL: The Sixth House, 1983), pp. 7–8.

62. Personal interview with Sam Abrahams, April 6, 1986.

63. Personal interview with Edward Cook, August 24, 1988.

3. The Selah Jubilee Singers (Thurman Ruth, lower left), c. late 1930s. Photo courtesy of Thurman Ruth.

4. The Rolling Stone Jubilee Singers, c. late 1930s. Photo courtesy of the Reverend John Leak.

5. The Norfolk Jubilee Singers, c. late 1930s. Photo courtesy of Ray Funk.

6. The Golden Gate Quartet, c. 1940s. Photo courtesy of Ray Funk.

7. Charlie Storey and the All Stars, 1945 (Charlie Storey, bottom center). Photo courtesy of Charlie Storey.

8. The Skylight Gospel Singers, c. 1950. Photo courtesy of Ray Funk.

Chapter 2
God Gave Me a Song
Learning and Repertoire Formation

When the renowned African-American scholar James Weldon John-son noted that nearly any four young black men could form a quartet because they found the harmony parts "naturally," he was comment-ing on the ubiquity of quartet singing in black southern communities during the 1890s. His choice of words, however, unfortunately rein-forces the stereotype that African-Americans possess some mysteri-ous, innate musical ability that simply emerges without prior experience or training. Contemporary students of culture and behav-ior would be quick to dismiss such an assumption as preposterous. And yet these kinds of racial myths persist in many sectors of Ameri-can life, often reinforced by insensitive mass media. Anthropologists argue convincingly that any musical activity, be it the ability to har-monize in four parts, to produce complex polyrhythms, or to orna-ment the melody lines of an a cappella ballad, is a learned behavior transmitted socially in culturally specific situations. Obviously there is nothing "natural" about the way African-American quartet singers find their vocal parts. Rather, like members of any cultural group, African-Americans learn the rudiments of vocal style primarily by lis-tening to and imitating other singers and occasionally with the assis-tance of written transcriptions. From an early age, southern black children absorb the fundamentals of harmony singing and other es-sential musical techniques in the home, church and school. Once young singers actually join a quartet they receive rigorous instruction during regular rehearsal sessions. Eventually the serious singers be-come part of an ongoing rehearsal process in which singing skills and

songs are collectively transformed into an active performance repertoire.

New York's African-American church singers believe that the ability to sing gospel is a gift bestowed on certain individuals by God. Just
as some are anointed to preach the Word, so others are called to
spread God's message through song. As Charlie Storey remarks:

Some people are born with different gifts. Some are born with the gift of
laughing, and some with the gift of talking. And some people are born with
the gift of preaching, and some with the gift of singing. In my family, I have
a sister who's an elder preacher, and a brother who's an elder preacher. My
father was a bishop. But my gift was singing. Now they can preach, because
that was their calling. But they can't sing like Charlie can, because that's my
calling. Singing is my gift.[1]

While quartet singers acknowledge the divine source of their talent, they also recognize that performing in a group with other singers
requires instruction, practice, and above all discipline. Indeed, they
would scoff at the notion that any four African-Americans without
proper training could "naturally" produce good quartet harmony.
The Reverend Floyd King, who has trained quartet singers for more
than fifty years, explains it this way:

Now some folks can just sing. But harmonizing together and just singing are
two different things. If you sing with nobody with you, it could sound good.
But if you get somebody else with you, you get more voices, then you have
to be taught how to do it. One can't sing one way and another voice off another way. You've got to be taught how to harmonize together, or the voices
won't blend. See, I teach my fellas how to blend.[2]

Upon reflection, most singers agree that certain experiences in
early life helped develop and accentuate their God-given abilities.
The church, family, and school are the three institutions in which
most southern-born quartet singers gained their initial singing experience. The first two are closely related. Since attending church in the
rural South was a family affair, most youngsters began singing in
church congregations, in choirs, or in Sunday schools with their parents, siblings, and other extended family members. It is common for
family singing groups to organize through a church or for a group
formed at home to become affiliated with the church. This was certainly the case with Charlie Storey's family group. The members began singing in the home, and by the time they moved to Brooklyn in
1928 they were competent enough to perform regularly in the

church pastored by their father. Clifton Johnson of the Golden Jubilees recalls that his family group from Lumberton, North Carolina, was actually formed in church:

In church, in Sunday school—a bunch of us kids just started harmonizing. And we heard different groups, so we decided to do the same thing, and that's how we got started. When we first started it was my two sisters, my brother-in-law, and me. We sang together for three or four years. I was fourteen then [1926]. It was the Holy Cross Baptist Church, so we called it the Holy Cross Jubilees. We sang plain a cappella, back then we called it "harmonizing."[3]

Wilburt Huntly of the Faithful Harmonizers recalls that his family group, which he joined at age ten, practiced in his home once a week, and sang in small country churches in the area of Monroe, North Carolina. Jordan Evans and Mason Young of the Heavenly Tones, and Bill Dobson of the No Name Gospel Singers began singing in similar family/church groups in their respective home communities of Eastcuff, West Virginia, Rocky Mount, North Carolina, and Kenansville, North Carolina.

This tradition continues today in New York City, as members of teenage quartets are often related, or belong to the same church. It is even common for pre-teen groups to form spin-offs from the Sunday school choir and to make special appearances on gospel programs held at their home church. Although such groups often lack musical experience, they are always greeted with a great deal of enthusiasm and encouragement. The church offers a safe, supportive atmosphere for the transmission and development of musical skills.[4]

In the South, many young quartet singers gained early musical experience in their public schools. Billy Walker of the All Stars recalls growing up in rural Arkansas:

My first singing was in public school. I used to lead the chorus, and run the chapels and assemblies. And when they had a play or something, several of us kids would sing a solo or something. We had a glee club, and then four of us started harmonizing. That was the first group I sang with. That was in 1951 or 1952—we won the championship in the National Farmer's Association Quartet Competition. We sang more or less gospel music, stuff like "Ezekiel Saw the Wheel" and "King Jesus Is a Listening." Like barbershop-style singing.[5]

William Kelly recollects similar experiences in North Carolina in the late 1920s:

I used to sing with a little school group in Mt. Holly High School, a quartet. We sang only gospel. We would sing in the morning, when we would have the devotional service. Two or three times a week they would call on us to sing. And sometimes we would sing at other schools, when they put on some type of program, like on a Friday night. We had no real name, so they'd just say "We'll now have a number from the ninth grade quartet."[6]

It is difficult to pin down exactly how young singers in the church, school, or home first learned their musical skills and songs. Casual imitation probably accounted for a good deal of their early learning experiences.[7] This usually occurred first in church settings, where group and congregational singing provided an initial exposure to spiritual and gospel music. In church, youngsters absorbed the basic elements of pitch, rhythm, harmony, vocal techniques, and body movement simply by watching, listening, and eventually repeating the behaviors of older singers. In the same way they learned other aspects of worship that resurface in gospel performance—preaching, testimony, chanted prayer and holy dance. A similar process undoubtedly went on in the home, where fledgling singers imitated the vocal patterns of their parents and older siblings who were accomplished singers.

Those who demonstrated "God-gifted" promise often received more formal instruction from recognized teachers. Shape-note singing was taught in some southern black churches. Many informants recall that their parents and grandparents "sang by note." While some of today's older singers remember learning shape-note singing as children, none of them retained the skill, and use of written notation is completely absent in the community today. However, early experience with shape-note singing probably introduced young singers to the basic concepts of four-part harmony, which forms the foundation of quartet singing.[8]

Choirs and glee clubs usually had a designated leader whose job it was to organize and instruct the singers. With the exception of shape-note singing, this teaching was done strictly by aural means. Similar techniques were practiced by instructors known as quartet trainers. These individuals, who were generally self-taught or who acquired their skills aurally from older trainers, specialized in teaching the basics of four-part harmony singing. They helped younger singers find their parts, blend their voices, and arrange songs. In the case of family groups, a parent or older relative often served as an informal instructor, assisting youngsters in finding voice parts and arranging songs. Jordan Evans, Mason Young, and Randy Swain, of the Heavenly Tones, all recall that their mothers taught them the fundamentals of harmony singing. The Reverend Floyd King recalls that his uncle, Samuel King, trained the first quartet that Floyd sang with in

Alabama, the Shilo Jubilee Singers. Samuel King, although a member of this group, also trained other young quartets and eventually passed this skill on to his nephew Floyd. Alton Griffin remembers that Melvin Smith, of Deep Creek, Virginia, trained young quartet singers in the area during the 1920s. Like King, Griffin later developed this talent and periodically trained quartet singers after he moved to New York.

According to King and Griffin, the first thing a trainer does with a group of young singers is to assess their vocal range, to make sure that each individual is singing the part that best suits his or her voice. This technique, known as "placing voices," is explained by King:

I start them with a scale. That scale is one, two, three, four. I do it in soprano (lead), tenor, baritone, and bass. So I go with these fellas quite a while, and I figure which one is best fitted for whatever voice. They have to listen to me and I tell them where to fit in. Otherwise it's like putting a screw in the wrong nut, the wrong screw won't go in the wrong nut! So if a man tells me he sings tenor, and I find out he can do soprano and lead best, then I'll put him on lead. So I'll do this until I get these boys so they can harmonize and know what they are doing.[9]

Once the voices are placed, the trainer helps the group members find their individual singing parts and eventually blend them together into the correct harmony. A successful trainer must possess a wide vocal range, including lead, tenor, baritone, and bass, to demonstrate parts to singers who may be having problems. And finally, trainers help shape a song's overall arrangement, making suggestions about harmony, vocal phrasing, rhythm, tempo, and so forth. On occasion, a group might bring in a song and ask the trainer to work up an arrangement on the spot. Griffin recalls his experiences with James Johnson, a well-known quartet trainer in Harlem during the 1930s:

If you had a song, he would arrange it and explain it for you, just how it would go. See, he would arrange the voices to fit the song—there are many different ways to set up a song, so it's not sung in the same manner. He'd set up the voices, and put an arrangement on the song for that particular group. See, another group couldn't sing it exactly that way, because they didn't have the voices.[10]

The use of quartet trainers was evidently quite widespread in the South, but with the exception of Johnson, no specific trainers were mentioned in connection with the New York community.[11] In many cases, however, one member of a quartet is recognized for her or his skills at placing voices and arranging songs, and such individuals often assume prominent roles during rehearsal sessions. This phenomenon occurred in the South, too, according to many informants who sang with quartets at an early age and who credit one of the older group members for teaching them the basics of harmony singing and voice control.

By the time most southern-born singers arrived in New York, they had acquired the basics of group singing through early experiences in the home, church, and school. Imitation and repetition of behavior patterns in large group settings and more individual instruction by a parent, trainer, or older singer account for this transmission process. But learning for quartet singers is a continuous process, and even the most experienced strive to hone individual vocal skills and tighten group harmony at their regularly scheduled practice sessions, known as rehearsals.

Most active gospel quartets rehearse at least once and sometimes twice a week. Rehearsals tend to be private in nature, usually held in a home, church, or workplace. For example, the Heavenly Tones and No Name Gospel Singers rehearse in small Brooklyn storefront churches, Charlie Storey's All Stars in his furniture store, the Wearylands in the basement of a hair-styling shop, and the Brooklyn Skyways in Willie Johnson's bus garage. During these sessions new songs are introduced and arranged, previously learned material is practiced and improved, and songs are organized for upcoming programs. Members usually take time to review their upcoming performance schedule and to discuss various business matters, such as the purchase of new uniforms and equipment or the state of the group's treasury. Sessions often end with socializing and refreshments. Rehearsals also show elements of sacred ritual as the singers are called to order by an opening theme and prayer and always close with a group prayer or benediction.

Between the opening prayer and closing benediction, a great deal of musical activity takes place. Initially a group warms up by running through several familiar numbers. One member may point out a mistake or trouble spot he or she noticed during a recent performance, and the group will pause to smooth over the harmony or correct an error in vocal phrasing, articulation, rhythm, or timing. If the group has an important engagement in the near future, an entire rehearsal session may be given over to planning and practicing the specific songs for that performance. A series of three or four songs will be performed as if an audience were actually present. In addition to the songs, the group also rehearses the chanted song introductions, the dramatic gestures and lyric enactments, and, occasionally, the choreographed dance routines. The entire program may be run through several times, until all aspects of song, speech, and movement are finely tuned to the group's satisfaction. Substantial portions of many rehearsal sessions are also spent learning new songs. A new piece, whether an original composition or a song gleaned from a recording or hymn book for rearrangement, is always brought into the rehearsal by an individual member—usually the person who intends to sing the lead vocal. The song will be considered the property of this individual, unless he or she chooses to turn the song over to another lead singer, making the song's ownership somewhat equivocal.

While the learning and rearranging process is complex, patterns do emerge. First, the song leader introduces the song to the group through a tape-recorded version, or simply by singing the basic melody through several times. The leader continues to sing while the background singers gradually fall in behind. The chorus and verses are repeated several times until everyone becomes familiar with the song's basic melodic, harmonic, and rhythmic framework. At this point the singing stops, and the members start making decisions about where the song will be pitched and which background singers will sing which harmony parts (high tenor, tenor, background lead, baritone, bass, etc.). This process is exhausting and time consuming; the group may run through a song a number of times, with different members switching parts, until they reach a satisfactory configuration.

Next, the actual background vocal parts are arranged. While the song leader often makes the initial suggestions about how the harmony should sound, the background singers are ultimately responsible for creating and coordinating their own vocal parts. In many groups there is one member—usually the unofficial trainer or song arranger—who will suggest individual vocal parts for any member who is having problems.[12] Like the previously described trainers, these singers possess sensitive ears for pitch and harmony, as well as a wide vocal range; their skills enable them to demonstrate the whole gamut of vocal parts. Hank Channel of Charlie Storey's All Stars, Phil Johnson of the Spiritual Voices, David Steward and Earl Ledbetter of the Wearyland Singers, Ralph Moragne of the Sunset Jubilees, Robert Todd of the Heavenly Tones, and the Reverend Floyd King of the No Name Gospel Singers all serve in this capacity. While these individuals act as the experts in placing voices and assisting in the formation of vocal parts, they do not completely dominate. The overall process is quite democratic and all members contribute ideas.[13]

Once the voices are placed and the background parts are roughly formulated, the group works on perfecting its harmonic chords. Ralph Moragne refers to this step as "teaching chords." He instructs members to hold one chord while he makes minor adjustments until they achieve the desired vocal "blend"—that is, until the voices are precisely in pitch and perfectly balanced in terms of dynamics and timbre. The goal is to get the voices as close as possible without any of the separate parts running into each other to produce unison rather than harmony singing. The group then practices the transitions from one harmonic chord to the next. Called "turns" or "changes" by the singers, these are critical points where all voices must move tightly together to maintain the correct harmony and blend. They may rehearse a particularly difficult passage dozens of times, often at a reduced tempo, until they turn the chord correctly. Finally, special sections of songs, such as introductions, endings, and improvised "drive" or "gospel" segments (see Chapter 4), are isolated and run through.

At this point the group will usually sing the entire song through several times, making periodic stops to adjust the harmony, tempo, vocal phrasing, articulation, and so forth. Here, the lead melody line may be slightly modified, while words, phrases, and entire verses may be altered, dropped, or added. Again, the song leader and background arranger tend to exert the most influence, but all members are free to add ideas and criticisms, and usually do. During this time the musicians will solidify the exact chordal arrangements, rhythmic patterns, and melodic riffs they will use to accompany the singers.

This entire song learning process is rarely completed in a single rehearsal session. A singer will often simply take ten minutes toward the end of a session to introduce the basic melody of a song to the group and to get some notion of how their accompaniment might sound. The other singers may tape the song and listen to it during the week, and make suggestions at the next rehearsal.[14] During this second session the group will work the song seriously for an hour or more, formulating the basic arrangement. They will probably spend several additional sessions fine-tuning the song before it becomes part of their active performance repertoire. A group may spend months working out an arrangement before going public with a song, and occasionally will simply drop a number that cannot be arranged to their satisfaction.

In a given rehearsal, a group practices a number of songs in various stages of development. The members spend some time tightening up the previously learned material that forms the core of their active repertoire. Arrangements for one or more recently introduced songs will be worked through in some depth, and finally a new song may be offered for the group's consideration. In this way groups maintain a set of well polished songs for public performance while they continually learn new material that may eventually enter into their active repertoire.

Rehearsals constitute an essential component of quartet music culture. In addition to providing older singers with the opportunity to maintain their singing skills, sessions serve as valuable training grounds for younger singers who wish to master the rudiments of quartet singing. While older singers and song arrangers tend to adopt the role of strict disciplinarian, they are generally patient with and supportive of new and younger singers. This transmission of musical skills is especially striking in groups with cross-generational membership, such as the Spiritual Voices, the Sunset Jubilees, the Brooklyn Skyways, Charlie Storey's All Stars, the No Name Gospel Singers, and the Wearyland Singers.

Rehearsals also offer a creative environment in which the song leader, the background song arranger, and the other group members can work cooperatively on innovative song arrangements. While the process is not without its tensions, the final song arrangement represents a fascinating balance of individual and communal concerns. The All Stars, for example, might refer to a song that Charlie Storey brought to the group as "Charlie's song," while attributing the overall song arrangement to the entire group.

But more than singing is practiced in rehearsals. The dramatic recitations and testimonies that connect songs are also rehearsed, with the lead singer (chanter/reciter) working out appropriate call-and-response patterns with the background singers and musicians to accompany her or his chanted words. The lead singer experiments with various gestures and dramatic actions, while the background singers choreograph appropriate hand movements and dance steps. Other special effects, such as switching leads mid-song, or having two leaders work together in a call-and-response pattern, are also arranged. The fact that groups rehearse speech and movement, as well as singing, suggests that all three modes of expression contribute significantly to the success of a gospel performance.

Rehearsal sessions also provide important opportunities for socializing and camaraderie, particularly before and after the actual singing takes place. Singers often come early and stay late. Social relationships are formed that often grow into life-long friendships. As a result, quartet members who have sung together for years form something of an extended family and are always ready to support one another in times of social or financial crisis.

And finally, the religious aspects of the rehearsal cannot be overlooked. Sessions always begin and close with a prayer and often include a Bible reading. The spiritual intensity of most rehearsals is remarkably high. In spite of the small audience, usually consisting of family members and friends, the singers often became quite emotional during particularly moving renditions of songs. Various manifestations of Spirit-induced joy are commonly exhibited, including shouting, hand waving, and murmuring "Thank you Jesus" at the end of a song. While singers rarely "fall out" into total states of ecstasy the way they do in church, they unquestionably "feel the Spirit" during a good session.

Not only are quartet rehearsals occasions for perfecting singing techniques and learning new songs: they also offer opportunities for intimate fellowship and spiritual solace. In this light the non-professional African-American quartet emerges as an important social unit whose purpose extends beyond simply making music, as Brenda McCallum suggests: "In many cases, the quartet group was, simultaneously, an extended social and familial network, a brotherhood or fraternal organization, a beneficial society and mutual aid association, and a convocation for spiritual fellowship."[15] Men and women join in rehearsal to share their gifts of song, to reaffirm their faith, and to enjoy one another's fellowship—all in preparation for public performance and spiritual mission.

The development of a gospel quartet repertoire is a fascinating process that draws from diverse sources. Along with essential musical skills, the words and melodies to many songs are learned in a singer's early experiences in church, at home, and in rehearsal sessions. As expected, the older folk hymns, spirituals, and revival songs are typically the first pieces to enter into the active repertoires of southern-born singers. Such compositions, referred to in the community as "old church songs," remain popular among today's New York quartet singers. For example, the Heavenly Tones simply rearranged the classic spiritual "Steal Away to Jesus" for five voices. The lead singer improvises short phrases while the background singers (whose vocalizations appear in parentheses) carry the primary lyrics.

I believe I'll—   (steal away to Jesus)
   oh I'll—   (steal away home)
Come on and—   (steal away to Jesus)
   oh yea—   (steal away home)
You ought to steal—   (steal away to Jesus)
   who-ah-ah-ah—   (steal away home)
Oh I—   (ain't got long to stay here)
   no I—   (ain't got long to stay here)

You know my God—   (my God, He calls me)
Well Lord—   (He calls me by the thunder)
You know the trumpet sounds—   (trumpet sounds, within my soul)
Soul,   (soul)
Soul,   (soul)
    (oh, oh, oh ain't got long to stay here)
Oh Lord—   (ain't got long to stay here)
Lord we ain't got long—   (ain't got long to stay here)
Oh Lord—   (ain't got long to stay here)
Oh Lord—   (ain't got long to stay here)
Mother's gone on—   (ain't got long to stay here)
We're down here by ourselves—   (ain't got long to stay here)
Oh Lord—   (ain't got long to stay here)
Oh Lord—   (ain't got long to stay here)
We're living down in a mean world—   (ain't got long to stay here)
Oh Lord—   (ain't got long to stay here)
Oh Lord—   (ain't got long to stay here)[16]

Other old church songs that retain strong currency among the local New York quartets are "Amazing Grace," "Swing Low, Sweet Chariot," "When the Saints Go Marching In," "Old-Time Religion," "This Little Light of Mine," "Pass Me Not Oh Gentle Savior," and "Leaning on the Everlasting Arms." While most singers remember segments of these songs from their childhood church experiences, they will often refer back to written hymnals or collections such as the *Gospel Pearls* to check words or to add additional verses.

Live performances by other gospel groups and quartets are important resources for songs and stylistic practices. Borrowing ideas from another group, however, is a sensitive issue, since original songs and innovative arrangements are highly valued, and no group wants to be accused of "stealing." Most singers will readily admit that they do get ideas for songs by listening to other groups, but qualify this point by explaining that such songs are rearranged into their own style. Thurman Ruth recalls that the Selah Jubilee Singers first heard "I Want Jesus to Walk Around My Bedside" during a live performance by the Soul Stirrers in Texas. Ruth and his group went on to rearrange and later record the piece. Rebert Harris of the Soul Stirrers, on the other hand, contends that the Selah Jubilee Singers simply "stole" the song from them.[17] In the post-war years, with numerous professional groups coming in and out of New York to record and perform, this borrowing (and subsequent rearranging) of songs became a frequent occurrence.

The electronic media were already pervasive forces in American life by the time the singers in this study had come of age. Radio broadcasts and recordings of sacred quartets had reached a broad African-American audience by the 1930s and served as valuable sources of songs and musical style. Not surprisingly, it is difficult to get specific information from singers on this issue, as they wish to avoid accusations of song theft. But the evidence suggests that pre-war recordings and radio broadcasts by the Southernaires, the Golden Gate Quartet, and the Norfolk Jubilee Singers provided the early New York quartets with a great deal of song material. In the post-war years, recordings by the Dixie Hummingbirds, the Soul Stirrers, the Swan Silvertones, and the Sensational Nightingales were particularly influential. Although many of the older folk hymns and church songs sung by the local New York groups were originally learned in church or at home, a significant percentage of the post-1930 gospel song repertoire came directly from commercial record-ings and radio broadcasts or from live performances by professional groups.

The Faithful Harmonizers' version of "King of Kings," apparently a rearrangement of a 1960s Dorothy Norwood recording, presents an outstanding example of how popular, mass-disseminated music can be reappropriated by community-based artists. Squarely in the post-1930 gospel mold, the song's lyrics take the form of a personal testimony, and by example urge the listener to seek spiritual salvation through Christ (the "King of Kings") in order to be transformed from a state of sin to one of grace:

Well it was a long, long time ago,
    my heart was troubled within,
My head bowed down in sorrow,
    the Devil had me wrapped in sin,
Lord I started out to seek salvation,
    then I had a hard time resisting temptation,
Well I kept on searching till I found,
    the King of Kings,
        the King of Kings.

And then He— (changed my heart so I could love right)
And He— (changed my mind so I could think right)
And He— (changed my tongue so I could talk right)
And He— (changed my feet so I could walk right)
Let me hear you say— (yes)

Let me hear you say—   (yes, yes)
Let me hear you say—   (yes, I found the King of Kings,
                              the King of Kings)[18]

Today a single song may enter a group's active repertoire through a combination of sources. Take the instance of an individual singer hearing an interesting song on the radio or during a live gospel program. From this initial stimulus he or she might consult a recording or printed version of the song for the exact words. Eventually the singer introduces the song to the group in a rehearsal session, where other group members help shape the final arrangement. Here members may draw on past versions of the song heard in church, on record or radio, or in live performances by other groups. Once a song has been substantially rearranged, an individual singer or the entire group often claim it as their own composition, thus further obscuring the true origin of the piece.

Original gospel songs, as opposed to the aforementioned rearranged compositions, crop up occasionally in the repertoires of local groups. Most singers believe that, like the gift of singing, the songs themselves come directly from the Almighty. They see themselves simply as conduits for His words.[19] Arthur McKoy of the No Name Gospel Singers reflects:

God has been dealing with me, that's why He gives me songs in my sleep, and I write them down. I know He's the one who is doing it, He saved me. Sometimes I wake up singing, I was saying thank you Jesus as I was laying in the bed. And I knew the song He gave me, so I just got right up then and cut the light on and started writing the song.[20]

Reverend King of the No Name Gospel Singers and David Steward of the Wearyland Singers also report that songs come to them in their sleep, sometimes as dreams. Others claim God sends them songs while they are working alone or at other times of seclusion. Randy Swain of the Heavenly Tones recalls how the song "I Got Something to Shout About" first came to him:

Songs come to me mostly when I'm alone. I sing to myself a lot on the job. I work by myself, see, I'm a maintenance man at Kennedy Airport. So this song came to me, it was about two years ago. I was on the job, putting up a fence. And everybody had left me there, and I was singing a song. And suddenly something went all over me, and the song just came out of my mouth: "Lord I got something to shout about." I just started singing it. And after that I got all the words together and brought it in here to rehearsal and we started singing it.[21]

Complete songs do not always come to singers at once; often ideas accumulate over a period of time. David Steward of the Wearyland Singers reflects:

For me, songs come in pieces, bits and pieces. In my mind, they would come, and I'd write them down. When I finished writing down the lyrics, then I'd figure out how I wanted the song to go. You know, I'd sing it in my mind, how I wanted to do it, before I go into rehearsal. Then when I get there, I'd have to get the musicians to paint a picture in their head of what I wanted. Then after that, I'd get the background set up, and that's it.[22]

Billy Walker of the All Stars acknowledges going through a similar process:

Songs come a little bit at a time. First you get a theme, or a title—what you want the story to be. It's like a sermon, really. Then after you get the beginning you work out the verses, and the rhythm you want. You just keep working at it. Sometimes it takes two or three weeks, sometimes a month. But you do it a little at a time. And lots of times when I get an idea, I can't work it out myself, so I have to get the background [singers] with me. And after I get what they are going to do, then I won't give them no more. I'll take it away and I'll go back and work on it myself. Then I'll come back and give them some more. So we keep working at it.[23]

One of Walker's recent compositions, "Pray a Prayer for Peace," is the result of extensive rehearsing with the All Stars. The song reflects a strong concern with contemporary social issues—health problems, hunger, poverty, racism, and war—and, in keeping with the gospel tradition, suggests that prayer and faith in the Almighty are the solutions:

Pray a prayer for those in the hospital,
    lying in their sick bed.
Pray a prayer for those behind bars,
    and no one to throw their bail.
Pray a prayer for the hungry children
    that's running through the streets.
Pray a prayer for those out there
    with no shoes on their feet.

We got to pray, pray,
    pray a prayer for peace,
Pray a prayer for everyone,
    please pray for me.

Pray a prayer for the races,
   to come together as one.
Join hands together,
   with the Father and the Son.
Christ died on Calvary Mountain,
   and he died to save us all.
Together we'll stand y'all,
   divided we'll fall.

Pray a prayer for the presidents,
   and the rulers of the lands.
Let them know that God holds all,
   all power in His hand.
He can destroy,
   and He will defend.
Why don't men start living right,
   stop that living in sin.[24]

The composition of original songs for community-based quartet singers is both an individual and a collective endeavor. Usually an individual will receive a basic theme or core idea for a song through some form of divine inspiration. The singer will gradually work through the lyrics in her or his mind, often writing down or tape-recording sections as they become solidified. Eventually a rough version of the song is brought into rehearsal, where the entire group contributes to the final arrangements. The original author tends to guide this process, but the background singers often implement changes in words, melody, phrasing, and so forth. While the final product is considered the property of the individual who first conceived of the song, it bears the mark of the entire group.

The repertoires of New York City's local gospel quartets are a mixture of old and new, of the anonymous folk and the commercially composed. Post-1930 gospel compositions, learned primarily from commercial recordings, radio broadcasts, song books, or live performances, form the bulk of most repertoires. Original pieces, usually conceived by one individual but melded into final form by communal input, are also popular. And finally, older spirituals, folk hymns, and church songs continue to be rearranged in a gospel style and performed for appreciative audiences. A single performance might include a standard gospel composition such as Thomas Dorsey's "Precious Lord," a more contemporary gospel song such as James Cleveland's "God Has Smiled on Me," a traditional spiritual like "Oh Mary Don't You Weep," an old church song such as "This Little Light of Mine," a hymn like "Pass Me Not Oh Gentle Savior," and one or more original compositions. The fact that the more traditional hymns, spirituals, and church songs have survived—albeit in rearranged form—speaks for the tenacity of these compositions and the continuity in the religious singing traditions of African-Americans. By reviving and maintaining these older songs as part of their active repertoires, younger singers appeal to elderly, more conservative church members, and ensure that these pieces will not pass out of tradition.[25]

Repertoire considerations lead naturally to questions of song lyrics and themes, and eventually to the deeper issue of meaning. The three texts quoted thus far reflect a thematic consistency common to post-1930 gospel songs and to many of the older spirituals and church songs that form the core repertoire of local quartets. The basic message centers on the New Testament promise of salvation through personal commitment to Jesus Christ. Songs urge the individual listener to transcend the burdens of this world and find eternal joy with God the Father, through Christ. "In gospel music Jesus Christ is Everything—Friend, Protector, and Liberator—because he is portrayed as the Ultimate Alternative to a world that is essentially nothing," concludes Jon Michael Spencer.[26] The words remind believers of their spiritual commitment, and challenge sinners to undergo conversion and join the flock.

Lawrence Levine notes that, like the older spirituals, twentieth-century gospel songs are filled with hope and affirmation, portraying God as an immediate, living presence. On the other hand, Levine argues that the lyrical content of gospel songs tends to be otherworldly in nature. The songs focus on the dependence of humankind on God and Christ, while depicting heaven as removed from our present earthly situation—a reward to be obtained only in the future. In further differentiating gospel songs and spirituals, Levine writes the following about gospel:

In terms of long-range solutions for Man's problems, the gulf between this world and the next had grown wider. There were few songs about Old Testament heroes, few songs portraying victory in this world. Ultimate change, when it came took place in the future in an otherworldly context. Christ, with His promise of a better tomorrow "sometime, somewhere, someday, somehow," was the dominating figure upon whom Man was almost totally dependent. No longer were temporal and spacial barriers transcended. This world was to be suffered; one had to take comfort from the blessings one had and from the assurances of the Almighty.[27]

Other authors stress the intimate relationship between God (Christ) and humankind, and the optimistic nature of gospel lyrics. Portia Maultsby's commentary summarizes these points:

Textual themes in composed black gospel music mirror messages communicated in sermons by black preachers. They express a belief in the teachings and powers of Jesus Christ. Emphasis is placed on the earthly relationship between God and man rather than Biblical themes from the Old Testament that dominated the spirituals. Many gospel songs convey the message that man's worldly problems, troubles, sorrows, and burdens can be overcome by having faith and believing in Jesus Christ.[28]

Critics concur on this key point: while gospel lyrics tend to focus on earthly hardship, trouble, and despair, they also offer a positive solution to these problems and the opportunity to transcend worldly burdens through a spiritual commitment. The overall tone of most songs is one of joy, celebration, and optimism. In addition to the need for personal salvation through Christ, other popular gospel themes identified by scholars include the joys of heaven and reuniting with deceased family and friends, the story of one's conversion experience, reminiscing over old-time ways of family life and worship, and reverence for parents (especially mothers) and elders.[29]

These patterns are clearly evident in the lyrics of the gospel compositions and older church songs favored by today's New York quartet singers. The need for individual salvation, as expressed in the previously cited rendition of "King of Kings," is often heard. Equally popular are songs portraying Jesus as savior, friend, and helpmate—the doctor upon whom humans can "lean," as the Reverend Floyd King relates:

Oh Lord,   (let me lean on you)
   let me lean on you.   (let me lean on you)
Oh, oh Lord   (let me lean on you)
   let me lean on you.   (let me lean on you)
My body is tired,   (my body is tired)
   my soul needs rest.   (my soul needs rest)
Oh Doctor Jesus,   (let me lean on you)
   let me lean on you.   (let me lean on you)[30]

Jesus is viewed an omnipresent force who will remain with an individual throughout his or her life. Clifford Williams of the Brooklyn Skyways sings:

Look where Jesus brought me from,
Church, look where Jesus brought me from,
Say He brought me from the cradle,
    way up to the present time,
Look where Jesus brought me from.
Look where He brought my mother from,
    ((repeat))
Look where He brought my father from,
    ((repeat))[31]

Ron Adams of the Spiritual Voices exclaims that no one but Jesus will
do for him:

Can't nobody,   (do me like Jesus)
Can't nobody,   (do me like the Lord)
Can't nobody,   (do me like Jesus)
He's, my, friend.

Listen—
Said He picked me up and He—   (and He turned me around)
Yes He did, good God almighty—   (He picked me up,
                                    and He turned me around)
And He—   (He picked me up,
              and He turned me around)
He's, my, friend.[32]

   While Jesus is seen as humanity's hope and salvation, the evil forces
of the universe are embodied in the person of the Devil, or Satan,
who is constantly nearby, ready to tempt the innocent believer. John
Goudelock of the Golden Jubilees reminds his audience of the Devil's
presence and the true Christian's ability to triumph over evil:

Got to keep moving,   (moving up the King's highway)
    every, every day we're—   (moving up the King's highway)
Oh yes we are moving,   (moving up the King's highway)
    Up the King's highway,   (moving up the King's highway)
Satan is on my track,
    and every day you know he's trying, to turn me back,
Got to keep on—   (moving up the King's highway)
    ah, ha, moving up the King's—   (moving up the King's
                                        highway)

You know I met, God one morning,
    I saw, Jesus kind of ..?..
Oh the Devil had lost this soul of mine,
    oh that he thought he had.
My hand got stuck on the gospel plow,
    and I wouldn't take nothing for my, journey now,
He-e-e-e— (moving up the King's highway)
    up the King's highways.   (moving up the King's highway)[33]

    The nostalgic yearning for bygone days when people allegedly took their religion more seriously is expressed in songs like the popular camp meeting spiritual "Old-Time Religion." Charlie Storey and the All Stars' rendition of "Meeting Tonight" actually evokes the imagery of an old time southern camp meeting:

There's going to be a meeting,   (meeting tonight)
    an old-fashioned meeting boys,   (meeting tonight)
Said a meeting,   (meeting tonight)
    old-fashioned meeting tonight y'all,   (meeting tonight)
There's going to be singing,   (singing)
There's going to be shouting,   (shouting)
There's going to be praying,   (praying in, the old time way)
There's going to be a meeting, boys,   (meeting tonight)
    old fashioned meeting tonight.   (meeting tonight)[34]

A related theme, the veneration of parents and elders is often heard in songs like Billy Walker's original composition, "Memories of Mother's Teachings":

Memories,
    of mother's teaching,
Oh they still,
    linger on.

When I was a young boy,
    in the early years of my life,
My mother would always teach me,
    about the love of Jesus Christ.

    ((repeat chorus))

She use to call me to her side and say—
Here's my Bible,
    take it in your hand,

Learn to read it my child,
    so you'll be able to understand.
Oh— (memories)
Those old memories— (of mother's teaching)
My mother use to teach me y'all, (oh they still)
Yes they still linger— (linger on)[35]

Many song lyrics describe the glories of heaven, the final resting place where believers will reunite with family and loved ones. Gospel compositions like "I'll Fly Away" and "By and By" reflect the singers' desires to transcend earthly hardships and achieve heavenly bliss in a land of eternal joy and peace. The Sunset Jubilees' rendition of "Meet Me There" offers a vivid image of what the chosen can look forward to:

The walls are made of jasper,
    the streets are of gold,
In that blessed homeland,
    up above.
And half of all his wonders
    will never be told,
Till then we,
    shall rest,
        in His Love.

Said meet me there, (meet me there)
    Lord meet me there, (meet me there)
Where life is so sweet,
    and fair,
I want you to be,
    in that home with me,
Oh promise,
    to meet,
        me there. (meet me there)[36]

Charlie Storey's version of Dorsey's "Peace in the Valley" describes Heaven as a land free from all earthly troubles:

Know the bear,
    will be gentle,
And the wolf,
    going to be tame,

Tell the lion,
    going to lie down,
Going to lie down.
    with the little bitty lamb.
Oh there'll be peace,   (peace in the valley)
    in the valley,   (peace in the valley)
For me, (for me one day)
    for me one day.   (for me one day)

There'll be peace,   (peace in the valley)
    down in the valley,   (peace in the valley)
For me,   (for me one day)
    and for you one day,   (for me one day)
No more sadness,   (no more sadness or sorrow)
    no more sorrow,   (no more sadness of sorrow)
No more trouble,   (no more trouble I'll see)
    I'll ever see,   (no more trouble I'll see)
There'll be peace,   (peace in the valley)
    down in the valley,   (peace in the valley)
For me,   (for me one day)
    for me one day.   (for me one day)[37]

When believers meet "over yonder" they will find not only peace and rest, but also much celebration, singing, and shouting, as Darrell McFadden describes in the Golden Sons' version of "Lay Down My Life for the Lord":

There'll be singing over yonder,
    singing, over there.
When the Saints get together,
    we're going to enjoy one another
And we're going to
    (lay down our life for the Lord),
I know we're going to
    (lay down our life for the Lord)

Lord there'll be shouting over yonder,
    shouting, over there,
When we all get together,
    going to enjoy one another,
And we're going to
    (lay down our life for the Lord)
I know we're going to
    (lay down our life for the Lord)

Won't it be grand,
    won't it be grand?
Won't it be grand church,
    won't it be grand?
We're going home, (going home)
    to live with Jesus,
Tell me won't it be grand,
    won't it be grand.[38]

While heaven is envisioned as an otherworldly place to be experienced in the future, song lyrics also stress the immediate rewards of
salvation here and now on earth. Songs extolling the joys of communal worship and the exhilaration of the Holy Spirit, such as the Heavenly Tones' version of "Talking About a Good Time," are common:

If you're talking about a good sing and shout,
        (we going to have a time)
    talking about a good sing and shout,
        (we going to have a time)
If you're talking about a good sing and shout,
        (we going to have a time)
    when we all get together,
        (we going to have a time)

If you got the Holy Ghost,
        (we going to have a time)
    if you got the Holy Ghost,
        (we going to have a time)
If you got the Holy Ghost,
        (we going to have a time)
    when we all get together,
        (we going to have a time)[39]

This brief survey of song lyrics reveals that local quartet singers, in
keeping with the gospel tradition, prefer songs that stress the joys of
personal salvation and the rapture of communing with the Almighty
and fellow worshipers—both in heaven *and* here on earth. But interpreting isolated texts without giving ample consideration to their social and historical context is risky. Levine readily admits this, noting
that any attempt to analyze lyrics without sufficient discussion of performance practices will "lose the essence and distort the experience
of gospel song."[39] Indeed, most who criticize gospel music for being
too "otherworldly" in vision base their conclusions almost exclusively

on verse/chorus lyrical analysis of songs such as "Peace in the Valley" or "Lay Down My Life for the Lord." Too often the equally vital aspects of performance are ignored—the chanted song introductions, the lengthy improvised "drive" sections, the dramatic movement, the intense performer/audience interaction, and, perhaps most importantly, the expectation of divine presence in the form of the Holy Spirit. Once a broader performance perspective is assumed, we realize that, for quartet singers and their audiences, the temporal and spatial boundaries separating humankind from the Almighty can be temporarily transcended and Christ's promise of victory can be achieved in this world, here and now. Charlie Storey and Darrell McFadden are not only singing about tomorrow's heavenly rewards; they are also paying homage to their southern ancestors, while simultaneously inviting their listeners to join with them in the immediacy of spiritual communion. Reaching such an understanding requires more than simply pondering the printed lyrics on a page of sheet music or transcribing words and notes from a commercial recording. Interpreting gospel quartet performance demands an intimate knowledge of the cultural setting in which the sacred drama unfolds—the gospel program.

Notes

1. Personal interview with Charlie Storey, October 1, 1986.
2. Personal interview with the Reverend Floyd King, March 2, 1986.
3. Personal interview with Clifton Johnson, January 1, 1986.
4. Burnim reports similar experiences among young choir members in Texas, Bloomington, and Indianapolis. For more on the training of choir singers see Mellonee Burnim, "The Black Gospel Music Tradition: Symbol of Ethnicity," Ph.D. dissertation, Indiana University, 1980, pp. 103–108.
5. Personal interview with Billy Walker, February 2, 1986.
6. Personal interview with William Kelly, November 11, 1986.
7. Alan Merriam suggests that imitation is the most important process by which casual performers receive musical training in most cultures. More formal learning occurs through a process he calls education, which involves techniques of instruction and a specific teacher, or agent. See Alan Merriam, *The Anthropology of Music* (Evanston, IL: Northwestern University Press, 1964), pp. 145–163. Jeff Titon reports that the Anglo-American Baptist church singers he studied in Virginia learned their gospel hymns by "imitation and example." See Jeff Titon, *Powerhouse for God* (Austin: University of Texas Press, 1988), pp. 232–236.
8. For more on the influence of black shape-note singing on early quartets see Lornell, *"Happy in the Service of the Lord"*, pp. 17–18.
9. Personal interview with the Reverend Floyd King, August 7, 1985.
10. Personal interview with the Reverend Alton Griffin, May 1, 1986.

11. For more on the importance of quartet trainers in the South see Lornell, *"Happy in the Service of the Lord"*, pp. 88–93.

12. To the best of my knowledge there is no emic title for the group member who is most active in placing voices and helping singers find parts. Because these individuals often speak of their talents in song arranging, I will refer to them as "song arrangers." The term "song leader" (also mine) refers to the individual who brings the song to the group and sings lead. In some cases an individual assumes both roles in rehearsal, as when Ralph Moragne, the primary song arranger for the Sunset Jubilees, leads a song.

13. Lornell reports similar observations in Memphis quartet rehearsals. See *"Happy in the Service of the Lord"*, pp. 101–102.

14. The significance of the portable cassette tape recorder as a learning device cannot be overstated. One or more of the group members taped nearly every rehearsal attended. Sometimes tapes were played back at the end of a song or session for group criticism. More often, however, members took tapes home to learn the words and vocal parts to recently introduced songs. New members unfamiliar with a group's repertoire were often given tapes and instructed to learn their parts for certain songs by the next rehearsal. By providing instant replay and long-term recall, cassette recorders have become indispensable to the song learning and arranging processes.

15. Brenda McCallum, "Songs of Work and Songs of Worship: Sanctified Black Unionism in the Southern City of Steel," *New York Folklore* 14 (1988): 19.

16. Recorded in rehearsal, Tingamen Temple, Brooklyn, NY, May 28, 1987.

17. See Harris's recollection of this incident in Heilbut, *Gospel Sound*, pp. 79–80.

18. Recorded at the New Mount Calvary Baptist Church, Harlem, NY, December 29, 1985.

19. Titon notes that Anglo-American gospel singers speak of "receiving a hymn from the Lord" and of the human composer simply being a "mouthpiece for the Lord." See Titon, *Powerhouse for God*, pp. 227–228.

20. Personal interview with Arthur McKoy, February, 1986.

21. Personal interview with Randy Swain, June 14, 1986.

22. Personal interview with David Steward, March 16, 1986.

23. Personal interview with Billy Walker, June 27, 1986.

24. Recorded in rehearsal, Charlie Storey's furniture shop, Brooklyn, NY, June 6, 1989.

25. David Evans notes the popularity of older church and gospel songs among younger singers in rural Mississippi. See Evans, "The Roots of Afro-American Gospel Music," p. 128.

26. Spencer, *Protest and Praise: Sacred Music of Black Religion* (Minneapolis: Fortress Press, 1990), p. 221.

27. Levine, *Black Culture and Black Consciousness*, pp. 176–177. See also Levine's entire section on gospel music (pp. 174–189) for further textual and performance analysis.

28. Portia Maultsby, "Afro-American Religious Music: A Study in Musical Diversity" (Springfield, OH: The Hymn Society of America, n.d.), p. 14.

29. See for example Richard Raichelson's discussion of gospel song texts in "Black Religious Folk Song," pp. 315–329. Also see Heilbut, *Gospel Sound*, pp. xxvii–xxiv; and Pearl Williams-Jones, "Afro-American Gospel Music," in

Vaden Butcher, ed., *Development of Materials for a One Year Course in African Music for the General Undergraduate* (Washington, DC: Department of Health, Education, and Welfare, 1970), p. 203.

30. Recorded in rehearsal, Brooklyn, NY, June 24, 1987.

31. Recorded at the First Freedom Baptist Church, Jamaica, NY, January 10, 1986.

32. Recorded in Central Park, New York, NY, June 29, 1986.

33. Recorded at the Benjamin Cardoza Junior High School, Far Rockaway, NY, March 22, 1986.

34. Recorded at Charlie Storey's Auditorium, Brooklyn, NY, March 8, 1986.

35. Recorded in rehearsal, Charlie Storey's furniture shop, Brooklyn, NY, January 22, 1986.

36. Recorded in Central Park, New York, NY, June 29, 1986.

37. Recorded at Charlie Storey's Auditorium, Brooklyn, NY, March 8, 1986.

38. Recorded at PS 40, Brooklyn, August 31, 1986.

39. Recorded at the Glorified Pentecostal Tabernacle Church, Brooklyn, NY, December 15, 1986.

40. Levine, *Black Culture and Black Consciousness*, p. 177.

9. The Golden Jubilees, Far Rockaway, 1986 (l to r: John Goudelock, Grayon Lee, Reverend George Tinsley, Clifton Johnson, and Joshua Hankinson). Photo by Ray Allen. Note that Reverend Tinsley, who had just joined the group, had not been issued an official uniform.

10. The Wearyland Singers, Manhattan, 1987 (David Steward front, Earl Ledbetter vocalist on far right). Photo by Ray Allen.

Chapter 3
Let's Go Out to the Programs
Sacred Quartet Singing in Context

In her discussion of the aesthetics of gospel music, Pearl Williams-Jones notes that one must "experience a gospel 'happening' in its cultural setting" to grasp the full emotional and spiritual power of the art form.[1] This is particularly true for live quartet performance, where singing, chanted words, music, and holy dance are intertwined in expressive worship. The gospel program described in the Preface offers the reader a taste of sacred quartet ritual, but a more detailed discussion of social setting and organization is necessary to fully appreciate the cultural, spiritual and aesthetic complexities of such gatherings.

Quartet singing programs are only one of a number of intensely-focused, readily recognizable events that make up the ritual life of African-American Protestants. Others are Sunday morning worship services, week night prayer meetings, and week night and weekend revival meetings. Though differing slightly in structure, all share a common goal. As ritual, they aim to render evangelical Christian doctrine intellectually valid and emotionally satisfying through shared worship experiences that include prayer, testimony, scriptural reading, singing, and preaching. Further, these gatherings serve as social occasions where participants may tighten communal bonds and celebrate their common heritage.

The Sunday morning service is the most important of these rituals, and has received a great deal of scholarly attention. Descriptions of Sunday morning services, such as those offered by Arthur Paris in his informative ethnography of a black Pentecostal church in Boston, point to a carefully ordered event. An opening devotional period consisting of song, prayer, scripture reading, and testimony precedes an offering, choir selection, sermon, and altar call. Announcements and a final benediction close the service.[2] Along with their Pentecostal and Holiness counterparts, many southern-influenced Baptist and Methodist congregations engage in a demonstrative style of worship. Emotional praying, testifying, preaching, and singing may invoke the Holy Spirit, which manifests itself through behaviors like shouting, weeping, holy dancing, and among some denominations speaking in tongues and healing. Singing, in the form of congregational hymns, the songs that preface individual testimony, and special choir selections form an essential part of these services. But the sermon is the centerpiece of the Sunday morning gatherings, since it is the vehicle through which the preacher delivers God's message to the congregation.

Regular Sunday morning worship services ordinarily feature choirs and soloists. Community-based quartets, on the other hand, appear primarily at specially designated afternoon and evening services known as programs and anniversaries. A quartet singing program is, in many ways, an extension of the Sunday morning worship service—an opportunity for people to "have church" on Saturday night or Sunday evening, with the quartet singer, rather than the preacher, taking center stage.

Interestingly, there are structural similarities between the twentieth century quartet singing program and nineteenth-century minstrel and vaudeville stage entertainment. For example, the olio section of a minstrel show featured a variety of short acts including singers, dancers, comedians, and acrobats. The modern quartet program retains this basic format, simply limiting the types of acts to groups of sacred singers. Further, today's gospel emcee serves as onstage director and humorous raconteur, roles based loosely on those of the minstrel interlocuter and comic endman.[3] The fact that jubilee quartets were active in 19th-century popular theater strengthens the plausibility of a connection between the minstrel/vaudeville show and the quartet singing program. The structural format, however, is where the parallel ends, since sacred quartet singers and their audiences shun all secular stage themes in order to maintain the spiritual integrity of their gatherings.

Before World War Two, New York's community-based jubilee quartets limited their public performing almost exclusively to church settings. No written record pinpoints the date of the earliest program devoted exclusively to sacred quartet singing. Thurman Ruth recalls that during the late 1920s many of Brooklyn's local quartets consisted of members of one church and did much of their singing at Sunday afternoon and evening services in that home church. The earliest quartet program Ruth remembers is the first anniversary of his Selah Jubilee Singers in 1928 or 1929. The affair, described in Chapter 1, featured seven or eight quartets. The fact that the Eastern Star quartet—a group that Ruth recalls consisted of older singers—was well established in Brooklyn by the time of the Selahs' anniversary suggests that the local jubilee quartet tradition probably stretched back at least to the mid to early 1920s.

Based on the recollections of Ruth and other older singers, it is safe to assume that by the early 1930s special singing programs devoted primarily to quartets were common in African-American churches throughout Harlem and Brooklyn. Unlike today's events, which may feature up to a dozen gospel groups, the scale of these earlier programs was small. The Reverend Alton Griffin recalls that his Golden Crowns often sang by themselves at Harlem churches, usually doing several sets of three songs each. On other occasions they sang with one, two, or even three other groups. William Kelly remembers that most of the Harmonaires' programs featured only one or two other groups. Evidently these programs were not commercial in nature: usually a free will offering would be taken and split fifty-fifty between the groups and the sponsoring church. Sometimes groups would sing without compensation. Charlie Storey recalls singing in the early 1940s:

Back then, more groups sang for free. They'd come and help your church, and your church would come back and help their church. That's the way they did it. Nobody said nothing about money in those days. When you spoke about some money, about getting paid, that was like a bad word—a curse word. They might take us up an offering, but whatever they raised, you didn't say nothing. Different today. The groups want to know before they sing whether they're drawing anything or not. They want money.[4]

Apparently many of these early quartet programs were staged for the benefit of small churches, to help them raise revenues and attract new members. The Reverend John Leak, leader of the Rolling Stone Jubilee Singers of Brooklyn, remembers how his group assisted one neighborhood church in the late 1930s:

Now the Saint Paul's Disciple Church, it was located on Bedford Avenue, in a storefront. They came to me, and asked us to help them build up. So we went up there and started singing [on Sunday afternoons], and in less than two months they didn't have standing room. People were standing in the street! So they purchased a small place on Gates Avenue, and it got overcrowded, so they bought a theatre across the street. And as long as the pastor lived he said that if it hadn't of been for the Rolling Stone Jubilee Singers they never would have been able to buy that building. People were loyal to support those causes back then.[5]

Programs during the 1930s and 1940s sometimes took on the format of song contests or battles. On such occasions several groups would come together to compete, with a group of judges to choose a winner. Reverend Griffin recalls:

Most of the time in a battle you had to sing [slow] harmony. There were a few times we went up against three or four groups, but most of the time it was a two-way battle, two groups. . . . The judges were usually people who knew music, maybe the organist of a church, or someone who was well trained and familiar with vocal singing. We used to sing a few songs they weren't judging on—they called it warming up. But then we got to the songs we were being judged on, usually we did two each, maybe three. . . . They judged in the techniques of the voices and how close the voices could blend. That's the way they did it—on your English [diction], and closeness of voices. They were judging everything, even the way you stand. We stood straight, we didn't move on those songs.[6]

Ruth agrees that these contests were dominated by slower, harmonizing songs, since the judges used harmony and articulation as the major criteria for choosing a winner. By the late 1930s, Ruth claims these song contests (which Griffin refers to as "song battles") were gradually replaced by "battles of song" where two groups would compete and the audience, by their applause, would choose the winner. Here there was more emphasis on all-around showmanship, recalls Ruth, rather than on strict harmonizing. In any case, Ruth, Griffin, and Storey agree that while these early song contests and battles were quite competitive in nature, rarely were there any hard feelings between the groups. Losers simply assumed they would take revenge at the next program. All competing groups usually shared the money raised by the offering, while the winner might also be awarded a trophy or a cake. Ruth and Griffin concur that a strong sense of cooperation existed among the local groups during those days. When a quartet had an anniversary, other groups would come to "help them out" without asking to be paid. The host quartet was expected to reciprocate during the upcoming year by performing at the other groups' anniversaries free of charge.

As the popularity of quartet singing skyrocketed after the second world war, quartet programs in New York increased in number and size. Larger churches, halls, theaters and auditoriums became the preferred venues. Promoters sponsored huge commerical extravaganzas, featuring up to a dozen acts, including the stellar professional groups that were touring the burgeoning gospel circuit in the 1950s. But the smaller, less commercial programs never waned in popularity, continuing to thrive in neighborhood churches and community centers.

Saturday evening and Sunday afternoon singing events became known as "gospel programs" and "gospel anniversaries" in the postwar years. Quartets dominated these gatherings during the 1950s and 1960s. Today's New York gospel programs occasionally include soloists and choirs, but small vocal ensembles still predominate. While churches continue to be the most popular settings, gospel programs may also be held at auditoriums, halls, or schools, or on sidewalks. There is little distinction between a bona-fide church and a school or auditorium, since participants make a point of transforming these secular settings into sacred ones in the opening stages of their ritual.

A gospel program may be sponsored by a group, a church, a church organization, or an individual promoter. Many of the smaller programs are organized to raise money or to attract new members for the host church. The pastor, choir, or some church organization—the Deacon Board, the Usher Board, the Women's Prayer Group—may sponsor a gospel program to raise money for the general operating costs or for a specific need such as a building fund. They will choose a gospel group, usually through a friend or family contacts, and invite them to organize a program and serve as the sponsoring or honored guests. This sponsoring group then invites several other groups to appear on the program. It is tacitly understood that invited groups will perform for no pay, while in return the sponsoring group will reciprocate for no remuneration at future programs. Over the years groups become friendly and form cooperative networks for the organization of such programs. If a church is in dire need, the sponsoring group may decide to donate all proceeds from the offering back to the church. In other cases, the sponsoring group receives some percentage of the offering, usually forty or fifty percent. These church-organized programs tend to be small in scope, with attendance varying from twenty-five to a hundred people. Performances feature up to a half-dozen groups and perhaps the host church's choir. Several hundred dollars may be raised through a free will offering.

Individual groups and local promoters also sponsor more lavish gospel programs, which take place in larger churches, auditoriums, and schools. Known as "ticket programs," there is a straightforward admission charge, and no offering is taken. Tickets are sold by the participating groups and at neighborhood record shops, barber shops, and restaurants. Upcoming ticket programs are advertised with small photocopied fliers known as "throwaways," which are distributed at other programs and through local shops. The groups are usually paid, although precise financial arrangements vary. The better known local groups may command a flat fee (usually between one and two hundred dollars), while others receive a percentage of the proceeds from the tickets they sell. Younger or lesser known groups may agree to sing for free to gain exposure. Such ticket programs often feature as many as eight or more local groups, and are attended by several hundred people. Since ticket prices tend to be high—often ten to twelve dollars—the sponsoring group or promoter stands a chance of clearing a small profit.

The gospel anniversary is the second type of singing event that features quartets. These commemorative programs honor groups or individuals for their service in the gospel field during the past year. They are usually ticket programs, often featuring up to a dozen groups in addition to the honorees. While financial arrangements vary, most of the proceeds go to the honored group. The guest groups usually sing gratis, with the understanding that the honored group will return the favor at their anniversaries. Occasionally the better known local groups will demand a fee, although this is a point of tension among groups that often leads to resentment. With sufficient publicity, a popular group can attract a large crowd and stands to turn a small profit on its anniversary.[7] Anniversary, appreciation, or birthday programs may also be held to honor individuals active in the community, such as solo singers, evangelists, emcees, and promoters. Like the groups, these individuals receive community recognition as well as a sizable portion of the ticket profits on their anniversary programs.

The local New York groups also appear at larger commercial programs, often referred to as "Gospel Extravaganzas" or "Gospel Explosions," that feature several professional gospel groups. Here, a promoter rents a large church or auditorium with a seating capacity of at least five hundred. Placards, posters, and smaller throwaways advertise the program throughout the community. Several professional out-of-town groups—perhaps the Dixie Hummingbirds, the Mighty Clouds of Joy, the Gospel Keynotes, or the Jackson Southernaires—serve as headliners, while the best semi-professional local groups fill out the program. A common arrangement is for the local groups to sell tickets and retain a percentage of the profits in lieu of a flat fee. This system, which many feel exploits the local singers, assures promoters a good crowd while keeping their costs low. Ticket prices are high, often as much as twenty dollars. Further, the sale of records, tapes, and pictures gives these larger programs the feel of a commercial show. But the local groups and their followers continue to play a central role in these commercial programs and help assure that even the biggest extravaganzas remain fundamentally religious in nature. This point will be taken up in further detail in Chapter 9.

Upon arrival at a program or anniversary, singers and audience members tend to congregate outside, in front of the church, or in the rear of the sanctuary or auditorium. There is a great deal of socializing, and the programs inevitably begin at least an hour after their advertised starting time. In churches and auditoriums with kitchens, meals are often sold before and during programs. The cuisine consists almost exclusively of southern or soul food specialties, including fried chicken, fish, or rib dinners garnished with corn bread, potato salad, cole slaw, collard greens, and pig's feet, with sweet potato pie and various cakes for dessert.

As the program begins, people gradually take their seats in the main sanctuary or auditorium. Since most sites lack backstage areas, singers usually take seats in the congregation and simply come forward to the front of the sanctuary when called on to perform. The master of ceremonies ("emcee") sits in one of the front rows, where he or she may easily step forward to announce the next group. In auditoriums and schools the main stage is the primary performance site, while in churches the area directly in front of the pulpit serves this purpose. But once a performance is underway, singers will move from this central stage area and walk down the aisles to interact more intimately with the congregation, thus blurring the distinction between performers and spectators.

While no two community-based gospel programs are exactly alike, all follow a standard format and involve prescribed social roles.[8] Like the Sunday morning service, a gospel program is divided into two parts. Programs always begin with a brief "devotional service," which includes congregational singing, prayer, scripture reading, and personal testimony. The second segment, the "song service," consists of a series of short performances (perhaps fifteen minutes) by each of the featured groups. The format of the Travelling Sons' anniversary held in Jamaica, Queens, on October 6, 1985, is typical:

I. Devotional Service
   1. Opening remarks and greeting by devotional leader
   2. Congregational song - "I Want to Be Back With Him"
   3. Chanted prayer by devotional leader
   4. Testimony period - with songs
   5. Congregational song - "This Little Light of Mine"

6. Introduction and greeting from Reverend Hurdle of the Travelling Sons
7. Introduction of Emcee

II. Song Service
1. Selections by Deacon Thomas and the Violinaires:
   -"Standing in the Safety Zone"
   -"Prayer Changes Things"
   -"Save Me Lord"
   -"I'm Thankful I Found the Lord"
2. Selections by the Angelettes
   -"Prodigal Son"
   -"If I Ever Need the Lord"
3. Duet by Reverend Evans and Brother Brown
   -??
4. Selections by the Golden Jubilees
   -"Lord Jesus Is Mine"
   -"Working for Jesus"
   -"Rise Again"
   -"Be What You Are"
5. Introduction and selections by the honorees, the Travelling Sons
   -"Dark Clouds"
   -"Tree of Life"
   -"I Have a Few More Tears to Share"
   -"Prayer Changes Things"
   -"I'll Fly Away"
6. Selections by the Inspirational Voices of Angels
   -"Operator"
   -"I'll Be Glad to Meet the Lord"
   -"When I Come to the End of My Journey"
7. Selections by the Wearyland Singers
   -"Try Jesus"
   -"How Great Thou Art"
   -"Working on a Building"
   -"I'll Surrender"
8. Closing Benediction

After the initial period of informal socializing, the program is called to order with the beginning of the devotional period. At this point the members of the audience take their seats and immediately join the devotional leader in a congregational song. The typical New York gospel audience is almost exclusively African-American, and approximately two-thirds female. While most of these women are middle-aged or older, there are often many young mothers with small children. Most of the men are older, and with the exception of the singers there is a marked absence of teenaged and young adult males. Further, in smaller programs and anniversaries, often up to half of the audience consists of gospel singers who either have just finished or are waiting to sing. At any given time during a service, the group up front is singing not only to an audience of appreciative fans but to their fellow singers as well. This heightens the competitive at-mosphere of gospel programs, since performers are well aware they are constantly being evaluated by their peers.

The role of the audience, from the opening congregational song to the closing benediction, is one of active participation. People are ex-pected to sing, move, clap, and stamp to the music, to spur the per-formers on with shouts of encouragement, and to experience the power of the Holy Spirit. If the congregation does not "rejoice in the Spirit" and "have church," they are chastised by the singers and em-cee for being "cold" and "dead." And if the groups do not succeed in "warming" them up and gaining their participation, the service will be considered a failure.

The service officially begins when the devotional leader picks up a microphone, greets the audience, and begins singing a familiar con-gregational song such as "This Little Light of Mine," "Glory Hallelu-jah," or "On the Battlefield for My Lord." At the close of this "opening up number," the devotional leader usually makes some brief remarks, welcoming the audience and reminding them that they are not gathered to be entertained, but rather to worship God, to "have church." As one leader put it, "Some people may have come expecting a show tonight, but they're in the wrong building. We're here to praise God!" After a prayer a Bible verse is often read. An-other congregational song may be offered, followed by a testimony period. Here congregation members take turns standing up to share with everyone how God has been working in their lives. Individual testimonies are generally preceded by singing a verse or two of a hymn, and sometimes end with specific prayer requests. There may be one final congregational song before the devotional leader intro-duces the emcee, who will host the remainder of the program.

The devotional leader is often a member of the sponsoring church—a deacon, bishop, or choir member. At larger programs, however, it is not unusual for a well-known visiting minister, a solo singer, or even a member of one of the featured gospel groups to serve in this role. The devotional leader may conduct the entire ser-vice, but often she or he will invite other individuals up to read scrip-ture, recite a prayer, or lead a congregational song. The singing is usually accompanied by several musicians who play drums, piano, electric guitar, and bass guitar. Their role is to provide the instrumental accompaniment for the congregational singing and to fill in behind prayer, testimony, and other spoken remarks.

The devotional service may vary slightly in format and length. It tends to be longer in smaller churches, where the more intimate atmosphere often encourages lengthy testimony periods. In larger settings with more groups scheduled to perform, the devotional service is shorter, perhaps with no scripture reading or testimony period. On occasion, if the first group or emcee is not ready, the devotional leader may have to stall for time by leading several more songs or encouraging the congregation to extend their testimony period. No program, however, begins without a minimal devotional period that includes congregational singing and prayer.

The purpose of the devotional period is two-fold. First and foremost, it sets a spiritual tone for the entire gospel program, reminding the participants that they have come to engage in religious ritual, not merely to see a show. A successful devotional period engenders a spiritual atmosphere befitting a religious service, as Reverend Kelly of the Faithful Harmonizers explains:

Well, a gospel program is a church service, it's not just something like a rock and roll concert. It's a church service, and you're going to worship—not just going to be seen or for a show or something like that. It's a religious service. You have devotion, and you should have prayer. Give God the glory, and help to build up the Spirit, bring the Spirit in. And when you get up to testify, and tell the goodness of the Lord, and how good He's been to you, and what He has done in your life, and that brings the Spirit in. If you go in a church, or in any building, and you just start singing, it's kind of hard, because it's cold. But if you keep talking about the Lord and His goodness, then you feel emotions—you feel good. And the Spirit stays, if it's really real. So that's why you have devotion.[9]

Second, the devotional period is meant to warm up the audience and to engage them physically in the performance through singing, clapping, testifying, and so forth. Devotional leaders are not shy about demanding audience participation. Between congregational songs one leader spoke:

We ask you now,
    to get into the service.
The more you put into it,
    the more you get out of it,
        Amen somebody!

I don't know about you,
>   but I'm feeling all right,
>   I went to church this morning.
Let me see the hands,
>   how many of you went to church this morning?
So let us get into the service this afternoon.
Let us not be ashamed,
>   to clap our hands and tap our feet or whatever.
Let us get into the service.
We want to loosen up and let go,
>   and let God come in and bless our souls.
I'm going to sing a song now.
Can I have some musicians?[10]

Devotional services can become extremely emotional, and during periods of song and testimony congregational members may "get happy" from the Holy Spirit.

When the devotional leader relinquishes the microphone to the emcee, the devotional period is over, and the song service begins. The emcee is usually a local radio disc jockey, evangelist, promoter, or well-known personality in the community who is particularly skilled as an orator. The emcee's role is not only to announce each group, but also to help the sponsor in ordering the program, to see that each group is present and ready to go on at the appropriate time, to acknowledge distinguished guests, and to keep the audience's attention between groups with stories, jokes, and announcements. Like the devotional leader, the emcee reminds the audience of the spiritual nature of the event and praises or chastises them depending on the extent to which they are participating in the service. However, the overall demeanor of the emcee is less serious than that of the devotional leader, for the emcee has license to tell jokes and stories at appropriate times. For example, Rocky Bridges, a well-known radio personality on New York's station WWRL, often greets his audience by asking them how they feel. If he is not satisfied with the volume of their response, he will quip that they must be "dead" and "ought to be buried." He may go on to share some family news, reflect on his recent trip to Africa (he often has the audience recite "Praise the Lord" in Swahili), and acknowledge the program sponsors or honorees (often telling a joke about them) before he introduces the first group. In the following remarks, Bridges demonstrates his abilities as entertainer, spiritual leader, and salesman:

For those of you who don't know me,
    I'm Mrs. Bridges second son.
She had one before me,
    and another one after me,
But I always tell her,
    she ain't had another one like me.   (laughter)
Well anyway,
    I'm happy to be here.
Now if you came out for a program,
    we won't have a program.
But if you came out for church,
    we will have church tonight.   (amen)
All right?
    we started out good.   (amen)
And for those of you who rushed out and didn't get any supper,
    let me tell you,
Go downstairs,
    they got some goood food down there.
They got some fish dinners,
    they got some ribs,
        tater pie,   (laughter)
            and collard greens,
What else you got down there?
    soda and coffee and everything else, right?
All right,
    we're going to have a good time.
So y'all go downstairs in between groups,
    and get some food for the body.
Then come on back up here,
    have some food for the soul,
        all right?
All right,
    let's have church,
        have a good time tonight.[11]

The emcee facilitates the smooth transition between groups by keeping the attention of the audience with a delicate balance of humorous and spiritual anecdotes. During a program in Brooklyn, emcee Sister Marie Wright had to ad lib between groups while PA systems were switched. Somewhat miffed at the audience's lack of enthusiasm over the Gospel Seven's performance, and hoping to stir them for the next group, Wright gibed:

Did you enjoy the Gospel Seven?   (little response)
Did you enjoy the Gospel Seven?   (yeah)
Come on, give them a hand then!!   (light applause)
Whoo—sure are some dead folks in here tonight
I'm sure,
  as we move down that line,
    somebody is going to wake up them dead folks.
I believe everything needs to be buried.
Somebody talk back to me—
Everything dead needs to be buried (all right)
If you dead,
  maybe we have an undertaker in here that will take time out
    and go bury you.
And then we'll come right back and have a good time in the name
of the Lord.

Y'all are just too quiet for me,
I don't like to emcee for no dead folks.
But you may be waiting on your favorite group,
  I'll tell you something,
God could be come and gone,   (ah yes, amen)
  While you're waiting.
They're going to get these mikes together in a while.
See the Devil always got a way of trying to get,
  in God's program.
Either something will go wrong with the PA system,
  or someone won't let someone use their microphones.
But we pray that we'll be able to get together in a little while,
  so that the rest of the Saints will be able to sing and enjoy this
  program.
We have another very fine group coming to sing for you at this
time.
The young man who is the leader of this group is known as the
Mayor of Fulton Street.
And I do not know a better person,
  than Brother Charlie Storey and the All Stars
Give them a big hand as they come.[12]

When announcing individual groups, Wright, Bridges, and other
emcees often tell funny stories about individual group members, adding light humor to the service. But during performances the emcee
must also act as something of a spiritual cheerleader, exhorting the
singers and congregation members to move more deeply into the rit-

ual experience. For example, when a group ends a particularly powerful performance, the emcee may try to keep the energy level high by encouraging the congregation to continue to clap, stamp, and shout until the next group takes the stage. Bridges explains:

The emcee must control the tempo and timing. In other words, when you come behind a group that has been driving, you don't go out there and let it die. You've got to hold that energy for the next group. Because if you let it die, they'll have to work twice as hard to build it back up again. A good emcee knows how to work that audience. And the groups like to work with me, because I build them up, I know how long to keep them out there.[13]

Once the emcee has announced the upcoming group she or he will ask for audience applause as the performers come forward and assume their position on stage or in front of the church, facing the congregation. One of the group members will greet the audience, and the performance begins. Some groups choose one individual—often a senior member—to serve as primary spokesperson and introduce songs and individual singers. Once a singer has stepped forward and assumed the position of lead singer, however, he or she becomes the center of attention.

The lead singer always stands in front of the background singers and musicians, an indication of his or her superior status. The lead singer is usually responsible for supplying an appropriate song introduction, unless this task has already been taken care of by the previous lead singer or the group spokesperson. Long testimonies and narratives, however, are most often delivered by the singer who is about to lead the next song. Once the actual song begins, the lead singer provides the primary melody line, directs the group by signaling certain vocal transitions, and brings the piece to a close. Most importantly, the lead singer has the primary responsibility for building the congregation's emotional energy in anticipation of the descent of the Holy Spirit. It is he or she who will move out among the audience, and try to stir them with testimony and song.

The background singers and musicians play a subordinate role to the lead singer. They usually stand in place, behind the lead singer, and rarely move out into the audience. Their main function is to provide the supportive harmonies and urge the lead singer on with shouts of encouragement. Sometimes one background singer known as a "utility man" will follow the lead singer when he or she moves out into the congregation, seeing that the microphone cord does not become tangled. The utility man also serves as a medium cooler, restraining and escorting the lead singer to the side if he or she becomes overwhelmed by the Spirit. While the roles of lead and background singers are clearly demarcated, most groups rotate them by switching lead singers from song to song.

A group usually sings two or three songs, depending on the size and time constraints of the program. A typical performance lasts between fifteen and twenty minutes. On small programs with only a few groups, each ensemble's performances may be slightly longer. The honored group at an anniversary or a special guest at a ticket program is usually allotted more time—often up to half an hour, usually coming in the mid to later portion of the program—during which they might sing five or six numbers.[14] And if at any point a singer or audience member becomes overwhelmed by the Holy Spirit, a song may be extended in hopes of drawing other participants into the experience. It is common for a group to sing two fairly short (three-to-four-minute) songs, and then extend their final number for ten or fifteen minutes in hopes of invoking the Spirit. This sometimes becomes a point of controversy, as other singers may resent a group's taking more than its allotted time if it means cutting short other performers' sets.

Once a group finishes its last song, the members return to their seats in the audience or move to the back of the church while the emcee thanks them and introduces the next group. This process is repeated as each group is called, in turn, to come forward to sing. The emcee sometimes takes time between groups to make announcements and to acknowledge distinguished guests—ministers, community leaders, local promoters and radio personalities, singers not on the program, visiting folklorists, and so on—who may be asked to come forward to greet and briefly address the congregation. If there is a free will offering it is usually taken midway through the program. Here the devotional leader or another singer leads a congregational song while the audience stands, pew by pew, and marches to the front of the church, where offerings are deposited in plates. Once the last gospel group has completed its set, the emcee asks the devotional leader or an available minister or deacon to come forward to deliver a final benediction. This marks the official close of the gospel performance, although singers and congregation members often remain afterwards to socialize.

There is an overall democratic tone to a gospel program, reflecting the deep collective structure that characterizes much African-American sacred ritual. Programs do, of course, involve a number of clearly recognized and somewhat stratified social roles—the congregation (audience), the devotional leader, the emcee, the lead singer, the background singers, and the musicians. However, there is considerable flexibility with regard to who may fill which slot, and participants are constantly switching these roles throughout a performance.[15] For example, while the role of devotional leader is often filled by an official of the sponsoring church or a respected minister or singer, it can be played by any number of people with skills at oration and singing. It is not at all unusual for a singer with one of the featured groups or a strong-voiced church elder to be asked at the last minute to lead the devotional service. Further, the devotional leader may at any point relinquish his or her controlling status by asking another congregational member to come forward to lead a song or prayer, or to read from the Bible. Three or four individuals may take turns playing the central role in a single devotional service. The role of emcee is more rigidly defined, particularly at larger events where a radio disk jockey or other media celebrity assumes the position. In small programs with only a few groups, however, the devotional leader, a member of the sponsoring group, or other church members may serve as emcee. In such instances the emcee duties are often rotated among several individuals. The role of singer can be wide open, particularly in small and medium-sized programs where little or no pay is involved. Anyone from elderly soloists to pre-teen youth choirs may be invited forward to offer a song between groups. Young or newly formed groups looking for exposure will be allowed to perform if time permits, even if they were not originally scheduled. This non-restrictive policy sometimes results in an inordinate number of low quality performances, but these are generally tolerated if the singers are judged to be sincere in their religious commitment.

The fact that a gospel program is structured to allow a large number of groups to sing for relatively short, equal time segments reinforces the communal nature of the event. During the devotional service and the early stages of the song service, most singers assume the role of congregational members, sitting in pews or standing in the back area of the church while awaiting their turn to sing. As each group is called forward, its members shed their role as congregational participants, assume the role of singers, and become the focus of attention. When they finish, they return to their seats and resume their role as members of the congregation. This constant rotation of performers reinforces a sense of equality among participants and tends to discourage any one group from dominating and assuming a star status.

Gospel singers and musicians do not by any means spend all their time seated in the congregation. In warm weather some may congregate outside the church or hall until the devotional service is over and the program is well underway. Some will eat during this period if food is being served in the basement or adjoining room. And if they have another program to attend, group members may leave immediately after finishing their performance. But most singers spend considerable time, particularly before and after their performance, as actively engaged members of the general audience. Although the spirit of competition is high, it is not unusual for a group waiting its turn to stand and shout encouragement during a moving performance by other singers.

Within the group itself, there is a strict hierarchy between the lead and background singers, with the former assuming the prominent role. However, since most groups feature several lead singers, these roles are constantly being switched, resulting in the sharing of the spotlight. And all singers, regardless of their status as lead or background, dress in the same perfectly matched outfits, reflecting a sense of equality among group members. Interestingly, a new singer while being broken in will not dress like the rest of the group (see photo 9). But once officially accepted as a full-fledged member of the group, he or she will be invited to purchase a matching uniform.

Perhaps the feature that most emphasizes the egalitarian nature of the smaller gospel programs is the seating arrangement. Nearly all participants will eventually find themselves assuming the role of congregation members, since there is rarely a backstage area large enough to accommodate all the performers. The devotional leader, emcee, singers, and musicians all spend some time sitting in the audience, where they are expected to participate in the service by interacting with whichever group is singing up front. Ultimately everyone is subsumed into the congregation. Individuals and groups emerge at designated times to assume temporarily specified performance roles, but eventually they return to their previous status as audience members.

The flexibility of roles, the constant rotation of performers, and the participatory nature of the audience makes for an event that is truly a collective creation. Like most sacred ritual, the gospel program imposes specific roles whose status and authority are organized in a somewhat hierarchical fashion. But as the performance moves toward the transcendent experience of the Holy Spirit, divisions in social status are minimized as distinctions between artist and audience diminish. Ritual participants may rejoice equally and collectively as they approach a state of "spontaneous communitas." The concept of communitas, as conceived by Victor Turner, refers to a ritualized experience of intense human interrelatedness and lack of social hierarchy that occurs during liminal (in between) phases of many rites of passage.[16] During spontaneous communitas an individual becomes "free from the culturally defined encumbrances of his role, status, reputation, class, caste, sex or other structural niche. Individuals who interact with one another in the mode of spontaneous communitas becomes totally absorbed into a single synchronized, fluid event."[17] Looking cross culturally, Turner contends that spontaneous communitas "appears to be frequently associated with mystical power and to be regarded as a charism or grace sent by the deities or ancestors."[18] We will return to Turner's model in the discussion on ritual and spirituality offered in Chapter 6. At this point it is clear that his notion of communitas accurately characterizes the heightened moments of gospel quartet performance when hierarchy disintegrates; singers and congregation members spiritually unite to summon the Holy Spirit into their presence. Communal ecstasy and the collective shout are the ideal results. The flexible, democratic organization of the gospel program unquestionably facilitates this process, but so does the patterning of individual quartet presentations, as the next chapter reveals.

Notes

1. Williams-Jones, "Afro-American Gospel Music," p. 376.

2. Paris, *Black Pentecostalism*, pp. 45–97. For other descriptions of Sunday morning worship services see Melvin Williams, *Community in a Black Pentecostal Church: An Anthropological Study* (Pittsburgh: University of Pittsburgh Press, 1974), pp. 101–108; Fauset, *Black Gods of the Metropolis*, pp. 16–19, 27–28, 64–65; Gerald Davis, *I Got the Word in Me and I Can Sing It, You Know* (Philadelphia: University of Pennsylvania Press, 1985), pp. 15–26; Thomas Burns and Stephen Smith,"The Symbolism of Becoming in the Sunday Service of an Urban Black Holiness Church," *Anthropological Quarterly* 51 (July 1978): 185–204; Horace Boyer, "An Analysis of Black Church Music, with Examples Drawn From Rochester, New York," Ph.D. Dissertation, Eastman School of Music, 1973, pp. 157–177, 208–216.

3. For more on the structure of minstrel shows see Toll, *Blacking Up*, pp. 52–57.

4. Personal interview with Charlie Storey, April 18, 1986.

5. Personal interview with the Reverend John Leak, July 8, 1989.

6. Personal interview with the Reverend Alton Griffin, April 24, 1986.

7. Several groups reported making up to five hundred dollars at their anniversaries. Even with a successful anniversary, however, the local groups in this study rarely bring in more than several thousand dollars for a year's worth of singing. Most of this money goes into a treasury to pay for uniforms, instruments, and travel expenses. What little money is left over may be distributed among the group members, or donated to charitable causes. Thus all singers and musicians remain dependent on their non-performing, day jobs for their livelihoods.

8. For further descriptions of community gospel programs and their relationship to church services see Lornell, *"Happy in the Service of the Lord"*, pp.

94–100; Patterson, "Going Up to Meet Him," pp. 91–93; and Feintuch, "A Noncommercial Black Gospel Group in Context," pp. 42–45.

9. Personal interview with the Reverend Vernella Kelly, January 17, 1986.

10. Recorded at Public School 40, Brooklyn, NY, October 13, 1985.

11. Recorded at the Rozier Temple, Harlem, NY, May 4, 1986.

12. Recorded at Public School 40, Brooklyn, NY, August 31, 1986.

13. Personal interview with Rocky Bridges, March 22, 1986.

14. Daniel Patterson reports that during the Golden Echoes' anniversary in North Carolina the honored singers scheduled themselves to appear during "prime time, after the audience has fully gathered and been warmed up by other groups but before the departure of those with weary children or early-morning jobs." See Patterson, "Going Up to Meet Him," p. 92.

15. Paris reports a similar collective structure to performance in his analysis of social roles in a Sunday morning Pentecostal worship service. See Paris, *Black Pentecostalism*, pp. 71–79.

16. Victor Turner, *The Ritual Process* (Ithaca NY: Cornell University Press, 1969), pp. 95–97.

17. Victor Turner, *From Ritual to Theatre* (New York: Performing Arts Journal Publications, 1982), p. 48.

18. Turner, *Ritual Process*, pp. 137–138.

11. Phil Johnson, manager of the Spiritual Voices, in front of his barber shop on Ralph Avenue, Brooklyn, 1989. Photo by Ray Allen.

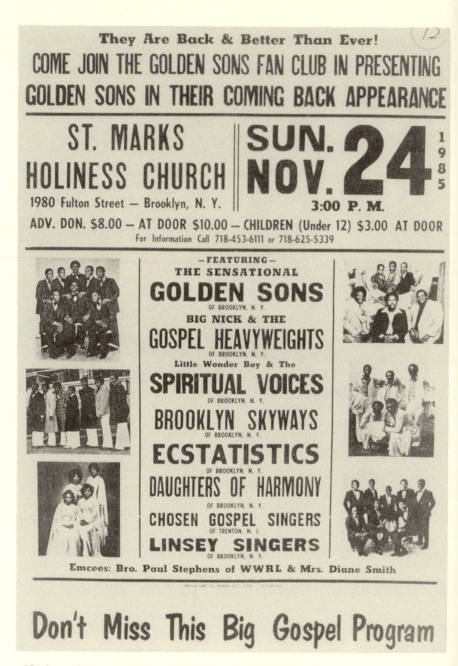

12. Gospel Program Flyer, 1985. Photo by Ray Allen.

Chapter 4
Shouting the Church
Quartet Performance Strategies

When members of a community gospel quartet stand before their local church audience, they aim to do more than simply entertain. If
their singing is strong and the Spirit is moving, they will touch a deep
emotional core and leave their listeners in a state of transcendent joy.
They seek to bring on the experience of the Holy Ghost, or, in their
words, to "shout the church." To achieve this goal, gospel quartet
singers employ a variety of expressive forms: song, narrative, gesture, and dance. During each group's fifteen to twenty minute performance slot these forms are organized into a series of dramatic
expressions, or performance strategies. For discussion purposes the
most prominent of these strategies have been grouped into three
broad categories: dramatic movement (processionals, gestures,
dance, and lead switching); spoken/chanted narrative (formal audience greetings, dramatic narratives, and song commentaries); and
song improvisation (variation in the rendering of lyrics, melody, and
rhythm, and improvised drive sections).

Dramatic Movement

Once the emcee formally announces a group and asks for applause,
the singers often come forward, in ceremonial fashion, from their
seats in the rear of the church. Many groups have their musicians
come on stage while the emcee is talking. As the group is announced,
the musicians begin to play while the singers march, swaying to the
music, down the main aisle to the front of the church. Sometimes a
group will actually begin singing its first song while still seated in the

audience—dramatically rising and continuing to sing as they process to the front of the church.

Similarly, groups will often process off during their last number, eventually reaching their seats or the back of the church while their musicians continue to play (see photo 13). Sometimes the lead singer will have to be escorted off, waving and shouting, if she or he has come under the influence of the Holy Spirit. Often groups choose to process off while singing a slow song. In such instances the background singers will proceed slowly down the aisle, often with hands on each other's shoulders, repeating the final chorus. Meanwhile the lead singer moves in front of them, improvising the lyrics, shouting and waving, often on the verge of tears. Singers may move all the way to the back of the church before completing the song and taking their seats. If the congregation is particularly responsive, singers may remain standing and repeat a final chorus or two.

These processionals serve the dual purposes of heightening dramatic tension and collapsing the symbolic space between the singers and their audience. By emerging from and returning to the congregation over the course of their performance, singers stress their oneness with the audience. Even in larger commercial programs, where groups may enter from a formal backstage area, they will often process off through the audience and exit from the rear of the church or auditorium. When they diminish the normal space between themselves and the congregation, the singers destabilize the traditional artist/audience hierarchy and facilitate the interaction.

In addition to processionals, movement in the form of swaying, walking, prancing, running, dramatic gesturing, acting out lyrics, and dancing in choreographed steps is integral to gospel quartet performance. Upon taking the stage, the background singers stand in a row, several feet apart, with the lead singer standing three or four feet in front of them. The non-singing musicians form a third row behind the background singers. Once the song begins, all of the singers tend to sway with the rhythm, often clapping their hands, patting their thighs, and/or stamping their feet. The lead singer remains relatively stationary at first, although he or she will also clap, pat, and stamp, as well as raise and wave hands, make sweeping arm gestures, or point at individual audience members while singing.

As the song progresses the lead singer may begin to move sideways, walking or prancing back and forth in front of the background singers. The lead singer will then move closer to the audience. If there is a raised stage, he or she will hop off it and approach the first row. In a smaller church with no stage, the lead singer will simply step forward, often moving down the center aisle. The "utility" background singer often will follow close behind, handling the microphone cord. Once the lead singer has penetrated three or four pews into the congregation, she or he may lay down the microphone (or hand it to the utility background singer) and move farther into the audience, while continuing to sing, chant, or shout, often waving both arms dramatically and sometimes touching or shaking hands with congregation members. The lead singer may work his or her way back down the aisle to rejoin the group in front or, if exhausted or overwhelmed by the Spirit, may be escorted back to the group by the utility background singer. Occasionally the lead singer will be so possessed by the Holy Spirit that he or she will run up and down the aisle and must be physically restrained by the other singers. At this point either a new lead singer takes over or the song ends.

Gospel quartets will often switch lead singers in mid-song, particularly during a group's final number (photo 14). The switch usually takes place during a drive section where lead singers engage in extended vocal improvisation (see the Song Improvisation section later in this chapter). The second leader simply steps forward at a prescribed time and takes the microphone from the first leader, who in turn steps back to take a place with the background singers. After the second leader has "worked" the song sufficiently, the first leader may step forward and resume the lead role. Sometimes the two lead singers will remain out front and perform a double-lead routine. Here they trade short, staccato vocal phrases in a rapid call and response fashion. The two singers will often face each other, rocking forward and back in time with the music, exchanging improvised lines (photo 15).

Lead switching and the use of double-leads add variety and intensity to the drama. Through the use of multiple lead singers a group demonstrates its vocal versatility while presenting an array of sound textures and stylistic interpretations in the performance of a single song. And there are other practical advantages to this strategy. During a long song, a leader may become emotionally or physically drained, or so overcome by the Holy Spirit that she or he can no longer sing. A second leader then takes over to maintain the emotional intensity and prolong the song in hopes of engaging additional congregation members in a communal shout.

Another important form of movement is the acting out of song lyrics. Although groups no longer perform the kind of song-skits that Charlie Storey and Thurman Ruth remember as being popular among prewar quartets, singers will often use simple dramatic gestures to enact their words. For example, when the Brooklyn Sky-ways sing "We got to go down on our knees and pray to the Lord above," they fall to their knees (photo 17a). When Ron Adams of the Spiritual Voices sings that he feels the Spirit "all in my hands" and "all in my feet," he shakes his free hand and then points to his feet and runs in place. David Steward wraps his arms around himself as he sings the lyric "Oh Lord, hold me, so tight." To personalize their lyrics further, lead singers will often point directly at themselves while singing a first person verse, or at specific congregational members when singing an interrogative phrase such as "I wonder do *you* feel the Spirit?"

Sometimes the background singers will work out a series of choreographed moves to dramatize the words to a chorus. For example, when the Faithful Harmonizers sing "King of Kings," the background singers point to their heads, mouths, chests, and feet as they sing:

And He changed my mind so I could think right,   [head]
And He changed my tongue so I could talk right,   [mouth]
And He changed my heart so I could love right,   [chest]
And He changed my feet so I can walk right,   [feet]

When the Ecstatistics sing "God shall wipe, all tears, away," all the group's members swoop their right hands down, wipe them in front of their eyes, and swish them to the side, as if to cast off tears.

Younger groups such as the Ecstatistics and the Spiritual Voices actually employ choreographed dance moves. These carefully prepared dance routines are worked out during rehearsals. Sometimes the singers will simply sway their arms and step in a synchronized movement during a chorus or special verse of a song (photo 16). At other times the dance steps will be highlighted, with all singing stopping while the vocalists go through their moves. Such exhibitions will often complement the lyrics, as in a routine used by the Spiritual Voices when they sing "When we get happy, might do the holy dance." Just as they complete this phrase, all four vocalists step forward and execute a synchronized forward and back shuffle-step while the drum alone keeps the beat. Such dramatizations are recognized by the singers and their audience as stylized representations of holy dance—that is, not the "real thing." But the Spiritual Voices feel their theatrics contribute to the power of their overall performance which, they hope, will culminate with possession by the Holy Ghost and "genuine" holy dance. As might be expected, many of the older singers look on such dance routines with a degree of suspicion, arguing that the singers are simply entertaining rather than truly moving with the Spirit. But church audiences generally approve, and such routines often bring them to their feet, clapping and shouting for more.

Spontaneous, "authentic" holy dance does occur when a singer and/or congregation members come under the anointment of the Holy Ghost. This frequently happens during a drive section, and often at the tail end of a presentation, when the singers are processing off the stage and the audience is standing, totally engaged in the performance. To elevate the emotional energy and pave the way for Spirit-induced holy dance the musicians will continue to play, often breaking into a rapid 2/4 rhythmic beat commonly associated with sanctified music. Urged on by the driving rhythms, the singers and/or congregation members may be completely overwhelmed by the Spirit and begin to dance in a fervid manner. Individual dancers, often with closed eyes and grimacing faces, engage in rapid, up and down foot motion, using short hops and/or low kicks. Hands and arms are held tightly to the sides. Hips and torso are generally kept tense and straight, although some individuals bend slightly forward at the waist. Dancers may remain in place, twirl about, or, space permitting, skip or hop up and down the aisles. These extended instrumental sections may continue for up to five minutes, with various singers and congregation members engaging in snatches of holy dance. The movement is physically taxing, and an exhausted dancer may pause, raise his or her hands in a shout or cry, and suddenly resume the dance. Occasionally a dancer may convulse or even collapse. When this happens, nearby worshipers immediately surround the individual to calm him or her and make sure no bodily harm occurs.

Dramatic movement, lead switching, and choreographed dance provide gospel quartet performance with a compelling visual element. Through gestures and enactments the singers underscore the immediacy and emotional depth of their message, and attempt to foster greater audience interaction. The movement of the lead singer into the congregation is of special import, as it represents a conscious effort to diminish the space between performer and audience, and thereby reinforces the participatory nature of the event (photo 17d).

Spoken/Chanted Narrative

Once a group has assumed its position in the performance space facing the congregation, one member will usually step forward to greet the audience. Introductions are usually prefaced with stock phrases such as "Giving honor to God, the pastor and deacons of [the sponsoring] Church, and all who have gathered here this afternoon." The singer responsible for introductions acknowledges and thanks the sponsor, host group, or anniversary honorees for inviting them to the service. If the group members are close friends of the sponsor, words of praise or a humorous anecdote may be offered. And, if time permits, the singer may tell the congregation about a recent trip or special singing engagement, or perhaps ask for prayers if a group or family member is sick or in need.

To express sincerity, a singer will again remind his or her audience they have come to "have church," rather than to put on a show or out-sing the other groups. He or she may give the congregation a chance to respond by asking them how they feel, or if they are ready to serve God. Occasionally a singer will ask all present who believe in Christ and who came out to worship to raise and wave their hands as a public show of faith, as Willie Johnson of the Brooklyn Skyways did one evening at the First Freedom Baptist Church of Jamaica:

Let me see the hands of those out there,
    that come out tonight to have church.
Now I don't mean,
    that somebody came out to see,
        who could sing better than the next person,
        or who can out-dress the next person.
Someone is here tonight,
    that believes there is a God up above.
Now I want to tell you something.
If you don't believe there's a God up there,
    don't even wave your hands.
But if you believe,
    there's a God up above,
        let me see you wave your hands.[1]

Once, when Charlie Storey was annoyed that a local program was billed as a "song battle," he stepped to the microphone as his group took the stage and made his intentions clear:

Are you enjoying yourself?
Give everybody a hand my friends.
And they say this is a battle of the song,
    but I'm glad I'm not on the battling side of the songs.
I'm here to just fill in some of the program.
Ain't but one thing I battle with,
    and that's a battle with Satan,
        he's trying to be what he's not supposed to be.

I believe in battling Satan.
As long as I'm battling for the Lord I'm happy today.
We hope you enjoy yourself.[2]

Such greetings assist the singers in establishing rapport with the congregation and are a catalyst for additional artist/audience interaction. Further, they are yet another vehicle for singers to affirm their spiritual intent and the religious nature of the program.

Following the formal audience greeting, a group may immediately begin its first song, or more words may be offered. Lead singers often use dramatic narratives and commentary to preface and connect songs. During the initial stages of a presentation the leader may simply recite the title and first lines of the upcoming song for the benefit of the background singers and musicians. But when a singer wishes to increase the intensity of audience participation, he or she may choose to offer a lengthy story or testimony as an introduction to the next piece. The longer narratives are often recited in a regular rhythmic cadence or delivered in a chanted vocal style similar to that of a preacher. Here the singer/chanter improvises around a core theme, weaving phrases into rhythmic, formulaic vocalizations that are often punctuated by instrumental riffs and shouts from the background singers.[3] The most effective narrators move into the audience to "testify" and "preach" their words, making generous use of the dramatic gestures described in the previous section.

Before we examine these narratives a brief word on transcription is needed. The spoken, chanted, and sung materials are purposely transcribed and presented in verse-like form, following the fundamental principles of ethnopoetics developed by Dell Hymes and Dennis Tedlock. Recurrent patterns of linguistic features (parallel grammatical construction, repetition, particle markers, elongation of vowels, shifts in tense, etc.) and paralinguistic features (vocal intonation, variation in pitch and loudness, timing, use of pauses, etc.) are used to clarify the internal structure of the verbal texts.[4] The bracketed notations in the right hand column are meant to differentiate—albeit roughly—the spectrum of speaking/chanting/singing styles encountered during a gospel quartet performance. *Ta* (talk) refers to regular speech patterns associated with everyday speaking in terms of rhythm and pitch. *Re* (recitation) refers to speech falling into a regular rhythmic cadence, marked by pronounced pauses and a slight rise in pitch and volume. *Ch* (chant) refers to speech characterized by strong rhythmic cadences, tense vocal constriction, raspy intonation, and a general rise in pitch and volume followed by sudden drops in pitch and volume at the end of each phrase (chanted speech is associated with African-American preaching). *Sch* (song-chant) refers to vocalizations showing more variation in pitch than chanting, but not the degree of organized pitch variation (melodic contour) to qualify as song (song-chant is associated with various vocal improvisations, such as drive sections, that occur during gospel songs). *So* (song) refers to vocalizations regularly associated with singing, characterized by highly organized changes in melodic pitch and tightly structured rhythms. These five notative terms should not be thought of as analytical, mutually exclusive categories; rather they are most useful as general points along a speech/song stylistic continuum.

Turning now to the narratives we see that certain linguistic and paralinguistic conventions that folklorists identify as "keys to performance" and "metanarrational devices" are used to frame and enhance the narrative text.[5] Devices such as opening formulae, parallelism, repetition, elongation of vowels, and variations in vocal delivery style call attention to the narration as an artistic performance while establishing and intensifying the relationship between the singers and the congregation. Take for example a story that Willie Johnson of the Brooklyn Skyways often tells to preface the final song of a presentation. His narration takes the form of a personal testimony, that is, a story recounting how the Lord has been active in an individual's life. Here Johnson recalls a life-threatening accident:

Thank you,   [Ta]
      we need an old fashioned talk with the Lord.
Let me see the hands of those out there,   [Re]
    that come out tonight to have church.
Now I don't mean,
    that somebody came out to see,
      who could sing better than the next person,
        or who can out-dress the next person.
Someone is here tonight,
    that believes there is a God up above.   (Yes)
Now I want to tell you something.   [Ta]
If you don't believe there's a God up there,   [Re]
    don't even wave your hands.
But if you believe,   [Ch]
    there's a God up above,
      let me see you wave your hands.   (yeah)
I feel pretty good tonight church.   [Ta]
I want to tell you my testimony before I go tonight.

You see me standing here right now.   [Re]
How do I look,
    do I look all right?
I want to tell you something.
June thirteenth,
    nineteen hundred and eighty-four,
        I was in a very bad explosion.
You hear them talk about it on WWRL for a long time.
Church,
    one Wednesday evening,
        I was around the garage.
Someone,
    I don't know what happened,
        put some gas,
            in one of the cans.
I picked it up church,
    and I went to throw it out.
But at that time,   [Ch]
the whole thing exploded,
    knocked me down to the ground.
I want to tell you something church.   [Ta]
My face,   [Ch]
    was burned like a burned potato.
My hands were burned like charcoal.
One year later,
    I didn't have no hair on my head.
But look at me right now,   (yeah)
But look at me right now,   (yeah)
Oh-h-h-h   (Oh Lordy)
Look at me now.
Who says God ain't real?
Who says God ain't real?   (Ain't He real)
Oh-h-h-h-h   (Ain't He real)
Look where,
    Jesus brought me from.[6]

Johnson's opening line, "we need an old fashioned talk with the Lord," is a reference to the preceding song. After reaffirming his intentions to "have church" (rather than out-singing or out-dressing the other singers) he uses an opening formula to frame his story: "I want to tell you my testimony before I go tonight." Moving through the tale he switches from a recited to a chanted vocal delivery and ends by emphatically repeating the rhetorical lines "But look at me right now!" and "Who says God ain't real?" His presence in the church, with no signs of scars or burns and a full head of hair, offers proof of God's wondrous healing power, proof that God is indeed real. This sets the stage for the next song, which, appropriately enough, is "Look Where Jesus Brought Me From."

One evening in Hartford, Connecticut, Keith Johnson (no relation to Willie) of the Spiritual Voices offered a similar testimony underscoring the Almighty's miraculous power:

See some of you out there know,   [Re]
You know the Lord,
  worked a miracle in the Spiritual Voices' lives.
Around, two years ago,
  we were on our way to Boston, Massachusetts.
And when we got up here in Hartford, Connecticut,
  it started to rain.
All of the sudden,   (oh yeah)   [Ch]
  a car came in front of us y'all,   [Re]
   yes it did.
We tried to stop,
  but the mean old Devil he wouldn't let us stop y'all.
So our van,
  went into a spin,
   yes it did.   (yes it did)
And the next thing you know y'all,   [Ch]
  we went over a cliff y'all,   (yes we did)   [Re]
   yes we did.
Our van went down that cliff,   [Ch]
  not one time, did that van turn over,
   not two times, did that van turn over.
That van kept tumbling, and
  tumbling,
  tumbling,
  tumbling,
  tumbling,
  tumbling.
We were in the hospital all night long,   (yes we was)
We were in the hospital all night long.   (all night long)
But look at us now.
Ain't the Lord real,
Ain't the Lord real,
Ain't the Lord real.

After blaming the near-fatal crash on the Devil, young Johnson builds his testimony to a peak by switching into a chanted voice and using repetition ("tumbling, tumbling, tumbling" and "Ain't the Lord real?") at the climax. As with the previous example, the group's presence, unharmed, is evidence of God's power to protect the faithful in times of danger. But Johnson is not satisfied with the audience response, and he switches out of narrating mode to address them directly:

```
I see,                                                    [Re]
    some of you sitting out there,
        acting like you don't know who I'm singing about.   (well)
I see there's some young people out there,   (yeah)
    sitting out there looking at me,
        laughing at me,
            because I'm up here singing for the Lord.   (yea)
But I can guarantee you one thing tonight,
If Michael Jackson was up here tonight,
    some of y'all be all over the floor.
Now some of the older people out there,
If James Brown was up here tonight,   (yeah)                [Ch]
    some of y'all would be a-a-all over the floor.   (yeah)
If Michael Jackson's got the nerve to sing "I'm Bad,"
    just leave me alone.
If James Brown's got the nerve to sing,
    "get it on the good foot,"
If James Brown had the nerve to sing please,   (please)
                            please,   (please)
                            please,   (please)

Let me tell you something—
I'm singing about somebody,   (yea)
    better than Michael Jackson.
I'm singing about somebody,
    who will never,   (never)
        leave you alone.
I'm singing about somebody,
    sometimes it'll make me get on the good foot.
I'm singing about somebody,
    when you're in trouble,
        then fall down on your knees,
Tell the Lord please,   (please)
                please,   (please)
                please,   (please)
```

I'm singing about somebody,
 who sits high,
  who look low.
His name is Jesus! (Jesus)
   Jesus! (Jesus)
   Jesus! (Jesus)

Some of you people out there, (go ahead)   [Re]
 looking at me.   (yes)
Say oh,   [Ch]
 he's from New York.   (well)
I know, (I know)   [Re]
 what all them young men be out there doing.
You know some people think they know everything anyway.
He probably be hanging out,
 all night long.
He probably be on the dance floor,
 all night long.
He probably be drinking,
 all kinds of whiskey.
He probably be smoking,
 all kinds of reefer.
But I can stand right here,   [Ch]
 and tell y'all tonight. (yeah)
I don't need no reefer, (yeah)
I don't need no cocaine, (yeah)
I don't need no crack, (yeah)
I don't need no crack. (yeah)
I'm already cracked up on—
I'm already cracked up on—
I'm cracked up on Jesus! (Jesus)
Jesus! (Jesus)
Jesus! (Jesus)
Jesus! (Jesus)
Anybody out there know him? (Jesus)
Anybody out there know him? (Jesus)
Come on and stand on your feet, (stand up)
Stand on your feet, (stand up)
Stand on your feet, (stand up)
Stand on your feet, (stand up)
Say yeah, (yeah)
Say yeah, (yeah)
Say yeah, (yeah)

Say yeah,   (yeah)
Wo-a-a-a-a-
[pause as instruments pick up rhythmic and chordal accompaniment]
Can't nobody,   (do me like Jesus)   [So]
Can't nobody,   (do me like Jesus)
Can't nobody,   (do me like Jesus)
He's, my, friend.[7]

Johnson chastises his audience with a secular contrast, implying they would be more receptive to James Brown or Michael Jackson than to a gospel singer like himself. He than declares himself above such secular temptations, for he has personally rejected the evils of nightlife, alcohol, and drugs so often associated with young African-Americans in cities like New York. Such vices are simply not necessary when you are "cracked up on Jesus" he chants. Note that the second half of this narrative is suffused with repetition and parallel construction ("I don't need no reefer, I don't need no cocaine," etc.). This, combined with his call and response chant with the background singers heightens the drama until he finally breaks into the next song, "Can't Nobody Do Me Like Jesus."

Another testimony depicting the dangers of urban life and God's willingness to "make a way" for His followers is offered by a guest vocalist with the Golden Sons. On this evening Darrell McFadden, who leads most of the group's songs, asks a friend to step forward and "tell his story." The young singer accepts the microphone and speaks:

Oh Lord, ha,   [Re]
      y'all looking at a young man here tonight.
The Lord,
      was on my side. ha,
It was about,
      a year ago.
I was on my way,
      coming home from work, church. ha,
A young man,
      came up to me. ha,
He said so-o-o-n, ha,   [Ch]
      o-o-oh son. ha.
Son do you have any money on you? ha,   [Re]
I looked at the young man I said mister, ha,
      I don't have anything.

The young man pulled out a gun y'all, ha,   [Ch]
    shot me five times. ha,   [Re]
Now y'all don't hear me, ha,
    y'all don't hear me.
Tell me ain't God good.   [Ch]
Tell me won't he make a way for you?
Look at me y'all, ha,
I got shot five times. ha,
But I'm able,
    to be with y'all tonight.
I'm able, ha,
    to wave my hand y'all.
Tell me ain't he good?
Yeah ain't God good?
Yeah!   (yeah)
Yeah!   (yeah)
Yea-a-a-h.
Yes He is!
Yes He is![8]

The singer begins with a relaxed recitation, and then moves to a chant as he elongates the "o"s in "so-o-o-n" and "o-o-h son." He then halts his story, moves back into a recitation delivery, and quips at his unresponsive audience, "Now y'all don't hear me." Again he breaks into chant as he finishes the story of his tragic shooting and triumphant recovery, proclaiming God's goodness as evidenced by his ability to come to church and "wave my hand y'all," in spite of five bullet wounds. Again we see chanted call and response, repetition of short phrases, and an elongated vowel (yea-a-a-h) occurring simultaneously at the climax of the narrative.

On occasion introductory narratives are developed into full blown didactic fables. Consider Darrell McFadden's use of a folk tale about an old billy goat whose perseverance enables him to overcome seemingly insurmountable odds:

Ain't He real tonight?   [Ta]
Can I take a little time and talk to y'all tonight?
Sister Wright I'm reminded of a story,   [Re]
    about an old billy goat.
A billy goat in a farmer's yard.
This billy goat,
    was an old worn out billy goat.

He done worked, and worked, and worked on a farm,
    so many years.
And the farmer knew,
    that this billy goat was old and feeble.
And the farmer didn't worry about him y'all.
Can I take my time and tell the story?   (yeah)
Can I take my time and tell the story?   (yeah)
One day,
    the farmer,
        went in the barn to take care of some business you know,
And the billy goat wandered off into the field.
And a few hours passed on,
And the farmer realized,
    that the billy goat was missing y'all.
The farmer had in the field what they call a dug well,
Those of you from down South ought to know what I'm talking
about when I say a dug well,
This billy goat,
    fell in the well y'all.
And the farmer went to the well,
    and saw the billy goat down in the well—
Is y'all with me so far?
He saw the billy goat down in the well,
He said well,
Guess I'll bury that billy goat down in the well,
    I don't have no more use for him.
And I'm too old to get that heavy billy goat out of the hole.
So the farmer went back in the barn,
    and he got a shovel.
Went back in the field,
    dug up some dirt,
        threw it down in the hole   (yes he did)
            on top of the billy goat.
But that was a smart billy goat you know.
Every time the farmer threw dirt on him,
The billy goat
    shook it off   [Ch]
    ((pause, much applause))
    and he packed it under   [Re]
Ah y'all don't hear me,   (yeah)
Y'all don't listen to me tonight.
This is a good example for all the Saints here tonight.

The farmer got some sticks,   (well)
    and threw it down in that well.
But the billy goat said oh no,   (oh no)
He just shook it off,
    and tucked it under y'all.   (yeah)
The billy goat shook it off,
    and tucked it on under.   (yeah)
He shook it off,
    and tucked it under.   (yeah)
After a while, you know that smart billy goat got
    hi-i-i-i-igh.   [Ch]
Yeah,   (yeah)
Yeah,   (yeah)
Yeah,   (yeah)
Yeah,   (yeah)
[instruments crash, then pause]
We ought to learn from that billy goat tonight,   [Re]
The more your so-called friends lie on you   [Ch]
Shake it off,
    and pack it under.
The more they talk about you,
Shake it off,   (yeah)
Shake it off,   (yeah)
Shake it off,   (yeah)[9]

From here McFadden moves into a brief testimony that he uses to segue into the song "Lay Down My Life for the Lord" (see Chapter 2). The tale undoubtedly strikes a familiar chord with older southern-born listeners. To them the billy goat may well symbolize the plight of an elderly rural African-American, worn out from a life of hard work and servitude and cast off by the master (in times of slavery) or the land owner (in times of sharecropping). But presumably by maintaining faith in God the heroic figure is able to "shake off" the earthly hardships and eventually emerge in triumph. Note also McFadden's use of rhetorical conventions to frame the story and engage his audience. He begins with an opening formula, "Can I take a little time and talk to y'all tonight? Sister Wright [the emcee] I'm reminded of a story." After introducing the farmer and the billy goat, he suddenly breaks the narrative line, stepping out of the tale to ask the audience, "Can I take my time and tell the story?" Apparently assured by their cheers and applause, he continues the narration. But halfway through he stops again to address his listeners directly: "Ah y'all don't hear me, y'all don't listen to me tonight" and declares that his story has an important Christian moral—"we ought to learn from that billy goat tonight." By pausing throughout the narrative to request audience support—or to admonish them for lack of support—McFadden reminds them of the closeness of the performer/audience relationship and encourages their participation. And finally the use of chant, background vocal/instrumental response, the elongated "i" in hi-i-i-igh, and repetition brings the story to a dramatic climax, driving home the message, "Shake it [earthly hardships] off," and trust in the Lord.

Not all narratives take the form of personal testimonies or fully developed didactic tales. Many are simply short moral commentaries or reminiscences that somehow relate to the theme of the upcoming song. For example, Charlie Storey prefaces the song "Peace in the Valley" (see Chapter 2) with sentimental memories of his old singing colleagues who have passed on:

Sometimes when I look around,   [Ta]
    think about the Selah Jubilee Singers, Brother Ruth.
And there were six of those fellows,
    and I went to mostly everyone of their funerals.
And all of them are gone but Brother Ruth.
And I had a group called Charlie Storey and the Jubilee Stars,
    it was five of us fellows.
And all of them are gone,
    all but me, one.
And they told me years ago when I started singing,   [Re]
    years ago they said "Son, you got to sing easy,
Because if you sing the way you're singing,
    you won't be here long."
Well, I'm not singing myself,
    when the little wheel begins to turn in me
                   [reference to the Holy Spirit]
And they're all gone,
    fifteen or twenty years ago.
And I'm still here,
    singing hard.
So that tells me if God got a job for you to do,
    don't worry about .. ? ..
This song—
    sometimes I begin to get tired and get worried,
This song comes on my mind,
    think about all the friends we got gone.
This song comes up—[10]

Song commentaries sometimes conjure up nostalgic visions of family life and worship from the old rural South. Robert Todd of the Heavenly Tones reminds his audience he is from Georgia, reminisces about his grandparents and the way they use to "have church," and recalls his own conversion. He goes on to exhort his listeners to "make a joyful noise" and prepare themselves for the coming of the Spirit, thereby setting the stage for his song, "Let the Holy Ghost Come on Down."

Time is now.   [Re]
Time to get in a hurry,
    to serve the Lord.
[reference to last song]
I'm just looking out here,   [Ta]
    my mind is going back.
You see I'm a Georgia boy,
And I remember,
    Grandmother and Grandfather,
      we called them Grandma and Grandpa.
They used to have church,
And that's when I found the Lord,
    back there.
And I told them,   [Re]
    every chance I got,
      I would serve.
But I don't believe,
    He'd be satisfied today with our service,
      so many times.   (amen, amen)
David picked up his pen and said,
    "Make a joyful noise,"   (yes he did)   [Ch]
Come on church,
    make a joyful noise.
And we're sitting here like we're listening,   [Re]
    for something spectacular to happen.
So we're going to ask just for that now,
    we're going to ask for that spectacular—
      whatever you're looking for.
But I'm going to ask the Lord to send the Holy Ghost,   (yes)
I don't know what you are looking for,
    I don't know what you expect,
      but I'm going to ask him to send the Holy Ghost.
Because I found out—
    I didn't find it back there when I was a child,

and I accepted the Lord.
But later on, through the years,   [Ch]
    I found out that I can't do nothing,
        until the Holy Ghost comes.
I found out I can do all things,
    through Christ,
        is standing by to tell me that.
So let's ask the Lord to send the Holy Ghost down,   [Re]
I want y'all to get together,
    let's have church,
        let's have church.
I don't know,
    may be my last time,
        I don't know.
I may not be here another day,
    there's no guarantee.
But if He sends the Holy Ghost down,
    everything will be all right.[11]

Other song commentaries take the form of brief sermonettes, where the singer/chanter expounds on a song's spiritual significance. At the close of the Faithful Harmonizers' rendition of "King of Kings" (see Chapter 2), the Reverend Vernella Kelly recalls her own search and spiritual conversion as a young woman in Florida, and "recommends Him" to those listeners who have yet to find the Lord. Kelly continues to chant thanks to Jesus as the group softly breaks into a slow hymn, "I'm Coming on Home."

Hey,   [Ch]
    hallelujah,
        hallelujah.
Kept on searching,   (yes Lord)
    yes I did.   (thank you)
Finally one Monday morning,
    down in the state of Florida,   (yes sir)
        Nineteen hundred and thirty-three,   (hallelujah)
Kept on searching,   (yes)
    I kept right on searching,   (yes)
        and one day I found Him.   (oh yes)
Thank you Jesus.   (thank you)
O-o-o-o-oh,   [Sch]
    yeah, yeah, yeah.

I'm sorry,   [Re]
    if you,
        if you didn't find him.
I'm sorry,   (thank you)   [Ch]
    if you don't know Jesus.   (glory)
        I recommend Him to you.
Because I know a man,   (yes)
    from Galilee,   (yes)
If you're in sin,   (yes)
    He'll set you free.   (yes)
I wonder do you know Him,   (know Him)
    I'm so glad I know,
        I know Him for myself,
Thank you Jesus,   (thank you)
    hallelujah.   (glory)

[The rest of the group now begins to sing]

I wandered Lord,   [So]
    away from God,
But now,
    I'm coming on home.
The path of sin,
    too long I have traveled,
Lord, I'm coming,
    coming on home.

[Reverend Kelly continues to chant over the singing]

Thank you.   [Ch]
It will get all over you,
    just like fire.
Thank you Lord,
    thank you.
As I grow older,
    I get stronger.
Thank you Lord,
    thank you Jesus.
Oh glory,
    oh glory.
One day we are going on home,
    it's later than we think.
Thank you Jesus,
    thank you Jesus.[12]

This sequence closes the group's performance. As the singers move from the front of the church toward their seats, Reverend Kelly continues her emphatic chant, "Thank you Jesus," while congregation members murmur, cry, and wave their hands.

Narratives and song commentaries function in several important ways. Structurally they connect separate songs into a cohesive whole: ideally one number flows into another as the performance builds toward spiritual invocation. Note, for example, how Reverend Kelly's sermonette connects "Kept on Searching" with the Faithful Harmonizers' closing hymn. Or turn back to the first narrative discussed in this section, where Willie Johnson's initial comments refer to the preceding song, while his testimony thematically and emotionally "sets up" the next. A full performance by the Brooklyn Skyways that follows shortly demonstrates how narratives and songs are interwoven to form a complete twenty-minute presentation. In addition, dramatic narratives and commentaries serve to personalize specific songs. Song leaders usually tell narratives in the first person, or manage to identify themselves with the main character of their story and upcoming song. The "good talkers" who exploit this technique are able publicly to share their intimate thoughts, feelings, and life experiences, thus confirming the sincerity of the presentation.[13]

The thematic structure of individual narratives further serves to tighten communal bonds between participants. In terms of diachronic plot structure, the most successful narratives create tension by offering specific instances of earthly hardship, thus reminding listeners of the suffering inherent in the human condition. The death of a loved one, an accident, sickness, poverty, drugs and crime in the streets, growing violence among young people, or a national (the loss of the Space Shuttle Discovery) or an international disaster (the Beijing massacre) are common themes. The tension is ultimately resolved as the singer reveals that through faith in Christ, listeners can overcome their worldly problems and receive unlimited joy. A shared sense of struggle and spiritual salvation is intimated. Further, when singers talk about their southern roots and their longing to go back to the "old-time religion" of their forebears, they are reaffirming a deep sense of common history with their audience, an issue that will be returned to in more detail in Chapter 7.

Similarly the synchronic or relational structure of the narratives is based on a sacred/secular contrast: Christ and redeeming grace are pitted against Satan and worldly temptations and hardships, with the former always emerging victorious. Worth noting is the amount of space that is devoted to the description of this world's troubles. While the solution to earthly suffering is spiritual transcendence, the singers must never lose sight of their listeners' everyday social and economic problems. The biblical teachings they exalt in song make the most sense when tied to concrete secular examples; Christian doctrine and faith must connect with the problems of poverty, sickness, crime, and drugs that many inner-city African-Americans face daily.[14] Again, recounting shared problems and a shared solution through dramatic narrative fosters a sense of shared group identity.

The rhetorical narrative structure and performance conventions also reinforce the collective nature of the event, while simultaneously increasing dramatic tension. Singer/chanters self-consciously work to diminish the distinctions between themselves and their listeners when they break the narrative line to elicit congregational feedback and support. Moreover, the co-occurrence of chanting, background/instrumental response, repetition of phrases, and elongated vowels signals a heightened dramatic moment that invites full participation. Singer/chanters and congregational members occasionally fall under the anointment of the Holy Spirit during the performance of a particularly moving narrative, but more often narratives set the stage for a spiritual crescendo that occurs during the following song.

Song Improvisation

Once the actual song begins, the lead singer is expected to bring his or her own personal interpretation to the composition through extended improvisation and special vocal techniques. The melody and lyrics of a gospel song are not fixed entities, rather they provide the singer with a basic musical structure that he or she is expected to embellish. The actual "form" of a gospel song, as Pearl Williams Jones points out, is "merely the framework around which improvisation could take place."[15] Vocal melodies are ornamented through use of melisma, glides, falsetto swoops, and the interjection of spoken or chanted phrases. Individual singers will alter the rhythmic attack of their vocal phrasing to add further variation, while background singers and instrumentalists are free to create new harmonic and rhythmic accompaniments.[16] Song lyrics may be expanded with the addition of stock phrases or the rapid repetition of lines or phrases from the song. Or the lead singer may choose to omit a line from a song and substitute a stock phrase, shout, or moan while the background sings the actual words. In the latter situation the lead singer may totally abandon the song's lyrics and improvise at will, as James Fitzpatrick does in the Heavenly Tones' rendition of "Steal Away to Jesus" (see Chapter 2) and Willie Johnson does during the Brooklyn

Skyways' interpretation of "By and By" (see the second half of this chapter).

Lead singers use a variety of devices to produce a rich mosaic of vocal sounds and textures. Smooth, legato-style, high pitched singing is generally favored for slow tempo songs. Here lead singers may make extensive use of melisma, glides, and swoops or jump into a falsetto voice. Faster songs tend to feature a shorter-phrased, rougher vocal delivery, characterized by a high degree of vocal rasp and often accompanied by shouts, moans, and cries. At times both styles are employed simultaneously—the lead singer may improvise in a rough, shouting voice while the background singers croon the chorus in a smooth, clean style. In many groups, one singer may specialize in leading the smoother, "sweet" songs, while another takes the rougher "gospel" or "hard" numbers. Exploiting a wide vocal range is another favorite technique. Singers are admired for their ability to jump an octave or more, to move smoothly between a regular and falsetto voice, and to hold an extremely high or low note over an extended period of time. For example, congregations often come to their feet, cheering and shouting, when a tenor singer holds a high falsetto pitch for an extended period or when a bass singer strikes a particularly low, resonant note. A skillful lead singer will use melodic or textual improvisation and dramatic vocal shadings as a way of placing his or her unique stamp on a song. Like the dramatic narratives discussed in the previous section, the personal song interpretation conveys a sense of spiritual sincerity and enables a singer to express his or her feelings in a more convincing manner. The importance of song personalization as a core aesthetic principle will be taken up in the following chapter.

Song improvisation is not limited to embellishing the melody and lyrics of the verse/chorus structure, for many pieces include extended segments of vocal improvisation known as "drive," "gospel," or "working" sections. A drive section begins when the instrumentalists stall on one chord while the background singers repeat a single vocal line over and over. At this point the lead singer begins to ad-lib, switching from his or her regular singing voice into a tense, high pitched, rhythmically repetitive chant [Ch] or singing chant [Sch]. Occasionally the background singers will drop out, leaving the lead singer to continue his or her vocal improvisation with only the instruments for accompaniment. Or, as described in the first section of this chapter, a second lead singer may join the first and throw improvised phrases back and forth in a tight, call-and-response format. Short drive sections are sandwiched in the middle of the verse/chorus structure of many songs. But extended drive sections usually occur during a group's final selection, where the lead singer's chanted vocalizations are frequently accompanied by a slight increase in tempo and volume, as the musicians and background singers help build the song. During these final drive sections leads are often switched, double-leads are employed, and unrestrained movement is exhibited as singers walk or run into the congregation, wave their hands, shout, or grimace.

The texts of drive sections consist primarily of short, repetitive words and phrases. Formulaic lines such as "Can I get a witness?," "I want to thank you Jesus," "I wonder can you feel the fire?" or "Said ain't God good?" are often simply plugged in and recited in a rhythmic chant. Extended repetition of these short phrases is a hallmark of the drive. Although lead singers use a chanting style similar to that of preachers, rarely do their words take the form of a sermon or narrative plot. Rather, extended drive sections often begin as a personal testimony about the lead singer's original conversion, and go on to expound on the joys of salvation and the exhilarating feeling of the Holy Spirit. Eventually the lead singer will address the audience more directly, extending the invitation to those who are saved and sanctified to join together and feel the Holy Spirit. Clifford Williams, for example, starts his drive section in "Look Where Jesus Brought Me From" by noting his original condition of sin and subsequent conversion:

He brought me up,	(He brought me up)	[Sch]
He brought me up,	(He brought me up)	
When I was down,	(He brought me up)	
He picked me up,	(He brought me up)	
Turned me all around.	(He brought me up)	
And I remember,	(He brought me up)	
And I remember.	(He brought me up)	
When I was in sin.	(He brought me up)	
Nobody but Jesus,	(He brought me up)	[Ch]
Nobody but Jesus,	(He brought me up)	
Nobody but Jesus,	(He brought me up)	
Nobody but Jesus,	(He brought me up)	
He picked me up,	(He brought me up)	
He turned me around,	(He brought me up)	

Next, Williams addresses the crowd, inviting them to stand and clap as proof they are born again and filled with the Holy Ghost:

Everybody,	(He brought me up)	[Ch]
Everybody,	(He brought me up)	
Stand on your feet,	(He brought me up)	
Stand on your feet,	(He brought me up)	
And let the world know,	(He brought me up)	
You been born again,	(He brought me up)	
You been born again,	(He brought me up)	
You been born again,	(He brought me up)	
Been filled with the Holy Ghost	(He brought me up)	
Been filled with the Holy Ghost	(He brought me up)	
Everybody,	(He brought me up)	
Everybody,	(He brought me up)	
Come on,	(He brought me up)	
Come on,	(He brought me up)	
Let me hear you,		[Sch]
clap your hands.		
Let me hear,		
clap your hands.		
Just clap them a little bit louder,		
Just clap them a little bit louder.		
Let everybody know,		
that you are not ashamed.		
You been born,		
with the Holy—		
with the Holy fire.		
You been wash, wash, a washed,		
You been a wash, wash a washed.		
All right,		
He's all right.[17]		

A similar pattern is followed by Darrell McFadden in the Golden Sons' performance of "Lay Down My Life for the Lord." He begins his drive by improvising with the lyrical theme of the song that talks about "going home" to heaven:

I'm going home,	(Oh yes I'm going home)	[Sch]
I'm going home,	(Oh yes I'm going home)	
What about you?	(Oh yes I'm going home)	
Do you want to go home,	(Oh yes I'm going home)	
What about you?	(Oh yes I'm going home)	
Do you want to go home?	(Oh yes I'm going home)	
Do you want to go home?	(Oh yes I'm going home)	

Do you want to go home?	(Oh yes I'm going home)
Sit down and rest a while,	(Oh yes I'm going home)
Sit down and rest a while,	(Oh yes I'm going home)
Talking with my Jesus,	(Oh yes I'm going home)
Talking with my Jesus,	(Oh yes I'm going home)
Lord I've been rebuked	(Oh yes I'm going home)
Lord I've been scorned	(Oh yes I'm going home)
Ain't going to worry about it,	(Oh yes I'm going home)
Ain't going to worry about it,	(Oh yes I'm going home)
'Cause I'm out here on the street,	(Oh yes I'm going home)
Resting for the weary,	(Oh yes I'm going home)
Lord you promised me,	(Oh yes I'm going home)
Rest for the weary,	(Oh yes I'm going home)
When I get to Heaven,	(Oh yes I'm going home)
When I get to Heaven,	(Oh yes I'm going home)
Looking for my mother,	(Oh yes I'm going home)
Looking for my father,	(Oh yes I'm going home)
Looking for my sister,	(Oh yes I'm going home)
Looking for my brother,	(Oh yes I'm going home)
Home . . ? . .	(Oh yes I'm going home)
I'm going to look for my Jesus,	(Oh yes I'm going home)
I'm going to look for my Jesus,	(Oh yes I'm going home)

The background singers eventually drop out and a second lead steps forward to echo McFadden's improvisations. At this point the second lead singer mentions his own conversion, and the two singers engage in a chanting duel about the Holy Ghost, asking the audience if they indeed feel the "power":

Let me tell you what He done,	(yeah)	[Sch]
Let me tell you what He done,	(yeah)	
Early one Sunday morning,	(Early one Sunday morning)	
Early one Sunday morning,	(Early one Sunday morning)	
Let me tell you what He done,	(yeah)	
Sanctified my life,	(oh yes He did)	
Sanctified my life,	(oh yes He did)	
Filled me with the Holy Ghost,	(filled me with the Holy Ghost)	
Filled me with the Holy Ghost,	(filled me with the Holy Ghost)	
The Holy Ghost,	(power)	
The Holy Ghost,	(power)	
The Holy Ghost,	(power)	
The Holy Ghost,	(the Holy Ghost)	

The Holy Ghost,	(power)
The Holy Ghost,	(the Holy Ghost)
The Holy Ghost,	(power)
Somebody,	(Holy Ghost)
Got that,	(power)
Holy Ghost,	
Somebody,	(anybody)
Got that,	(got that)
Holy Ghost,	(power)
Holy Ghost,	(power)

Next the second lead drops out, and while the music continues, McFadden exhorts his audience to stand, clap, shout, and finally come forward and shake his hand. The second lead rejoins McFadden as a number of audience members run to the stage to shake hands, while others begin to shout and dance with the Spirit:

Wait a minute,   [Re]
Wait a minute,
I know our time is about up here.
But I want to ask somebody here tonight,
    that know God been good to you.
If y'all know God been good to you,
    the ones sitting down in your seat,
If y'all know God done something for y'all that y'all like,
    let me see y'all stand on your feet, come on.
        ((pause with music))
That ain't all.
If y'all know that God is good,
    let me here you clap your hands.
Come on.
    ((hand clapping increases))
That ain't all.
If y'all know,
    that God can save your soul,
I wonder if I can get about,
    five people to come down here,
        and shake my hand.
Huh?
    Is that all right?
If y'all know it's all right,
    then let me here you say yes,   (yes)

Say yes,   (yes)   [Ch]
Say yes,   (yes)
Say yes,   (yes)
Come on and shake my hand,   [Sch]
Come on and shake my hand,
If ya'll know He's all right,   (know He's all right)
    come on and shake my hand,   (come on and shake my hand)
The ones that been born again,   (been born again)
If you been born again,   (been born again)
    come on and shake my hand,   (come on and shake my hand)
Don't be shamed at all,   (don't be ashamed at all)
    don't be ashamed at all.   (don't be ashamed)
Don't be shamed at all.   (don't be ashamed)
What about you,   (about you)
    if you been born again,   (if you been born again)
Come on and shake my hand,   (come on and shake my hand)
Come on and shake my hand,   (come on and shake my hand)
Come on and shake my hand,   (come on and shake my hand)
Oh yeah,
Yeah,[18]

McFadden challenges his audience to become active participants in the performance as proof of their faith, and they respond accordingly.

Improvised drive sections allow lead singers to express their own personal feelings of Spirit-induced joy while simultaneously inviting their listeners to share in the experience. During the climax of extended drive sections distinctions between performers and audience blur, as the lead singers are most likely to set down their microphones and walk or run into the audience of clapping, shouting worshipers. Combining extensive repetition of short phrases, a chanted/sung-chanted vocal delivery, and demonstrative movement, drive sections serve as rhetorical devices that exhort the audience members to unite with the singers in the collective oneness of spontaneous communitas. Not surprisingly, the various manifestations of Spirit-induced behavior often reach their peak toward the end of extended drive sections. While singers and their listeners claim they may feel the Spirit and begin to "get happy" at any time in a gospel service, it is during extended drive sections that they are most apt to shout, cry, holy dance, and completely "fall out" into states of Spirit possession. Singers may become so engrossed in the Spirit that they must be helped off the stage by fellow group members and, on occasion, may come running back to the front of the church to continue to sing or testify, only to be ushered off again. Moreover, it is during long drive sections that singers actually make reference to their original conversion and imply their desire to re-experience those feelings, collectively, with fellow worshipers.

Not all local quartets use the above outlined spectrum of dramatically enacted, spoken, chanted, and sung performance strategies in a single presentation. Moreover, many of the older groups tend to shy away from what they consider to be flamboyant theatrics— the preached song introductions, extended drive sections, choreographed dance, and rhythmic jam sessions. But the middle-aged and younger groups who were reared on the postwar hard gospel sound make use of the full range of strategies. For them, these stylized behaviors form a repertoire of expressive components that, in various combinations, produce an aesthetically pleasing and spiritually fulfilling performance.

Two final points need to be made about the overall organization of gospel quartet performance. First, most groups combine expressive strategies in a way that gradually augments the emotional excitement and participation of their listeners. The singers actually refer to this process as "building" or "setting up" the church. Their initial songs and testimonies are meant to stir up the feelings of the congregation, while their final number aims to bring these emotions to a climax through the invocation of the Holy Spirit.

There are two ways in which groups culminate their performances in order to reach this desired goal. The first aims at an ecstatic experience and uses an up-tempo song featuring driving rhythms and an extended drive section. After completing several short songs, the lead singer will warn the congregation that the group's time is nearly up, but he or she wishes to depart with a final thought. This is often followed by a lengthy and spirited testimony that serves as a preface to the final song. During the last drive section, the sung, chanted, and dramatic components of the performance will reach peak levels, as the singers strive to call down the Holy Ghost and pave the way for spiritual ecstasy. Singers finally process off or are helped from the performance floor as the musicians continue the heavy rhythms.

A second technique tries to create a more mournful atmosphere. There is a final processional in which singers walk slowly off the stage and through the audience singing a slow, soulful song. Such a piece is usually begun at the front of the church, but after singing several verses, the group will move out and walk slowly down the aisle, with the lead singer out front, singing and testifying dramatically. Between pleas and sobs the leader may actually lean into the audience, shaking hands and hugging individual congregation members in a show of love and emotional sincerity. The aim here is not so much to induce unrestrained shouting and dancing as to move the congregation to a state of tears. Groups may also combine fast and slow songs in culminating their performances. As a successful extended drive section of the fast song winds to an end, the group may jump abruptly into a slow song and begin to process off. This dramatic shift often serves to cool down an ecstatic congregation, gradually returning them to a more composed state. Emotions continue to stir, but the more emphatic shouting and dancing will slowly subside, giving way to moans and cries.

Worth noting is the degree of spontaneity involved in the way a group organizes any given performance. Singers stress that while the order of their songs are often planned in rehearsal, they are never completely sure how their presentation will develop until they reach the program and evaluate the situation. The nature of the audience and its response to other groups may lead them to make last minute substitutions. For example, if the congregation consists primarily of younger and/or Holiness individuals, another up-tempo song may be added. On the other hand, if the audience is mainly older, more sedate Methodists or Baptists, additional slow hymns may be in order. And singers must leave themselves open to last minute divine guidance, as the Spirit may inspire a certain song at any given time. In short, singers must be highly attentive to the mood of their audience and to the emotional and spiritual atmosphere of any given situation. Flexibility and spontaneity are essential qualities of all successful performances.

This leads to a second point concerning the organization of the performance. While the goal of each group is to build toward a climactic spiritual experience, there is an overall sense of open-endedness in any given performance, as there is in the entire gospel program. For example, although each group is usually told to limit its presentation to two or three songs, it is understood that if the "Spirit is high," additional songs may be sung or the final song may be extended. Narratives connect songs, resulting in a continual flow of performance rather than a distinctly segmented presentation where a clear break separates one song from the next. Drive sections seem to roll on relentlessly, ending not through some logical narrative resolution, but simply when the lead singer becomes too exhausted or overwhelmed with the Spirit to continue improvising. Singers may begin to process off the floor, signaling the close of their performance, and suddenly run back up front to sing an additional verse or perhaps to begin an entirely new song. They must often be escorted off, only to break away once more to attempt a final verse or engage in a few steps of holy dance. It is often difficult to know exactly when a performance is actually over, and for the believer who is high in the Spirit, it may never be.

The entire gospel program—itself an event consisting of a series of individual yet connected performances—also reflects a sense of non-resolution. The level of intensity of a given program tends to surge and abate, rather than build up gradually to a climactic point when the final group takes center stage. Emotions may erupt during performances by groups early or midway through a program, subside for a while, and finally resurge toward the end. At this macro-level, there is usually no single point of culmination or resolution to a gospel program. The event seems to unfold continuously, to move along in a syndetic flow marked by fluctuating levels of emotional involvement.[19] Gospel programs are notoriously long, often lasting for four, five, or even six hours, usually with no official intermission. There is no sense of final closure; the song service comes to an end simply because of time constraints. One senses that the performance could go on indefinitely, that only one segment of an ongoing series has been witnessed, that things will be continued next week. And they usually are.

This open-endedness allows participants to transcend the temporal and spatial boundaries of the event itself. Audience members leave a good gospel program with a sense of spiritual and aesthetic fulfillment that stays with them for some time. They speak of flashes of spiritual happiness as songs from a Sunday afternoon program roll through their minds throughout the week. Singers will often recount and evaluate a particularly striking performance for days to come. Like a well-preached sermon, the impact of a moving gospel performance may carry beyond the confines of the immediate ritual and into the participants' everyday lives.[20]

Examining a full performance by a single gospel quartet demonstrates how the above strategies and principles of performance organization are implemented. A sample performance by the Brooklyn Skyways recorded at a medium-sized Holiness Church in Harlem serves this purpose. Approximately two hundred people are in attendance at Rozier Temple on Saturday evening, April 5, 1986. The program, with a ten dollar ticket admission, features a soloist, a choir, half a dozen local gospel groups, and two semi-professional guest quartets from South Carolina. Although scheduled to begin at 7:30, the opening devotional service does not get underway until approximately 8:30. By the time the emcee, Rocky Bridges, calls on the

Brooklyn Skyways, a soloist and six other groups have performed. It is nearly 11 o'clock. Emotions are running high, as the previous three groups have put on moving performances during which a number of congregation members became overwhelmed by the Holy Spirit. Several women are standing, waving their arms and shouting "Thank you Jesus," as the Mighty New Tones leave the floor. Rocky Bridges looks in their direction and calmly notes, "That's all right. When you are in church, you let the Spirit have its way." As the congregation quiets down and the women regain their composure, Bridges begins talking about the Brooklyn Skyways, recalling how he has traveled with them to the Carolinas and to Bermuda. Seeing that the musicians are ready, and that the singers are poised in the back of the church, Bridges asks the congregation to give a warm welcome to the Brooklyn Skyways. On this cue the musicians begin a snappy, 4/4 tempo instrumental piece as the four singers, Willie Johnson Sr., Willie Johnson Jr., Clifford Williams, and Leverne Robinson, come forward from the back of the church, swaying slightly to the beat. The singers take their places in front of the musicians, facing the congregation, and Willie Johnson Sr. steps forward to greet the audience as the music ends.

Addressing the audience in a speech mode normally associated with everyday, non-expressive talk, Johnson mentions that the group members are tired because they have just returned from a lengthy trip to Tampa, Florida. He assures the audience that the group is ready to have a good time, and turns the microphone over to Leverne Robinson, who immediately begins the first song, "There's a Better Way Church." The song, rendered in a medium 4/4 tempo, is a plea for people all across the world to strengthen their faith and return to God:

There's a better way church,   [So]
    there's a better way.
There's a better way church,
    there's a better way.
We've got to live,
    live together,
        down here.

Robinson, a natural tenor, stands well in front of the background singers while leading the first two choruses of the song. He then calls on "Brother Williams," steps back, and hands the microphone to Clifford Williams, who steps forward to lead the song in a deeper, slightly gruffer baritone voice:

All this country needs,   [So]
   (is a little more faith),
Church, all, that we need, right now, y'all,
   (is a little more faith),
Well all that we need, yeah,
   (is a little more faith)
We need an old,
   fashioned talk,
     with the Lord.

By the second verse Williams has become quite animated, waving his free arm as he sings, and falling down on one knee, arm stretched upward at the appropriate line in the verse:

One more thing I'd like to say if you don't mind,   [Sch]
People in America,   [So]
   Russia and China too,
Let me tell the world,
   just what we all should do,
Church we should go down on our knees,
   church and pray to the Lord above,
If the world could do that church,
   we'll have better luck.
We need an old,
   fashioned talk,
     with the Lord.

Williams hands the microphone back to Robinson, who steps forward to finish leading the song.

As the song ends, Robinson returns the microphone to Willie Johnson Sr., who again steps forward and speaks to the church. He relates a story of how his son, Willie Jr., recently returned to the Skyways after touring with another group. The tale is touching, ending with the father and son vocal team happily reunited. Shortly after beginning the narrative, Johnson Sr. switches from a talking mode into a slightly more rhythmic style of recitation:

My son was on the road,   [Re]
   he was traveling with Willie Black and the Messengers.
And I got a little worried,
   I didn't even know what to do,
And I said to the Lord,
   I said,

I brought my son into the world,
>to grow up to be a man,
And he's out there helping somebody,
>when I need him myself.
One Father's Day,
>that Sunday morning around about six o'clock,
>>he called me from Oakland, California.
He said happy Father's Day,
>happy Father's Day.
And he said, pop,
>in three weeks,
>>I'm going to be home,
>>>and I'm going to help you.
And I'm happy for him,
>and he's doing a beautiful job.
That's Willie Johnson Junior,
>give him a big hand.
We got this song together,
>he's doing a part in it.

Willie Johnson Sr. then asks for a round of applause for his son and moves into the song "By and By," featuring a prominent high tenor harmony sung by Willie Jr. The background singers croon the song's slow, sweet chorus, while Willie Johnson Sr. interjects snatches of lyrics in a rough, semi-chanted voice.

Sing it now, sing it.   (By, and by, Lord,)   [Sch]
>Lord, thank you Lord.   (when, the morning comes.)
You know church, all God's children,   (All God's children,)
>gathering,   (are going to gather home.)
And I'll be able—tell the story,   (And we'll tell, the story,)
>When I get over there,   (of how, we overcome,)
Listen—oh-h-h,   (And we'll, understand it better,)
>One of these old mornings y'all,   (by and by.)

He hands the microphone back to Leverne Robinson, who steps forward to lead a verse. The song ends with Johnson Sr. again resuming the lead and improvising over the final chorus.

Willie Johnson Sr. remains forward. He asks the congregation how they feel, noting that they have been "having church" during the previous group's performance. He then launches into a version of the personal testimony examined earlier in this chapter—the narrative about being burned in a gas explosion and miraculously healed with

no facial scars or other physical disfigurements. Approximately halfway through the testimony he switches from a slightly rhythmic style
of recitation into a tense, high-pitched chant similar to that associated
with preaching. Beneath his rhythmic vocalizations the instruments
strum, and the background singers punctuate his cries with shouts of
"Yeah" and "Oh-h-h y'all." Johnson prances back and forth in front
of the singers, arm outstretched. Finally he puts down the microphone and runs down the aisle, shouting and waving both arms frantically.

There've been people burned,   [Ch]
    have scars all over their face,
I don't have no scars on my face,
Look at me,
    look at me right now.
Ohhh—   (ain't God good?)
Ohhh—   (ain't God a good God?)
Ohhh—   (He's good tonight, y'all)

Johnson scurries back to the front of the church, continuing his impassioned chants while the background singers echo "Ain't God
good?" By this time most of the audience members are on their feet,
waving and clapping as Johnson hands the microphone over to Clifford Williams. The musicians pick up a steady, rocking 4/4 beat and
Williams begins leading "Look Where Jesus Brought Me From":

Look where, Jesus brought me from,   [So]
Church, look where, Jesus brought me from,
He brought me from the cradle,
    up to the present time,
Just look where, Jesus brought me from.
One more thing—
[repeat chorus]
One more thing, church—
Look where, He brought my mother from,
Church just look where, He brought my mother from,
Said He brought her from the cradle,
    church up to the present time,
Just look where, He brought my mother from.

After several verses Williams moves into an extended drive section,
switching into a chanted/sung vocal pattern as the background singers repeat "Jesus brought me up" over and over again. He then refers

to his earlier state of sin and how Jesus picked him up, implying his salvation. As Williams improvises he moves back and forth across the front performance area and penetrates several rows down the center aisle. The congregation continues to stand and clap.

When I was down,	(Jesus brought me up)	[Sch]
He brought me up,	(Jesus brought me up)	
He picked me up,	(Jesus brought me up)	
Turned me all around,	(Jesus brought me up)	
He placed my feet,	(Jesus brought me up)	
On higher ground.	(Jesus brought me up)	
Can I get a witness?	(Jesus brought me up)	[Ch]
Can I get a witness?	(Jesus brought me up)	
Oh yeah,	(Jesus brought me up)	
Oh yeah,	(Jesus brought me up)	
Well early one morning,	(Jesus brought me up)	[Sch]
One, one morning,	(Jesus brought me up)	
One fine morning,	(Jesus brought me up)	
Church one fine morning,	(Jesus brought me up)	
When I was sick,	(Jesus brought me up)	
When I was in sin,	(Jesus brought me up)	
Nobody but Jesus,	(Jesus brought me up)	
Nobody but Jesus,	(Jesus brought me up)	
Nobody but Jesus,	(Jesus brought me up)	[Ch]
Nobody but Jesus,	(Jesus brought me up)	
He picked me up,	(Jesus brought me up)	[Sch]
He picked me up,	(Jesus brought me up)	

Suddenly Willie Johnson Sr. leaps forward and grabs the microphone from Williams. He chants a four-line verse as the background drive continues, hands the microphone back to Williams, and runs down the center aisle shouting. With arms flailing, head shaking, and sweat dripping from his brow, he appears to be high in the Spirit and on the verge of falling out. At this point Willie Johnson Jr. steps forward to take over the lead. The background singers drop out as Johnson Jr. continues to rhythmically improvise in style midway between chant and song. He again exhorts the congregants to stand, wave and clap their hands:

Said ain't the man all right?	[Sch]
Said ain't the man all right?	
Said if you know He's all right,	

Said let me see you wave your hands,
Said let me see you wave your hands,
Come on let's wave your hands,
If God ever done anything for you,
      you ought to stand up on your feet,
Said let the world know,
      that you been born again,
Said let the world know,
      that you got the Holy Ghost,
Come on and just clap your hands,
Everybody just clap your hands,
Come on just clap your hands,
Let me hear you just a little bit louder,
Let me hear you just a little bit louder.

Next Leverne Robinson steps out from the background and works a double-lead routine with Johnson Jr. The two singers face each other, and as Johnson Jr. sings "Ain't God all right?" Robinson responds in time, "All right." Johnson Jr. begins chanting about the Holy Ghost as Robinson answers "power":

Ain't God all right tonight?   (all right)   [Sch]
Ain't God all right?   (all right)
Can't He make a way tonight?   (all right)
Ain't God good?   (I know He is)
Oh God will make you move,   (hey, hey)
Ain't God all right?   (all right)
Can't He make a way tonight y'all?
We-e-e-e-l,
I wonder,
      have you got,
Said the Holy Ghost,   (power)   [Ch]
Holy Ghost,   (power)
Said I wonder,   (power)
Got the Holy Ghost,   (power)
Said I wonder,   (power)
Said the Holy Ghost,   (power)
Have you got?   (power)
Got the Holy Ghost,   (power)
Have you got?   (power)
Got the Holy Ghost,   (power)
Power,   (power)

Robinson, who now seems to be quite high in the Spirit, returns to the background. Upon a signal from Johnson Jr., all instruments but the drums cease, and the vocalists sing in unison:

If the Lord ever done anything for you,   [So]
    you better stand up on your feet,
But if He never done nothing for you,
    you ought to stay right in your seat.

Willie Johnson Jr. improvises a few more lines, and the song come to an end. The instruments continue to strum and riff as Leverne Robinson grabs the lead mike and begins to chant, asking the audience to say "yeah." After several extended moans, he begins singing a slow, soulful number, "He Keeps on Blessing Me." The background falls in behind him, and after singing two choruses and a verse the entire group slowly processes down the center aisle while the instruments continue to play. Robinson, completely overwhelmed by the Spirit, does not want to leave the floor. Willie Johnson Sr. finally takes the microphone and begins to escort Robinson, who is shouting exuberantly, off the floor. About half way down the aisle Robinson suddenly breaks loose, runs back to the front of the church, and grabs the microphone to sing one final chorus:

I want to say it again,   [Ta]
    if you don't mind—
He keeps on blessing me,   [So]
If the Lord ever done anything for you let me see   [Ta]
    you wave your hands,
He keeps on blessing me.   [So]
I know we got to go, but listen—   [Ta]
He, keeps right on blessing me,   [Sch]
    over and over again.   [So]

Again Robinson is escorted off, hands outstretched, on the verge of tears.

At this point Rocky Bridges takes up the mike, and is about to call for applause, when he notices that Willie Johnson Sr., Leverne Robinson, and several congregation members are still shouting and waving their arms. He signals to Angelo Akin, the Skyways' band leader, to break into a fast, sanctified beat. The musicians respond, and suddenly the entire congregation rises up, stamping and clapping to the driving beat. Three or four women break into spontaneous holy dance, hopping up and down in their pews. Willie Johnson Sr.

charges up the aisle to the front of the church and dances for about thirty seconds. He skip-steps back down the aisle, head cocked upward, waving his hands. The music continues for several minutes as the congregation members shout and clap. The women dancers, exhausted, finally collapse in their seats. The church slowly calms as Rocky Bridges picks up the microphone to announce the next group.

This particular example demonstrates the variety of gospel quartet performance strategies and their overall flexible organization. The Brooklyn Skyways use a range of expressive behaviors in creating a performance that gradually builds toward a climactic peak, yet remains basically open-ended in nature. No precise point of closure is ever reached; the group could easily have ended after the drive section of "Look Where Jesus Brought Me From," or after singing several verses of "Keep on Blessing Me." They did not come back to the front of the church following the sanctified rhythms and Willie Johnson's holy dance, but they certainly could have. Apparently the Skyways were too high in the Spirit to return a third time to cool the congregation down, so Bridges simply allowed the music to continue until the energy naturally subsided. The relentless, ongoing character of the performance is well established.

Reviewing the thematic content of the spoken, chanted, and sung expressions and the kinesic patterns that constitute gospel quartet performances sheds further light on the meaning of gospel songs. Specifically, notions that gospel songs are thoroughly otherworldly and future oriented—due to the verse/chorus lyrical emphasis on humankind's rewards in heaven (see Chapter 2)—have been over-exaggerated. When the full range of aural and visual communication is taken into account, gospel songs rendered by quartets suggest ultimate victory for the believer in this world as well as in the next. Chanted narratives and song lyrics remind listeners of their common southern roots and their shared historical struggle. But there is also a strong emphasis on the peace and joy that salvation brings to the individual's present situation. While daily life is filled with burdens and hardships, the believers contend that their personal relationships with Christ bring about an immediate sense of happiness, enabling them to transcend earthly misery. And finally, improvised drive sections exhort listeners to feel the power of the Holy Spirit and literally to "get happy" here and now. When this calling is played out through ritualized performance, the experience of the Holy Spirit is immediate: participants do not have to wait for heaven to rejoice.[21] Taken as a whole, movement, speech, chant and song express a sense of temporal continuity among the past, present, and future experiences of evangelical African-American Christians. Believers are urged to remember their heritage, to experience the Almighty in the immediate present, and to look forward to a glorious future in heaven.

An intensely demonstrative gospel quartet performance is likely to appear disorganized and even chaotic to cultural outsiders. But close inspection reveals that gospel programs are highly structured events where participants assume prescribed roles and play out sacred drama in an orderly and predictable fashion. In these ritualized settings groups like the Brooklyn Skyways skillfully combine rhetorical expressive strategies to produce satisfying "spiritual entertainment." The complex process, however, requires far more than the mechanical manipulation of behavioral conventions. Gospel quartet performance is simultaneously art and religion, and is thus informed by a critical aesthetic philosophy and a sophisticated system of supernatural belief. The best gospel quartet singers must be masters at balancing these concerns.

Notes

1. Recorded at the First Freedom Baptist Church, Jamaica, NY, January 10, 1986.

2. Recorded at Public School 40, Brooklyn, NY, August 31, 1986.

3. For more on the spontaneous generation of oral formula in the African-American performed sermon, see Davis, *I Got the Word in Me*, pp. 49–64.

4. For more on ethnopoetics and its usefulness in text transcription, see Dell Hymes, *In Vain I Tried to Tell You* (Philadelphia: University of Pennsylvania Press, 1981), pp. 309–341; and Dennis Tedlock, "On the Translation of Style in Oral Narrative," in Richard Bauman and Americo Paredes, eds., *Toward New Perspectives in Folklore* (Austin: University of Texas Press, 1972), pp. 114–133.

5. See "The Keying of Performance" by Richard Bauman and "The Story in the Story: Metanarration in Folk Narrative" by Barbara Babcock in Bauman, *Verbal Art as Performance*, pp. 15–24 and 61–79.

6. Recorded at the First Freedom Baptist Church, Jamaica, NY, January 10, 1986.

7. Recorded at Capitol Hall, Hartford, CT, April 15, 1990.

8. Recorded at Capitol Hall, Hartford, CT, May 7, 1989.

9. Recorded at Public School 40, Brooklyn, NY, August 31, 1986.

10. Recorded at Charlie Storey's Auditorium, Brooklyn, NY, March 8, 1986.

11. Recorded at the Westminster Bethany Church, Brooklyn, NY, April 4, 1986.

12. Recorded at the New Mount Calvary Baptist Church, Harlem, December 12, 1985.

13. Spencer notes an interplay between spoken and sung utterances during Pentecostal worship, where "Singing smoothly connects one act of testifying to the next." The result, as in the gospel ritual, is "the continual flow of

sound." *Protest and Praise*, p. 186. Roger Abrahams has pointed out the tendency of African-American story tellers consciously to identify themselves with the hero of their tales. See *Deep Down in the Jungle: Negro Narrative Folklore from the Streets of Philadelphia* (Chicago: Aldine, 1970), pp. 58–59. Gerald Davis notes a similar tendency in African-American preachers who attempt to personalize their sermons in *I Got the Word in Me*, p. 90.

14. Gerald Davis points out that the most successful African-American sermons connect biblical doctrine to the secular needs of the congregation. See Davis, *I Got the Word in Me*, pp. 61–64.

15. Williams-Jones, "Afro-American Gospel Music," p. 379.

16. For further discussion of variation of time, text, and pitch in gospel singing, see Mellonee Burnim, "The Black Gospel Music Tradition: A Complex of Ideology, Aesthetic, and Behavior" in Jackson, ed., *More Than Dancing*, pp. 162–165.

17. Recorded at First Freedom Baptist Church, Jamaica, NY, January 10, 1986.

18. Recorded at Public School 40, Brooklyn, NY, August 31, 1986.

19. Anthropologist Robert Plant Armstrong suggests that much traditional West African art is structured syndetically; that is, through the repetition of small, similar units in an open-ended fashion (as distinct from synthetic ordering which process through the resolution of oppositions). The parallels seem striking here, as the entire gospel service moves along in a continuous, syndetic fashion. See Robert Plant Armstrong, *The Powers of Presence: Consciousness, Myth, and Affecting Presence* (Philadelphia: University of Pennsylvania Press, 1981), pp. 3–20 and pp. 66–72. For more on the open-ended nature of African-American performance see Abrahams, *Man-of-Words*, p. 186.

20. Gerald Davis notes that "the weight of a well-preached sermon is to be carried into areas of life beyond the temporal and physical space occupied by the performance of the sermon." See Davis, *I Got the Word in Me*, p. 33.

21. The notion of spiritual liberation as an immediate presence is well developed by James Cone in "Sanctification, Liberation, and Black Worship," *Theology Today* 35 (July, 1978): 139–152.

13. Reverend Floyd King (front, with cane) leading the No Name Gospel Singers in a processional, Brooklyn, 1986. Photo by Ray Allen.

14. James Fitzpatrick and Randy Swain of the Heavenly Tones switching leads, Brooklyn, 1986. Photo by Ray Allen.

15. Darrell McFadden and Ed Johnson of the Golden Sons, working a double-lead, Manhattan, 1987. Photo by Ray Allen.

16. Choreographed dance by the Ecstatistics, Brooklyn, 1988. Photo by Ray Allen.

17a. Willie Johnson, Reggie White, and Clifford Williams of the Brooklyn Skyways singing "We should go down on our knees and pray to the Lord above," Brooklyn, 1988. Photo by Ray Allen.

17b. Willie Johnson (front) taking over the lead.

17c. Willie Johnson, in the Spirit, dropping the microphone and running into the audience, passing a woman in a striped dress.

17d. The woman in the striped dress catching the Spirit and beginning to shout ecstatically, surrounded by congregation members to prevent injury.

Chapter 5
Express Yourself
Aesthetics from the Singers' Perspective

The atmosphere at local gospel quartet programs can be fiercely competitive. Although today's singers seldom engage in the kind of song battles or contests that were popular in the past, most readily admit they are trying to out-sing one another. As Ralph McLemore put it one evening during a rehearsal of Charlie Storey's All Stars:

See, today, it really doesn't matter if they call it a song battle or not, because everybody is going to try to out-sing everybody else anyhow. Regardless of what you call it, if my group is going to be at this place, and your group and his group are going to be there, then I'm going to try and have my group prepared so we come out on top. It's not like we're enemies, it's just that you want to be the best! And if a group sings in front of you, when you come up behind them, you want to top them. And the group that comes up behind you wants to top you. So it all boils down to a battle anyway.[1]

Even the most devout quartet singers consciously assume the responsibilities of performing artists whose presentations are open to audience evaluation.[2] While spiritual commitment is essential, they will also be judged on their ability to sing, speak, and move in accordance with a culturally defined set of aesthetic norms that are readily recognized by the African-American church community. A number of studies to date have focused on the aesthetics of African-American gospel music, but there is little information available concerning evaluation from the singers' perspective. Most authors approach the discussion in terms of western categories of melody, harmony, rhythm, vocal timbre, group organization, and other stylistic traits. Dynamic rhythms, antiphonal structure, repetition, variation in vocal tone and timbre, communal participation, and individual and collective improvisation are commonly identified as the hallmarks of gospel performance.[3]

A different approach is assumed here. The term "aesthetics" is not used in reference to western notions of art and beauty as recognized by an elite group of philosophers and critics. Rather, aesthetics, or better "ethno-aesthetics," is taken to be the principles by which a community organizes and evaluates its own expressive behaviors. The point is to discover the specific properties that enable cultural forms and practices to evoke deeply felt emotions and values or, as Robert Plant Armstrong argues, that empower works and events with an "affecting presence" within their specific cultural context.[4] The standards used by members of a given community in judging the quality of their own performance become the central concern.[5]

When asked what makes good gospel quartet performance, local singers inevitably talk about spiritual commitment and openness to the guiding power of the Holy Ghost. Singers claim they must be "God gifted," strong in their religious faith, and living a clean, moral life if they are to be successful. On the other hand, they acknowledge that a mastery of certain expressive skills—particularly those performance strategies discussed in the previous chapter—enable them to stir their audiences and set the stage for collective spiritual ecstasy. In short, the congregation is judging a group's ability to demonstrate musical and dramatic competence, to express emotional intensity, and to voice a genuine "spiritual feeling." This is best accomplished, the local singers reflect, through the delicate balancing of originality and personalization with cooperation and control.

In her study of gospel choirs, Mellonee Burnim remarks that "at the heart of the Black aesthetic is the acceptance of and, more important, the expectation of individual interpretation or personalization of performance."[6] Likewise, local gospel quartets are greatly admired by their audiences, and by each other, for original song arrangements and the unique interpretations they bring to an individual piece or performance. These criteria, in fact, are usually the first ones a singer will raise in evaluating a performance. Regardless of a song's origin— a hymn book, a recording by a professional group, or an old church song recalled from one's youth—it will inevitably be rearranged in rehearsal to fit the style and abilities of a particular quartet. Melodies, tempos, and harmonic structures are freely altered, and lyrics are often added or dropped. On occasion, the resulting piece may differ so drastically from the original source that the group will claim the song as its own composition. The most egregious error a group can make is to imitate another group's exact arrangement or to copy a recorded version of a song by a well-known professional quartet.

This penchant for innovative song arrangements is only one part of a larger sensibility that extols originality. Every group consciously strives to develop an overall unique style that cannot be confused with that of other groups. Clifton Johnson of the Golden Jubilees explains:

> We want our own style. We don't want to copy after nobody else—we want our own sound, and our own arrangements. If we sing like the Dixie Hummingbirds, you're only helping them, you haven't done nothing for yourself. We want to sound like the Golden Jubilees. Anytime we come out on stage and sing our theme song, "Jesus Is Mine," everyone knows it's the Golden Jubilees.[7]

The distinct sound and style of a lead singer often becomes the hallmark of the group. The texture of the voice is particularly important here. Some lead singers, usually referred to as "gospel men," "rough," or "hard" singers, are revered for their ability to shout, moan, and cry in a compelling manner. Others, sometimes known as "soft" or "sweet" singers, are respected for their smooth, flowing delivery. Those few singers who successfully vary timbre and demonstrate versatility in a range of vocal textures are held in especially high regard. The primary concern is that the lead singer have an uncommon vocal quality. In complimenting fellow singer Billy Walker, Charlie Storey notes:

> As a lead songster, Billy has a unique sound. Very few people have a voice like Billy's. He's got something in his voice that rings out, understand, that gives a feeling to you that's thrilling. Now his voice is something on the order of Sam Cooke. But then you really listen to him, and you know that it's not Sam Cooke, there's a different ring there.[8]

By comparing Walker to Sam Cooke—a singer who is venerated by many local singers as one of the greatest quartet leads of all time—Storey is paying a high compliment. Yet the fact that he immediately qualifies this judgment by noting that Walker's voice has a different "ring" to it emphasizes the value placed on uniqueness. To sound exactly like another singer, even the immortal Sam Cooke, is not acceptable.

Lead singers are expected to bring their own, personal interpretation to each song. Mason Young, who sings bass and lead for the Heavenly Tones, raises several interesting points in this regard:

When you hear me lead a song, I want it to be me! I arranged it, I originated that song the way it is. Now if I try and sing like the Clouds of Joy, or whoever, it just won't come out right for me—I won't feel anything because I'm impersonating someone else. Now if I hear it, and I like a song, I'm going to change something about that song, so it's me. It might be the same lyrics, or I might change them some, you know especially during the gospel [drive] section. But there will be something different about it—the beat, the tempo, the timing might be different, whatever.

When I first started singing, I learned through Jimmy Jones [Harmonizing Four] and William Bobo [Dixie Hummingbirds]. So I got some things from them, until I got it my way. But now if I sing one of Jimmy Jones's songs, I don't do it like him, I do it my way. People enjoy my way, and they enjoy Jimmy Jones. So it's like two different songs, even though it's the same song.

I believe that God gives you songs to sing. Now you learn them through someone else, but if you sing it your way, that's the way God intends you to do it, and it will work out better for you. If you try and copy someone else, it just won't work.[9]

Young's strong identification with his rearranged song—"I want it to be me"—is the ultimate statement of personalization. Through manipulating various structural aspects of a song—rhythm, tempo, text, melody—lead singers like Young transform the materials of others into their own creations. What was once a Jimmy Jones song is now something altogether different; it is now Young's song, actually a part of Young himself. And by evoking God's intent, Young justifies the entire process with divine approval. During part of a performance when Young or other lead singers succeed in adding their own touch to a song—perhaps through an effective melodic ornamentation, a compelling swoop or shout, a unique textual variation, or an overtly dramatic gesture—they are said to be "profiling," "styling," or "staring."

Of course these singers are speaking of ideal aesthetic standards that are rarely fully attained. The knowledgeable listener can often identify the commercial source of a community-based quartet's arrangement, or detect the marked influence of a professional singer on a local's vocal phrasing. In fact, the degree to which local quartets succeed in creating truly original song arrangements is a topic of much debate. Individual singers and groups constantly criticize one another for "copying behind" other quartets or for "stealing" someone else's song or arrangement. Ample borrowing, particularly from the professional quartets, unquestionably occurs, but so does a great deal of creative reinterpretation. Most importantly, wholesale copying is severely frowned upon and is relatively uncommon.

Part of personalizing a song is to sing with such compelling emotion and intensity that the congregation believes the singer sincerely knows what the song is about; that she or he has truly experienced the message and can therefore convey a genuine feeling about it to others. Like the preacher and blues singer, quartet leads do not simply recite poetic lyrics, but rather express deep sentiments from their personal lives that they know their peer audiences will relate to.[10] As Leverne Robinson of the Brooklyn Skyways states:

I always pick a certain song that I can relate to, a song I can feel, that is meaningful to me. If it ain't meaningful to me, I get lost trying to get people to listen to what I'm trying to say. If it's true to my life, and people enjoy it, it touches some people out there. It might be true for somebody else.[11]

Song introductions and testimonies, as pointed out earlier, are instrumental in this process of personalization. One evening after a rehearsal, Bill Dobson and Willie Davis of the No Name Gospel Singers commented on the effectiveness of Willie Johnson's testimony about his gasoline accident (see Chapter 4):

Willie's testimony is strong, because it [the accident] really happened to him. See, he's letting the people know what happened to him, and how he overcame it now. Because he has overcome it, and he's telling it now, to take him into his song. That actually happened to him, he's not up there lying—he's going on with the truth.

Right, you can really feel it. See, when he's up there I know what he's going through. He wants to express himself. And every time he thinks about that—his face could have been destroyed, but it wasn't. And I'm thankful—see I was burnt too, there was fire all over me. But there's no scars on my face either—I'm thankful my face wasn't ruined. So I know how he feels, he wants to get up there and tell somebody about it.[12]

The final aim is to personalize the song not only for oneself but for the whole audience—to give them "something they can relate to," as the singers say.

The best lead singers possess the ability to read their audiences. They must carefully choose their testimonies and songs if they are to reach listeners in a genuinely personal way. This often requires careful preliminary observation, as Willie Johnson of the Brooklyn Skyways explains:

A good lead singer, he's like a preacher. When you go to a place [service] you kind of look over the people, and you listen. This group does something, and this guy might not do something right. See, you've got to be smart enough to know as a lead singer how to analyze the way the people accept this song or that song, or accept the way a guy might move this way or that way. When I get up there, I'm going to do something different. Because when you see a guy in the service, and this guy ain't did it, then you get up there and do it. You capitalize on his mistakes.[13]

Once a song begins, a singer must constantly be attentive to audience feedback in order to know how to proceed, as Leverne Robinson of the Brooklyn Skyways reflects:

A lead singer always has to think. In other words, when he sings a song, he's concentrating at the same time on exactly how everybody is reacting to what he is doing. And if he is not getting the reaction he wants, he should be smart enough to stop that particular song and start another song, and see if that works. And then he can go on and build his program around that. So when you sing one song, you concentrate and see if the song is really taking to the people, if they're accepting it.[14]

The most effective lead singers know how to "set" (choose the order of) their songs and when to preach and testify to "build" the spiritual energy to finally "get over" with their audience. They must, of course, have the gift to speak and sing with great "feeling," "power," and "soul," and further exhibit the ability to "move with good action" and "demonstrate how you feel" to the congregation. In other words, the best lead singers know how and when to use their vocal, dramatic, and improvisatory talents to personalize their performance and to express the emotional intensity needed to inspire the other singers and the audience. The Reverend Edward Cook of the Mighty Gospel Giants sums these points up succinctly:

A good lead singer, he's what we call the gospel man, the Spirit getter. . . . He has to be smart. He has to know where to go to get the audience aroused. He has to know how to push the song, how to rev up the background, rev up the musicians. He's constantly thinking, he's constantly moving. He has a powerful voice. He's more of the preacher type, the shouting preacher type.[15]

The singers' attitudes about originality and personalization are not devoid of religious concerns. Mason Young's previous comments are typical: most singers believe that God wants them to sing a song "their way" and not to impersonate another singer. To express one's God-given gift of singing in a unique, personal style is interpreted as a sign of spiritual authenticity, while imitating others is often associated with an affected show. It is hardly surprising that a religious community whose doctrine demands a personal commitment to the Almighty that is to be achieved through a personal conversion experience should produce expressive products that take the form of highly personalized statements. And yet, because these personalized interpretations are perceived to be divinely inspired, the individual interpreter/artist remains tightly linked to the larger spiritual whole. Further, since singers are believed to perform best while under the guiding influence of the Holy Spirit—an unpredictable force—they are expected to demonstrate some degree of spontaneity and variation from performance to performance. Gospel performers who sing and move exactly the same way each time they render a certain song will automatically be suspected of engaging in a pre-choreographed show rather than truly singing as the Spirit directs them. The aesthetic principles of originality and personalization find support and justification within the singers' system of belief.

A powerful lead singer who can interpret songs in an innovative and personal manner is essential to any successful quartet. Singers are quick to stress, however, that good quartet performance also demands complete control and cooperation among all group members. Lead singers are expected to convey great energy and emotion when they sing, and yet they must preserve a certain degree of vocal control or they will be criticized for simply "blaring," "blasting," or "hollering." Their diction must be clean so their words are clearly intelligible. And while they may shout, testify, run, or dance, they must always maintain some semblance of order and control. If a lead singer becomes so overwhelmed by the Spirit that he or she can no longer continue to sing, he or she will immediately hand the microphone over to a second lead singer who will literally take control. The first lead singer may be assisted or even restrained by the "utility" background singer who serves as a "medium cooler" and maintainer of order.[16] Once the singer has regained composure, he or she may again resume leading. On the other hand, lead singers or entire groups who become so wild that their songs break down in mid-performance are dismissed as insincere fakes.

The lead singer is responsible for coordinating the entire group throughout the performance. He or she must see that the song is pitched in the correct key, that everyone begins together, and that a steady tempo is maintained throughout the piece. The lead singer "points" and "directs" the group through "turns" and "changes" in the harmony, using a series of vocal cues such as pick-up notes, bends, slurs, and subtle changes in dynamics. The lead singer may employ visual signals such as hand gestures or eye contact to alert the rest of the group to an upcoming verse or chorus, to indicate that a drive section is to begin or end, or to bring the song to a close.

Although the primary responsibility for directing the group lies with the lead singer, the background singers play a crucial supportive role. Their harmony, timing, vocal phrasing, and articulation must be perfectly coordinated or the lead may be thrown off. The key term background singers use in describing good harmony singing is "blending." In order to blend, each group member must first be placed in the right voice—bass, baritone, background lead, tenor, high tenor, and lead.[17] When the harmony parts are close, each singer is precisely on key, the voices are perfectly balanced in terms of dynamics and timbre, and the vocal timing and phrasing are impeccably synchronized, the voices are said to "join" and "blend." Well-blended voices are often referred to as "music" and may be compared to a chord on a piano or guitar. In Jordan Evans's words:

Because we sing such close harmony, it's hard to tell who is singing which voice—all those voices blend together. And when those voices are blending, I always say, "It fits like a glove." Once those voices hit and come together, it's right there, you know?[18]

Once the desired vocal blend has been achieved, the background singers must go through the song as a closely knit unit, always keeping their correct pitch, timing, and phrasing. Cooperation is essential. In addition to maintaining a perfect vocal blend, background singers must support and encourage their lead singer in building the emotional and spiritual energy in the congregation. Background singers often speak of "pushing" and "charging" the lead. Reflecting further upon the relationship betweeen the background and lead singers, Arthur McKoy of the No Name Gospel Singers comments:

I would say that the background is like an ocean. And the leader is riding on the top. Its like we're holding that leader up. And as he tries to go forward we push him on, we help him out. In another words, if we help build him, then he will sing longer, stronger. If a leader has good harmony behind him, he sings stronger, and he will be able to express himself more.[19]

Nearly all lead singers agree on this point. A strong, tight background gives lead singers the freedom to improvise with unrestrained passion. In contrast, if the background is listless and "dead," or the harmony or timing is slightly off, lead singers become distracted and unable to sing with full exuberance.

Although lead and background singing demand slightly different techniques and skills, ultimately all singers must work together as a tightly coordinated team. While the lead singer sets the songs, builds the energy, and points and directs the group, the background must be there for support at every turn with well blended harmony and emotional enthusiasm. Again bass singer Mason Young comments:

The most important thing for a group is you have to be all on one accord—it's togetherness, see? You have to concentrate on what you are doing, nobody tries to be an individual, one has to count on another. It's like a chain reaction, you all have to be as one. . . . Each one [singer] has to know what the other one is going to do. Everybody has to be able to sing in their own way, but everybody has to pull together.[20]

Young's emphasis on group cooperation at the expense of individuality is significant, particularly in light of his earlier comments about the need for a highly personal interpretation by the lead singer. Yet there is no contradiction here. The gospel group and overall performance is structured to support the creative expression of one individual, the lead singer, but within a collective frame. When an individual assumes the role of lead singer and steps "out front," he or she is allowed to present an innovative, highly individualistic interpretation. He or she becomes the momentary center of attention, the soloist who will "star" and "profile" in a unique style. Yet at no time is the lead singer completely independent from the background singers and musicians, for only through total cooperation and control can all the voices "blend" and "join" to create the desired sound. And the fact that lead and background parts are constantly rotated within a group allows some members to contribute in both capacities. The impulse for individual innovation and collective participation are well balanced; the contribution of each is recognized and appreciated. Only when aesthetic concerns for originality, innovation, and personalization are brought into harmony with those of cooperation and control can successful quartet performance ensue. In Young's words, everybody must be able to "sing it in their own way," while simultaneously being able to "pull together" on "one accord." Individual creativity finds an outlet, but intragroup competition and hierarchy are downplayed and the principles of communitas are not violated.

The importance of cooperation and control can of course be extended beyond the confines of the gospel quartet proper to include the entire congregation. As previously outlined, the physical participation of the audience through singing, clapping, stamping, and shouting is essential for successful gospel performance. Only through active audience feedback can singers know whether or not their emotional and spiritual message is having the desired impact. Singing to a "dead" church, on the other hand, is extremely difficult. At the highest level of organization, all the participants—the lead and background singers, the musicians, the emcee, and the congregation—must work in cooperation to build the spiritual and emotional atmosphere in order to produce a successful performance.

A number of scholars have underscored the importance of originality, improvisation, and personal interpretation in gospel performance.[21] Their investigations, in addition to studies in various genres of other black music, verbal arts, and material culture, present persuasive evidence that improvisation and spontaneous innovation constitute a major aesthetic paradigm for the traditional African-American arts.[22] What prior studies of black aesthetics have failed to stress, however, is the significance of cooperation and control. Previous discussions of gospel music, for example, note the communal nature of gospel performance in terms of audience participation, but pay little attention to internal group dynamics and coordination. Clearly in quartet performance lead and background singers must work together as a tightly supportive unit if they are to gain the favor and eventual participation of their audience. As stressed earlier there is nothing unselfconscious or "natural" about good gospel quartet singing: it demands practice, precision, and discipline on the part of all group members.

Of equal concern is the popular misconception that demonstrative gospel quartet singers are constantly raging out of control. Again, the evidence argues to the contrary. Singers stress that, no matter how deeply involved they become in a performance, they never lose control of their voices and actions. Even at the height of spiritual ecstasy, when a lead singer may be on the verge of falling out, the power of the Holy Ghost, it is believed, will see that she or he never misses a beat or turn in the harmony. And if a singer should become too high in the Spirit to carry on, she or he will be physically restrained by other singers in an attempt to restore a state of calm and composure. Such built-in control mechanisms prevent the lead singer from violating the prescribed boundaries of proper behavior—that is, not losing control and stability—thus assuring that the patterned performance will not degenerate into chaos.

Something akin to Robert Farris Thompson's notion of an "aesthetic of the cool" appears to be operating during a gospel quartet performance. In his work with African sculpture and dance, Thompson identifies an overarching aesthetic attitude stressing control, composure, stability, and balance.[23] This concept of the "cool" has been successfully applied to music by John Chernoff in his work with West-African drum ensembles and dancers. He states:

Dagombas say that "music cools the heart," and coolness in a musical situation calls for mediated involvement rather than concentrated attention, collectedness of mind rather than self-abandonment. . . . Without balance and coolness, the African musician loses aesthetic command, and the music abdicates its social authority, becoming hot, intense, limited, pretentious, overly personal, boring, irrelevant, and ultimately alienating. . . . The feelings the music brings may be exhilarating but not overpowering, intense but not frenzied. Ecstasy as we [westerners] see it would imply for most Africans a separation from all that is good and beautiful, and generally, in fact, any such loss of control is viewed by them as tasteless, ridiculous, or even sinful.[24]

This is not to suggest a complete or conscious retention of the African trait of coolness. But clearly the attitudes of coolness, control, and balance do inform gospel quartet practice among urban African-Americans. Quartet singers, like the members of a drum ensemble, must perform with compelling intensity and exhilaration, but they must likewise maintain command and stability if they are to function as a group. The highly emotive dynamism of the lead singer—often misinterpreted as wild, reckless abandonment by cultural outsiders—is, in fact, prescribed, controlled behavior that conforms to the demands and expectations of church audiences.

Rehearsals and gospel programs are rich with talk about music. The terminology and metaphors employed by singers in their discussions of gospel performance reveal additional insights into their evaluative system and the relationship between aesthetic and religious concerns. Lead singers, for example, are frequently complimented for their ability to sing with "feeling," "power," "energy," "force," "strength," "life," "authority," and "soul."[25] They speak in terms of a vital, life-giving force that must well up from within a singer's heart and be injected into a song. Singers are constantly encouraged in rehearsal to put more "feeling," "soul," or "power" into their performance. Younger singers are often instructed to "put yourself into the song," or reminded that "you can't get nothing out of a song if you don't put something into it." Songs are perceived as empty vessels for performers to fill with the life forces of feeling, soul, and power. In other words, the song or testimony has no inherent power in its own right. It only becomes meaningful, takes on an affecting presence, when empowered by emotion emanating from the performer who is inspired by divine forces. Regardless of how enduring a particular song may be with its striking textual imagery and beautiful melodic contours, its effect on the audience will be negligible unless the individual singer charges it with sufficient personal energy. Hence, when performers are said to be singing with "feeling" and "soul," they are expressing the intensity and sincerity necessary to render a song in a unique and personal way.

In addition to concerns with energizing and empowering songs, the following set of verbs are used by performers in reference to good gospel quartet singing:

attack	pull
build	push
burn up	ride
charge	ring
click	roll
drive	set on fire
elevate	squeeze
fly	stir up
get down	swing
get off	tear up
hit	turn loose
jump	walk
kick	warm up
move	work

In most cases these verbs are used in constructions where the singer is the subject and the song the object. For example, one commonly hears compliments such as "He was really pushing (or working, hitting, kicking, rolling, tearing up, burning up, etc.) that song" in reference to a strong performance. The emphasis here is on generating physical force, power, heat, and aggressive action, as the human voice is metaphorically likened to a force that can attack, fly, tear, burn, hit, stir, and so forth. This is in keeping with one of the stated goals of performance, which is to "move" and "get over" with the audience and to "wreck" the church.[26]

While good gospel singing is spoken of in terms of activity, dynamism, and power, poor performance is usually referred to in relation to inactivity and death. Singers who fail to put sufficient energy into their performance are commonly rebuked for "dragging" a song. The ultimate criticism is to say that a group's singing is "lifeless" and "dead," or that a singer "killed" a song through an uninspired interpretation. In a similar vein, singers often refer to unresponsive audiences as "cold" and "dead." However, the lexicon of negative evaluative terminology is not as rich or extensive as the positive. In rehearsals, poor singing is usually criticized in terms of its lack of positive attributes. Rather than insulting a singer by calling a listless performance "dead," fellow group members will comment that his or her song "needs more feeling, soul, or power." Likewise, they might encourage him or her to "attack, hit, drive, or push" the song in a more forceful manner. The life/death, active/inactive oppositions that form the foundation of the evaluative system usually find expression

through positive metaphors of life, action, and energy. Critical remarks are generally couched in terms of the absence of such vital
forces.

The above terminology is used mostly in reference to the demonstrative, shouting vocal style associated with hard gospel songs. Another smaller, though significant set of evaluative terms comes into
play with regard to the softer, harmonizing songs. Here the entire
group is praised for its ability to sing in a "sweet," "smooth," "mellow,"
"touching," "soulful" manner. In opposition to these adjectives that
imply gentleness, the terms "raggedy," "scratchy," and "strained" are
often used in reference to harmony singing that is flawed in terms of
pitch, timing, or timbre. Those who cannot control and balance their
voices with other singers are criticized for "blasting" and "blaring."
On the other hand, the verbs "blend," "join," "meet," and "make music" are used with regard to the way the voices come together in perfectly synchronized, "tight" harmony. Again, it is the positive
terminology that prevails, as groups with questionable harmony are
usually criticized in terms of their lack of "blend" or their inability to
"make music" or "join" their voices. Because of the limited vocabulary
in this realm, it is difficult to pin down an oppositional base that generates the evaluative metaphors for these softer, harmonizing songs,
or for background singing in general. Cooperation and control certainly are implied, for without precise coordination the voices could
not "blend," "join," or "meet" in a "smooth," "sweet," "tight" fashion.

Surveying this evaluative terminology raises several significant
points about the relationship of aesthetic and spiritual matters. First
is the emphasis on feeling, force, power, heat, life, and activity that
characterizes so much of the gospel evaluative lexicon. Just as matters
of empowerment and emotion are essential ingredients of good gospel quartet performance, so are they central to traditional African-
American religious thought and worship.[27] The evangelical Christian
teachings promise "new life" to those who will open their hearts to
the "power" of God and His Spirit—while those who do not receive
the power are thought to be in a state of eternal spiritual death.
Comprehending the intellectual tenets of biblical doctrine is a basic
necessity for faith, but the true believer must also experience and
re-experience the feeling and power of God's presence during communal ritual (see Chapter 6). Those who have not "felt the fire" of
the Holy Ghost cannot be among the ranks of the saved and sanctified. As a product of a religious community that stresses the emotional and experiential components of faith, it is not surprising that
gospel quartet singers are concerned first and foremost with the expression of feeling and power in their performance.

The overlap in discourse about musical and spiritual matters further underscores this point. Singers often use the same terms and metaphors in describing good gospel singing as they do in speaking about the power of the Spirit. For example, the term "feeling" is constantly evoked in reference to compelling singing as well as the exhilarating experience of the Holy Ghost. Performers explain that they "sing with feeling" when they get a "spiritual feeling" and vice versa. Similarly, when gospel singers speak of "building" a song, technically they refer to the subtle increases in tempo and volume, and the elevation of the harmony parts to a higher register. Their aim is not to simply "build" the song, but further to "build" the spiritual energy of the singers and congregation. When singers express themselves and "give vent to their feelings," they enthusiastically convey emotional intensity and the feeling of the Spirit. In this regard a group may "work," "charge," or "drive" a song so that the Spirit will "work" and "charge" the congregation and "drive" them into a state of ecstasy. Likewise, a singer or churchgoer may be "hit," "struck," or "smacked" by a song, just as he or she may be "hit," "struck," or "smacked" by the power of the Holy Spirit. These often happen simultaneously.

The nature and use of evaluative terminology reinforces the thesis that artistic and religious matters are inseparable dimensions of gospel quartet singing. When singers are praised for their ability to "sing with feeling," to "put power" into their presentation, or to "express themselves," they are actually being complimented for achieving both aesthetic and religious ideals. They render their material in a highly expressive, original, and personal manner, while exhibiting group cooperation, control, and harmonic blend; they aptly choose performance strategies to build and captivate their audience; and finally they remain open to the guiding influence of the Holy Spirit. When groups boast of "moving" or "getting over" with an audience, they refer to their success in reaching their listeners with a spiritual message delivered with outstanding artistic competence. As Willie Johnson of the Brooklyn Skyways sums up:

If the music is beautiful, and the harmony is beautiful, then that will make the Spirit more free. People will just sit there and feel the good harmony, and sweet music, it just makes them feel good. . . . When everything is right, then the Spirit will come. Because if the music is good, and the singing is good, it makes the Spirit come within, through that. If the music and singing aren't right, that can kill something within a person, so that can kill the Spirit—the Spirit dies. It takes the heart out of you, because the people know nothing is there. Everything is dead. But when a person gets up there and the music sounds good, the guitar sounds good, and the singing sounds good, the Spirit just comes alive.[28]

The following chapter will suggest that, during local programs where financial matters tend to be downplayed, the spiritual component takes precedent over aesthetic concerns. There are, however, limitations to the degree that groups can violate prescribed aesthetic norms and still produce an acceptable performance, even if their spiritual commitment is sound. Groups are not likely to reach their listeners with a "spiritual feeling" if they lack innovative arrangements, the ability to express themselves in a personal, compelling manner, or the discipline and control necessary to produce well blended harmony. While poor but sincere performances are politely tolerated, groups who consistently fail to demonstrate aesthetic competence are usually short-lived and rarely go beyond the confines of their own home churches. The unspoken assumption is that those individuals who do not truly possess the "gift to sing" should use their other talents in serving God.

Notes

1. Personal interview with Ralph McLemore, January 22, 1986.
2. Taking responsibility for audience evaluation of communicative behavior is Richard Bauman's primary criteria for performance. See Bauman, *Verbal Art as Performance*, p. 11.
3. Ricks, *Some Aspects of Religious Music*, pp. 292–313; Tallmadge, booklet for "Jubilee to Gospel"; Pearl Williams-Jones,"Afro-American Gospel Music"; Horace Boyer, "Contemporary Gospel Music, Part 2: Characteristics and Style," *Black Perspective in Music* 7 (Spring 1979): 22–58; Burnim, "The Black Gospel Music Tradition"; Maultsby, "Afro-American Religious Music."
4. See Robert Plant Armstrong, *The Affecting Presence: An Essay in Humanistic Anthropology* (Urbana: University of Illinois Press, 1971), especially pp. 3–33.
5. This ethno-aesthetic approach is further informed by anthropologically oriented ethnomusicologists who view such native systems of aesthetics as one component of a larger cognitive scheme by which a group or community conceptualizes its musical practices. See for example Feld, *Sound and Sentiment* and "Flow like a Waterfall: Metaphors of Kaluli Musical Theory," *Yearbook for Traditional Music* 13 (1981): 22–47. See also Keil, *Tiv Song* and *Urban Blues*; and John Chernoff, *African Rhythm and African Sensibility* (Chicago: University of Chicago Press, 1979).
6. Burnim, "The Black Gospel Music Tradition," p. 162.
7. Personal interview with Clifton Johnson, September 10, 1986.
8. Personal interview with Charlie Storey, October 1, 1985.
9. Personal interview with Mason Young, September 10, 1986.
10. Charles Keil notes that African-American preachers and bluesmen occupy roles in their communities where they are expected to give "public

expression to deeply felt private emotions." The gospel singer should be added to this list. See Keil, *Urban Blues*, p. 164.

11. Personal interview with Leverne Robinson, October 10, 1986.

12. Personal interviews with Bill Dobson and Willie Davis, February 2, 1986.

13. Personal interview with Willie Johnson, March 24, 1986.

14. Personal interview with Leverne Robinson, October 14, 1986.

15. Personal interview conducted with the Reverend Edward Cook, August 24, 1988.

16. This role of medium cooler is also played by specially designated "nurses" who surround and calm congregation members who become excessively high in the Spirit.

17. The term "background lead" is used by singers in reference to a background vocal part that mirrors the basic lead melody. With this harmonic arrangement the lead singer (or "front man") is free to improvise with the original melody and text or switch into a chanted vocal style while the background lead continues to carry the song's melody line. The device facilitates creative improvisation on the part of the lead singer.

18. Personal interview with Jordan Evans, January 20, 1986.

19. Personal interview with Arthur McKoy, February 2, 1986.

20. Personal interview with Mason Young, January 1, 1986.

21. The early work of Pearl Williams-Jones points to the vital role played by improvisation in gospel performance, arguing that the form of the gospel song simply provides a loose framework around which improvisation can take place. See Williams-Jones, "Afro-American Gospel Music," pp. 381–382. Mellonee Burnim has also stressed the importance of individual song interpretation and personalization for the gospel singer. See Burnim, "The Black Gospel Music Tradition," pp. 162–165.

22. See for example Abrahams, *Deep Down in the Jungle*, pp. 97–113; John Vlach, *The Afro-American Tradition in Decorative Arts* (Cleveland: Cleveland Museum of Art, 1978), pp. 1–5; Robert Farris Thompson, *Flash of the Spirit* (New York: Random House, 1983), pp. 207–222; Evans, *Big Road Blues*, pp. 106–166.

23. See Robert Farris Thompson, "An Aesthetic of the Cool," *African Arts* 7 (1973): 41–43, 64–67, 89–92; and *African Art in Motion* (Berkeley: University of California Press, 1974), pp. 43–45.

24. Chernoff, *African Rhythm and African Sensibility*, pp. 140–141.

25. The term "soul" is an important concept in African-American culture. Charles Keil identifies it as a key metaphor connoting identity and solidarity among blues singers and their audiences, and the larger black urban community. He notes the following native interpretations of the religious nature of the term: "the breath of life," "something you feel in your heart," and "a concrete and physical sort of spirituality." It is in this latter sense that gospel singers appear to use the term. See Keil, *Urban Blues*, pp. 164–190.

26. Other researchers report emic terminology suggesting physical force and dynamism as positive attributes of gospel singing. Anthony Heilbut, for example, notes that good gospel singers "tear up," "clean," "demolish," and "burn." Mellonee Burnim offers the verbs "blow," "jam," "get in," "cook," "burn," "tear up," and "get down." See Heilbut, *The Gospel Sound* p. xxxiii; and Burnim, "The Black Gospel Music Tradition," pp. 157, 159.

27. For more on the role of the Holy Spirit and emotionalism in African-American worship see James Cone, *Speaking the Truth: Ecumenism, Liberation, and Black Theology* (Grand Rapids, MI: William Eerdmans, 1986), pp. 17–34; and Arthur Paris's descriptions of worship services in *Black Pentecostalism*, pp. 45–80.

28. Personal interview with Willie Johnson, October 10, 1986.

Chapter 6
Singing in the Spirit
The Holy Spirit and Sacred Ritual

> The main thing is, when the Spirit hits you singing a gospel song, automatically you have to move. It's like a spiritual feeling. Sometimes you hardly know what you are saying—this is the Lord giving you the words to say. The spiritual feeling, this is what they call the burning of the Holy Ghost. It's like the song said, "Like Fire Shut Up in My Bones." If the fire hits you, you're going to move, you're going to holler, understand?
>
> Ralph Moragne, Sunset Jubilee Singers

When the power of the Holy Spirit descends in the midst of a gospel quartet performance, there is indeed a great deal of "moving" and "hollering." In the church community, quartets that perform under the influence of this power are said to be "singing in the Spirit." As Ralph Moragne explains, the Holy Spirit manifests itself in various ways. Participants may be moved to shout, cry, utter prophetic speech, run, or dance. Not all gospel performances culminate with the cathartic intensity of the one cited in Chapter 4, but gospel quartet singers always strive to call down the Spirit and share the ecstatic feelings with their listeners.

There is an abundance of literature devoted to the connection between spirit possession and various forms of music, dance, and prophetic speech found in organized worship. Much attention has been paid, for example, to the phenomena of glossolalia (speaking in tongues) and spirit possession in religious ceremonies involving drumming and other highly rhythmic forms of music.[1] There are numerous references to African-American preachers and worshipers being "struck" or "seized" by the power of the Holy Ghost during a forceful sermon.[2] Unfortunately, most researchers in this area fail to take seriously the beliefs and supernatural explanations of those who actually engage in spiritual practices. Scholars too readily posit neurophysiological, psychological, linguistic, communicative, and cultural/functional explanations for such phenomena. Similar problems arise with regard to the role of the Holy Spirit in African-American gospel singing. While most commentators acknowledge some connection between the fervor of gospel performance and the musical practices of the sanctified church, they tend to attribute the former's demonstrative nature to showmanship and entertainment. In his insightful work on African-American Pentecostalism, Arthur Paris underscores the dangers of applying such reductionist approaches to religious studies:

Unless a theoretical perspective takes seriously the world or definition of reality (and Weltanschauung) of the group with which it deals and which it attempts to understand, it will invariably misunderstand, or worse, debunk the world religious believers inhabit, and in doing so, will debunk the believers as well.[3]

A number of folklorists share Paris's concerns, and are looking more seriously and sympathetically at folk belief in the supernatural.[4] Several recent ethnographies have examined folk cosmology, spiritual experience, the patterning of ritual worship forms (preaching, testifying, praying, singing, etc.), and the relationship of sacred belief and practice to the social and historical conditions.[5] While no such account has been published for community gospel performance, the work of Morton Marks, based on the analysis of commercial gospel recordings, does provide a useful reference point for exploring the spiritual dimensions of gospel ritual. Though his application of sociolinguistic communication methods to sacred ritual is somewhat mechanical, Marks convincingly ties African-American gospel performance to older Afro-Caribbean and West African religious practices involving music and communal spirit possession. He argues that the gospel lead singer takes on the role of a preacher when he or she switches from a singing mode into a trance-generated, chanted vocal delivery. This code switching from a more European (sung) to more African (chanted) vocalization style, he claims, signals spirit possession. The lead singer's highly irregular, trance-generated vocalization clashes with the steady rhythms of the background singers and musicians, producing what Marks calls "paradoxical communication." This in turn may induce trance in the congregation.[6]

Marks's model will be returned to shortly, but first the quartet singers' descriptions and explanations of personal encounters with the Holy Spirit will be considered. Their accounts of "singing in the Spirit" offer a fascinating glimpse into the mystical dimensions of Afro-Protestant worship, raise intriguing questions concerning the spiritual authenticity of certain performance practices, and point to a pervasive sacred/secular tension within the church community.

Most working class, churchgoing African-Americans in New York City adhere to religious doctrines and practices deeply rooted in the traditions of southern Protestant revivalism. Be they Baptist, African Methodist Episcopalian, or some branch of the Holiness or Pentecostal movement, they believe in a strict interpretation of the New Testament that stresses a personal and total commitment to Christ. In order to become saved and sanctified, the individual must first go through a personal conversion experience in which he or she totally surrenders to Christ and eventually becomes filled with the Holy Spirit. While different denominations vary in the precise manner and number of stages an individual must go through to achieve final sanctification, all stress the necessity of experiencing the feeling and power of the Holy Ghost. Their doctrine is enacted through fervent worship practices in which participants become possessed by the Holy Spirit and engage in various ecstatic behaviors including shouting, speaking in tongues, and holy dancing.[7] Members of the African-American church community do not abandon these basic religious beliefs and practices at the close of their Sunday morning worship service. They are carried over into other realms of believers' lives, including additional ritual activities such as gospel programs.

Every sincere quartet singer will quickly explain that the Holy Spirit is a necessary ingredient for good gospel performance. Only when a singer is saved, sanctified, and open to the guiding force of the Holy Spirit can he or she truly "sing in the Spirit." When singers speak admirably of a recent performance they will often comment that "the Spirit was high." If there was a great deal of "shouting" and "hollering," the congregation was probably "getting happy" and the whole church was "falling out." Posters advertising upcoming programs invite the public to "Come Out for a Hallelujah Time," and to "Bring Your Shouting Shoes." These references are indicative of the centrality of spiritual matters to gospel quartet singers. Putting the experience of the Holy Spirit into words, however, is not an easy task for all singers. Some politely avoid the issue by claiming that the Spirit is simply ineffable, something one must actually experience to comprehend fully. This is not surprising, for language does not always provide a sufficient lexicon to fully describe the nature of supernatural and spiritual phenomena.[8] Moreover, those who do reflect at greater length on the subject tempered their remarks by emphasizing that the Holy Spirit, like the Almighty, works in ways that cannot always be predicted.

Those singers who are able to find words to express the experience speak of the Spirit as a real, physical presence, as something that "gets on" them. As suggested earlier, metaphors of power, energy, and fire are frequently used, as the Spirit is perceived as something that must be "built up," a force that can "strike," "hit," or "smack" a singer or bounce from person to person like electricity. Once the energy level peaks, the spiritual power may be passed on from singer to singer, from singer to congregation member, and vice versa. In the following interview excerpts six singers attempt to articulate the feelings they experience when they become "high in the Spirit."

Willie Johnson (Brooklyn Skyways): I feel good. Now I don't drink or smoke, but you hear people who take drugs, they say that when you get that shot or that sniff or whatever, it makes you feel like you want to fly. I don't know how it makes them feel, but it makes me feel that way when I feel the Spirit. It makes you feel like you're just floating on cotton or air, that's the way it makes you feel. You feel light, you feel just like a feather blowing around in the air. That's the Spirit, that's the way it works.[9]

David Steward (Wearyland Gospel Singers): It's really an inner feeling that is hard to explain. All I know is that when the Spirit takes over in my life I feel good. I feel light as a feather, I'm not worried about anything. When the Spirit takes over, I have no problems. I guess it's like somebody when they get drunk. They think they feel good. But being high with the Spirit is extraordinary. It's beautiful, it's a wonderful thing, better than anything I know.[10]

Robert Todd (Heavenly Tones): The Holy Spirit is indescribable, really. It's just something you sort of get out of yourself. You don't even think about who's listening, or who's around you. It's just a thrill, the Holy Spirit is there making you shout, anointing you with blessings. . . . There was a time when I had pain in my limbs and joints. But when I get the Spirit, I don't feel that pain. When the Spirit comes you just let yourself go and loosen up and give it to the Lord. You forget all your problems. . . . Jeremiah described as fire shut up in your bones. In another words you just can't keep your peace. It's like a flash of heat.[11]

Floyd King (The No Name Gospel Singers): You feel like sometimes you could just run away. You don't know where you're going when you run, but you're running. You can't help yourself. When the Lord anoints you with the Spirit, you might cry, you might start singing, or you might start talking and can't stop. You might just shake, you might do anything. You don't know how the Spirit of the Lord is going to handle you. See, under the anointing of the Holy Spirit, you don't know what you're going to say. Whatever the Spirit puts on you to say, you might say it. I may say something different from the song, but that's what the Spirit put on my mind. That's God talking through you, to you, through songs.[12]

Charlie Storey (All Stars): When you get into the Spirit when you start singing, you lose sight of self, understand? When the Spirit comes in and takes control, you feel like you're in a different world, altogether. Happy, rejoicing, that's what it feels like. . . . When the Spirit fills you, it fills you with words. It's like the words come right out. You open your mouth, and speak one word, and He'll keep speaking through you. The words just come without any thinking. When you get one out of your mouth, there was another one, fitting right into place. That's the way it is, the words just keep on flowing.[13]

Vernella Kelly (Faithful Harmonizers):A spiritual feeling is a good feeling, one you can hardly explain. You feel so uplifted, so good, like you really are flying on into heaven. Sometimes you feel hot, that's why you can't sit still. It's like Jeremiah says, it's just like fire, shut up in my bones. You can't sit still. It's like fire burning on the inside, it makes you move, and it makes you praise the Lord. You feel like running, feel like shouting, feel like clapping your hands, feel like really praising the Lord. But it's not like a sensation of being burned by fire—not burning to hurt—but burning to make you feel good, and move for the Lord.[14]

These and similar testimonies reveal a number of significant patterns. First, all singers describe the experience of the Holy Spirit in terms of extraordinary pleasure. They feel immense joy and happiness, in conjunction with a sense of being totally unburdened and relieved from all pain and worldly problems. Many report sensations of light-headedness, and on occasion feel as if their bodies are actually flying or floating away. Many also claim to experience a flash of heat or fire, making reference to the biblical verse from the book of Jeremiah (20:9) concerning "fire shut up in my bones." This heat is not described as uncomfortable, but rather as an energizing force.

In an attempt to convey further the intensity of their spiritual joy, a number of singers use secular metaphors and analogies. Being high in the Spirit is likened to taking narcotic drugs, getting drunk, flying through the air, floating on cotton, being pricked by a needle, falling in love for the first time, and receiving a surprise gift as a child. Singers perceive the Holy Spirit as a source of infinite power and energy; hence the common analogies to fire, electricity, and lightning. When one is hit by this energy, he or she may be moved to run, preach, or sing with great fortitude and stamina. Performers often claim that the Spirit gives them the strength to sing indefinitely, which may explain why lead singers occasionally refuse to surrender the microphone and must be physically removed from the performance area.

While singers report that spiritual feelings tend to build gradually, once the power reaches a certain threshold, they become totally possessed. Some blank out or feel as though they have been transported to another world. Many contend that the Spirit actually takes control of them and directs their actions. During the most intense moments the Spirit may actually seize a singer's voice and speak through him or her, as Ralph Moragne describes in the quote that opens this chapter. Following such experiences singers are often unable to recall their utterances, declaring they simply opened their mouths and the words flowed out.[15]

These reports offer convincing evidence that gospel quartet singers do experience similar feelings and physical sensations when under the influence of the Holy Spirit. Whether these feelings and accompanying behaviors are truly the manifestations of supernatural forces—or rather, as some social scientists imply, simply the result of neuro-physiological activity or social learning—is not of central concern here. The point is that "singing in the Spirit" is recognized by singers as a distinct and readily identifiable phenomenon. The fact that so many share in this experience, and that their individual descriptions closely correspond, indicates we are not dealing with the idiosyncratic visions of an eccentric few. Rather, gospel quartet singers perceive the Holy Spirit as a powerful reality, a presence essential to their singing ritual. Their supernatural experiences and beliefs are firmly grounded, as David Hufford would argue, in "empirical data [that] have been dealt with rationally by those who have assimilated these experiences to their world views."[16]

By most accounts, the spiritual feelings experienced during quartet performance are identical to those realized in a devotional, prayer, or Sunday morning worship service. In fact, the true believer can feel God's Spirit anywhere, at any time, as Charlie Storey reflects:

If you're living the right kind of life, the Spirit can hit you anywhere. Sometimes I feel the Spirit when there ain't nobody around me. I feel the Spirit when I'm talking to you about what God did for me. You can be walking in the streets, you can be riding in your car. And when you think about the goodness that God has given you, from where He brought you from, sometimes you feel that quickening power. Sometimes you can be in your room, sitting down thinking of the goodness, singing a song to yourself, and bring tears to your eyes. That power, that Spirit on high, will quicken your body. That is if you live the right kind of life.[17]

From the singers' perspective, God uses a number of channels to bring down His Spirit—the preaching of a minister, the testifying of a congregation member, or the singing of a gospel performer. Since the true Spirit only comes from God, for a singer to take too much personal credit for bringing it on would be blasphemy. Singers see themselves as merely one of several conduits through which the Almighty transmits His message. "Singing in the Spirit," then, appears to be one subcategory of the broader cultural domain of "being in the Spirit."

In the gospel song service, there is no question that the most powerful behavioral manifestations of the Holy Spirit occur during extended drive sections and final processionals. During these periods, singers are most apt to succumb completely to the Spirit and utter prophetic speech, shout vociferously, weep with joy, or engage in frenetic holy dance. The singers, however, tend to downplay this aspect of their performance when talking about their spiritual experiences. They emphasize that since they are constantly being directed by the Spirit, they can "get happy" at any point during a performance. Most singers describe this as a gradual process: they must first build up a "spiritual feeling" before becoming totally overcome. They often report feeling the Spirit prior to their performance, while sitting in the audience during the devotional service or when listening to other groups sing. Once they step to the front of the church, if the congregation is receptive and the energy is high, singers claim they begin to feel the Spirit immediately. This energy builds, often culminating in the extended drive or final processional. Sometimes, however, singers become overwhelmed in the Spirit during a chanted testimony or the sung verse or chorus of a song. According to them, the experience of the Holy Spirit is not something that can be confined simply to a particular segment of a song or moment of performance. The force is pervasive and can manifest itself throughout a gospel program.

Lead singers generally exhibit the strongest behavioral signs of Spirit possession. He or she is the one who runs, shouts, holy dances, and chants prophetic speech and may require the assistance of other singers in leaving the floor. Many lead singers claim that they have their deepest feelings of the Spirit when they are "out front," leading a song. Willie Johnson of the Brooklyn Skyways comments:

See the Spirit can hit you anyplace [lead or background], but usually it does more to you when you're out front, doing it yourself, telling about the goodness, singing the song. I feel the song, that I was burdened down, troubled, hurt, whatever. By singing the song it uplifts me, and makes me feel good. So if you're singing lead you maybe feel good until you have to put the mike down and just walk away, you couldn't sing. You get so full and feel so good, till you just can't do nothing, until they come back to you and you go on to finish the song, or one of the other guys will take it.[18]

Many agree that the lead singer is usually the strongest in the Spirit, but stress that all singers feel the Spirit throughout a performance. In fact, a number of singers who split their time between lead and background duties report there is essentially no difference in the level of spiritual feelings they experience. No clear consensus was reached, as members of the same group sometimes disagree over the matter. It does appear, however, that while all singers "feel" the Spirit when they sing, the background singers are more constrained by their role of maintaining the harmonic framework of the song. This duty inhibits them from engaging in the more unrestrained manifestations of the Spirit such as holy dancing or running into the audience. But the lead singer, who is usually improvising over the background's steady patterns, is freer to surrender totally to the Spirit without breaking down the structure of the song. The differences in how lead and background singers experience the Spirit is not so much in terms of inner feelings and physical sensations, but rather in the liberty the former has to express those feelings in behavioral terms. In Jordan Evans's words:

The background doesn't move as much as the lead singer, because the fact of it is, if the background moved or walked off like the lead singer, you wouldn't have any harmony. It wouldn't be as good as when you are all together. Not that the background doesn't feel it. See, when a lot of people get happy, they express it in different ways. But they all feel the Spirit, see? Some may laugh, some may cry, some may stand on their feet and clap. They all don't *react* the same way, but they *feel* about the same.[19] [emphasis mine]

The manner in which the spiritual feeling is passed between participants at a gospel program is a function of the complex interaction between the lead singer, the background singers, and the congregation. Morton Marks's model, as presented earlier, posits a basic unidirectional communication scheme. That is, when the lead singer "gets happy," he or she enters into a trance-like state and begins to chant irregular vocal patterns. These in turn become trance-inducing to the congregation. In comparing gospel performance to Afro-Caribbean drumming ceremonies, Marks summarizes:

Within gospel performance, it is customary to combine trancers with non-trancing performers. The ban on the drummers' trancing behavior mentioned earlier has its equivalence here in a similar restriction on gospel instrumentalists entering that state. They, along with supporting vocalists, assist the leader in entering trance, and then provide a steady and often highly intricate rhythmic framework within which the trance-generated vocalizations of the lead singer are displayed. The more these features clash with the rest of the ensemble, the more the total musical message becomes trance-inducing [to the audience].[20]

The ethnographic data from the New York community confirm Marks's basic model, but suggests the necessity for further refinement. All singers agree that the lead vocalist plays a central role in the spiritual process. The leader is primarily responsible for "building" the energy and "driving" the songs in order to bring on the Spirit and "get over" with the congregation. He or she is most apt to be "hit" first and hardest by the Spirit. A good lead singer can "fire up" the congregation and other group members. But the background singers and congregation also play essential roles in helping the lead singer bring on the Spirit. Earl Ledbetter, who coordinates the background for the Wearyland Gospel Singers, says that, while the spiritual feeling may initially hit the lead vocalist, the background singers will also feel it and must urge the leader on:

See, the lead singer always gets the Spirit first, because he's the one leading the song. The background is just following him. But once we get into it, the background starts feeling good too. Once we start pushing him, he can really get out there and shout, do whatever he wants, he feels even better. We would push the feeling back up to him. He would hear me in the background, saying "sing your song, son," or "take your time," and that would give him something to push on. If the background pushes the lead singer, he can do even more. But if the background is dead, it makes it hard for the lead singer.[21]

Arthur McKoy, bass singer for the No Name Gospel Singers, expresses similar sentiments:

In other words, if the background helps build him [the leader], he will sing longer, and harder. Its like we know he's getting into a spiritual mood, and we can see that he's expressing himself, that God's been good to him. You [the background] want to express it [the Spirit] too. You want to give him the feeling you're with him, that you know what he's saying is true. And when he can feel us expressing it back here, that's what you call the feedback, and that's going to make him sing harder.[22]

The background vocalists must not be considered strictly as "non-trancing performers," as Marks suggests. While they usually do not exhibit the extremes of emotional behavior that lead singers do, they still claim to be under the influence of the Holy Spirit. They must encourage the lead singer and assist her or him in passing the feeling on to the audience. Further, towards the end of an extended drive section where the background vocals may drop out, or during a final processional where all the singers are marching out together, the background singers often show stronger signs of the Spirit, as they may shout, cry, or holy dance.

The lead and background singers collaborate in building and passing the spiritual energy on to the congregation. The Spirit is often compared to electricity or fire as it jumps from one believer to the next. Lead singer David Steward explains:

The Spiritual feeling is like a chain, like a chain reaction. If somebody out there in the congregation knows something about God, about the Lord, and you [the singer] know something about it, it's like a chain reaction. If I feel it, they [the audience] will feel it too, eventually.[23]

The congregation, however, are not simply passive receivers in this situation: they must be active and receptive to the group's efforts. Audience members must clap their hands, stamp their feet, and shout back words of encouragement to the performers. It is difficult, nearly impossible, state the singers, to raise the Spirit in a congregation that does not become both physically and emotionally involved in the performance. As Charlie Storey remarks:

See, if that congregation is dead, and just sitting there looking at you, you ain't going to be able to do but so much. But if the congregation pushes you, like they're enjoying it, that will make you do more. A congregation can help build you, can help give you more determination to sing. It can make a guy sing longer, make him do more pushing. See if the people are enjoying it, it helps you too, you know the Spirit is there. But if the congregation is just looking dead, then you're going to die too. They got to have some fire in them.[24]

The Reverend Vernella Kelly points out that like a preacher a gospel singer requires response and support from his or her congregation:

Now if the congregation is pushing you and enjoying you, then that makes you enjoy more to. But if you are singing to a dead place, it looks like the Spirit doesn't come in and dwell in no dead place. Its just like when you preach and nobody ain't out there saying "amen" [responding to you]—the Word ain't getting across to the people, the Devil is trying to kill the Word. But any time you get support [from the congregation] it helps you, as a preacher or singer. It makes the Spirit come in, when they're with you. When the Spirit comes in it will go from left to right—hit you, you, and you. Then everybody is enjoying, when the Spirit is there.[25]

As the congregation begin to feel the Spirit, they can bounce the power back to the singers, who in turn may generate and transmit an even stronger emotional feeling back to the congregation, and so on. Rather than a linear, dyadic frame where the active lead singer (sender) simply transmits the feeling of the Spirit (information) to the passive congregation (receiver), there appears to be a complex feedback loop operating among all participants during a gospel program. The lead singer may initiate the process, but as a performance proceeds all singers and congregation members act simultaneously as senders and receivers, building the spiritual feeling in each other. To borrow from Ray Birdwhistell's terminology, the communication demands continuous feedback, as the singers and congregation members trade sensory information through both the audio-acoustic (aural) and kinesthetic-visual channels.[26]

The need for continuous audience feedback and validation in preaching and other forms of African-American performance has been discussed by Gerald Davis. He contends that, once the African-American performer has introduced an ideal traditional form (song, sermon, dance routine, etc.), the audience may accept, reject, or modify the interpretation. If it is rejected, the performer must readjust the presentation to render it more acceptable to the audience before proceeding to improvise a more personal interpretation.[27] A similar process appears to be operating during gospel performance, as the lead singer cannot proceed to shape a song into a compelling personal statement without constant validation and encouragement from the audience. Indeed, this circular organizing structure may be an underlying principle for much traditional African-American performance.

At this point it should be clear that various patterns of speech, song, and movement in gospel ritual serve as manifestations and evocations of spiritual possession. The entire process, however, cannot be understood solely in terms of a simple uni-directional communications model or reduced to a single stylistic code switching (from singing to chanting). Rather, singing in the Spirit is a complex phenomenon involving the conscious manipulation of performance strategies, continuous audience/artist interaction, and the expectations of transcendent intervention that participants carry to a gospel program. Ultimately, spiritual and aesthetic concerns converge to support one another, as the ritual structure reinforces sacred belief and facilitates the spiritual experience.

In his provocative cross-cultural survey of music and trance, Gilbert Rouget argues that music and dance cannot themselves automatically induce spiritual trance, for participants must first have expectations of divine communication before a transcendent state can be attained.[28] The latter is certainly true for African-American quartet singing. All participants—singers and audience members alike—come to gospel programs consciously anticipating a spiritual experience. Lest someone should forget, the devotional leader and emcee constantly remind all present that they are gathered to "have church" and "let the Spirit have his way." Throughout the program singers admonish those listeners who are not "letting loose" and "getting happy." The expectation of divine intervention, of a Spirit-induced communal "shout," is clearly established. Conversely, if the Holy Spirit does not make its presence felt, the program will be considered a failure. This does not necessarily mean that the sung and chanted words themselves have no divine or inherent mystical power, as Rouget implies. Church singers contend that good music, singing, testifying, and preaching can indeed "bring on the Spirit." Moreover quartet singers believe that their utterances are divinely inspired and that at certain moments the Holy Ghost, speaking through them, can induce Spirit possession in their listeners. For them, music and singing are gifts from God and can never be fully understood in mere social or behavioral terms.

On the other hand, there is a deep-seated tension among New York's quartet singers concerning the issues of spiritual authenticity and commercial showmanship. The Reverend Floyd King of the No Name Gospel Singers warns:

Now let me tell you this—if I said everything you see at gospel programs was the Holy Ghost, I might lie. You know why? There are some fellahs that sing and drink whiskey. The Devil tells them what to do. Now when you see a singer who might have had a drink, you might not tell nothing. He can go all up and down the aisle and fall out, whatever he wants. But then someone might come behind him who is under the anointment of the Holy Spirit— you get a different feeling from that singer than from the first one [that had a drink]. See the anointing of the Holy Spirit is different than what the Devil does.[29]

King's remarks are not unusual, for questions are constantly being raised concerning which gospel performers are truly singing in the Spirit and which—perhaps under the influence of alcohol, drugs, or the Devil—are simply putting on a show. When discussing the phenomenon of the Holy Spirit, singers inevitably caution that all the activity and emotions one witnesses during a gospel program are not necessarily the manifestations of the Spirit. Accusations of acting, clowning, and showboating are commonly leveled against other groups or individual singers.

The older singers in particular, who recall the days of the jubilee and harmonizing quartets, are fond of criticizing the younger singers for too much preaching, dancing, and running around, and not enough quality singing. Some dismiss these exaggerated behaviors as showmanship, arguing that, if a group is truly in the Spirit, an audience of believers will instinctively feel their sincerity without all the antics. Sam Abrahams, who sang with the old Skylight Singers, sums up these feelings:

These singers today claim to be spreading the word of God, but they're not living it. It's just a plain, fake story they're telling. Let me explain one more thing. If you are right with God, and you live for God, then you don't have to preach a sermon to convince people. They will automatically see it through you, and feel it on you. As you go to sing or speak or whatever you do, somebody will join you right away, because they feel what you are doing. But today it's so phony, until everyone is trying to convince somebody else that they are what they are.[30]

Most of the middle-aged and younger singers who engage in the more demonstrative and theatrical performance practices counter these charges by claiming they are simply trying to bring on the Spirit.

Another common criticism is that too many local groups emulate the professional gospel singers. In doing so the former compromise their spiritual commitment in favor of entertainment and financial concerns. Jordan Evans of the Heavenly Tones reflects on this dilemma:

A lot of local groups will go out and watch what the professional groups do. They watch their movement, and a lot of times they'll come back and want to do what they [the professional groups] want to do. But the thing about it is, to me this is wrong, because most of the professional singers are out there for a show. But when we go around to different churches, singing, we're not going for a show. We go and try and sing God's praises! And to me, if you are singing with the Spirit, you don't have to do all that stuff [move around like the professional groups]. If you sing with the Spirit, and sing like you're supposed to, and the Spirit is there, people are going to feel it. Understand what I mean?[31]

Since the Spirit can move people to run, cry, and shout, the obvious question arises as to how one distinguishes between singers who are sincerely in the Spirit and those who are simply putting on a show or singing for money. Many singers claim they can make this differentiation, arguing that once you have experienced the power of the Spirit yourself you can tell whether another group is real or not. They are often skeptical of groups who go through exactly the same moves and routines every time they allegedly "get the Spirit." Since the true Spirit is perceived as being spontaneous and unpredictable, singers who fall under its influence never know how they will be moved, and rarely behave in the same fashion each time. When questioned about a specific testimony—one accompanied by a great deal of shouting and running—that a well-known Brooklyn singer often gives, Jordan Evans responded:

That's like a show, like an act. If you see him sing tomorrow, he'll probably do the same thing. Today you may shout, but the Spirit is not going to always have you running all over the place and carrying on. The Spirit don't work that way. Now I can see you may get happy and shout, but the next time he sings he does exactly the same thing? Every time you sing you're not going to feel the Spirit that way. You can walk into a church and sing your heart out, and people might just sit there and look at you. And next Sunday, you go into that church, and sing the same song, and maybe when you hit the first one, you've got five or six people up there shouting. That's the way the Spirit does.[32]

Bill Dobson of the No Name Gospel Singers questions the sincerity of groups who engage in pre-choreographed routines:

Some groups have a dance they do, and they are just entertainers, you know? Every time you see them they do the same thing, the same way, the same dance, over and over. See, when the Spirit hits you, you don't know what you're going to do. It's no routine thing, understand? I've been in that situation, and when you don't get up there and do the same thing each time. God doesn't work like that. I'm not saying it might not happen a few times, but not every time![33]

This debate over spiritual authenticity reveals certain tensions among gospel groups and the larger African-American church community. Age is certainly a factor, especially for older singers who lack the energy and physical stamina to keep up with their younger counterparts and tend to prefer more restrained presentations. Denomination may also come into play, as Holiness and Pentecostal singers (and audiences) are generally more accepting of extremely demonstrative performance than are some Baptists and many Methodists. But most importantly, the question of spiritual authenticity underscores the rivalry between quartets as well as the tensions arising over the issues of professionalism and money. There is a strong sense of competition among the local groups, as well as the constant temptation to emulate the professional stars they hear through the media and see at larger commercial programs. Paradoxically, while local singers revere professional groups like the Dixie Hummingbirds, the Mighty Clouds of Joy, and the Jackson Southernaires for their extraordinary singing talents, the professionals' concern with money often calls their spiritual sincerity into question. Many local singers see the professionals as showmen who are more concerned with financial gain than with spiritual commitment. Since there is such a fine line between "shouting the church" and simply putting on a show, jealous local singers are quick to accuse their competitors of entertaining and imitating the professionals rather than singing for the Lord. Money, predictably, becomes a central issue. When certain local groups begin to demand higher payments to appear on an anniversary or ticket program, they are often chastised by their competitors for abandoning their spiritual mission. The point that "salvation is free" is often stressed by singers like Jordan Evans and Charlie Storey, who look askance at others who demand exorbitant fees to perform on local programs.[34] The tense but interdependent relationship between the local and professional quartets will be returned to in Chapter 9.

The extent to which gospel performers are morally justified in questioning the spiritual commitment of their fellow singers over the issues of money and showmanship is itself a topic of controversy. Some singers refuse to indulge in such talk, claiming only the Almighty is qualified to stand in judgment. But others do, often expressing sentiments that border on petty jealousy. The issue of spiritual commitment becomes exacerbated if one or more members of a group are suspected of not being strong in their faith, or of indulging in some immoral activity such as drinking, drug abuse, or sexual promiscuity. In short, performers are expected to "live the life" they sing about. If a group's spiritual reputation becomes severely tarnished, they may be dismissed as simply "singing just to sing," rather than "singing for the Lord," and may no longer be invited to perform at local programs.

A final point concerning spiritual authenticity relates to Reverend King's earlier remarks concerning singers being guided by the Devil rather than the Holy Spirit. The Devil is constantly being invoked during gospel programs and other African-American church-related rituals. While Christ always triumphs over His evil counterpart in sermon, song, and testimony, the faithful are constantly being warned of the Devil's omnipresent, tempting Spirit. Satan has the power, it is believed, to enter and to disrupt a worship, prayer, or gospel service. The Devil is blamed for nearly everything that might go wrong at a gospel program—from a singer being late or having a sore throat to the instruments going out of tune or a PA system malfunctioning. The ultimate fear is that the sacred gospel program will degenerate into secular entertainment if it is taken over by unsaved singers who are under the influence of the Devil's evil Spirit (and possibly alcohol, drugs, etc.) rather than the true Spirit of God. This may explain in part the constant reminders of the devotional leader, the emcee, and the singers themselves that everyone has gathered at the gospel program to "have church" and to "sing God's praises" rather than for entertainment or financial gain. The latter two, of course, are seen as manifestations of the Devil attempting to take over and destroy the true Spirit of the service.

The final question of who is and who is not genuinely in the Spirit can never be answered satisfactorily by an ethnographer who does not share the beliefs and experiences of evangelical Christians. The singers' testimonies suggest that some performers are genuinely "having church," while others are simply playing at having church in order to produce an entertaining show. Both are evidently happening, at times simultaneously. That is, on some occasions singers who are not truly "in the Spirit," but rather are motivated by ego, money, alcohol, or perhaps Satan himself, do perform at gospel programs. And further, there will always be a certain percentage of audience members who simply come to be entertained by good singing rather than out of religious conviction. The frequency of such occurrences is probably higher at the larger, commercial gospel extravaganzas where money is of major concern. However, genuine spiritual commitment is strong among many, perhaps most, at the smaller, local programs. In these settings the financial component is downplayed, and local singers take pride in boasting they are motivated by a genuine spiritual mission. The Reverend Vernella Kelly explains:

When I have a program it's not just entertainment, it's a spiritual filled program, to uplift someone. See when people come to programs, they have certain problems, and sometimes a certain song will relieve that problem and uplift them. . . . And it's the words in the song that really count. And maybe somebody will even be saved, listening to those words. Ain't everybody out there at programs saved! See something in a song might follow you, will go home with you. When you constantly think about that, you might live a different life, you might change your way of living. No, everybody out there ain't saved, but the words of a song can help you, can save you, I believe.[35]

Local gospel singers like Kelly see themselves as purveyors of God's word: they aim to uplift the believer and to confront the sinner through song. Unlike their secular counterparts who are primarily concerned with entertainment and financial gain, community-based quartets perform as part of their Christian duty. Many, like Arthur McKoy, actually envision their singing as something of a job:

When I'm in the house of God, I'm doing what He wants me to do. And He gave me a song, and I have to give it to the people. It's like a job God gave us to do. Those who are saved, they can see your good work. So we are letting our light shine so the Christians can see your good work. And so the sinners can also see your good work, and they might come in. Maybe the sinner might feel the vibrations, so he might want to come up and sing or testify. It might uplift him—he might want to change his way of living.[36]

The spiritual mission described by Kelly and McKoy is actually two-fold in purpose. Through their testimonies and songs they hope to strengthen the faithful while challenging the sinner to repent and join the church. With regard to the former, singers seek to support the faith of believers by constantly reminding them, through spoken and sung words, of God's goodness and His promise of salvation. They offer their listeners spiritual fortitude through messages of Christian love, salvation, and the possibilities of liberation from the burdens of an often hostile world. Jordan Evans explains how a song can stay with a Christian throughout the week, imparting the strength to cope with daily life:

When we sing, we try to touch somebody's heart. Sometimes we call it food to feast on. When you sing a song and a person will get that song, and get the feeling, and get the Spirit, they may be all next week singing the song for themselves. And that song can do a lot of things for you, set your mind at ease while working, you know?[37]

Some singers view their role as similar to that of preachers—that is to spread God's word and nurture the needy. Willie Johnson comments:

We're trying to deliver a message. It's a message to people about how God can save you, how God can heal you, how He can open doors for you, how He can make a way for you. How if you are burdened down you can be uplifted by song. If you've got trouble in your home or on the job, God can fix it. Stuff like that. That's just like being a preacher.[38]

In keeping with the evangelical Protestant tradition, gospel singers, like preachers, are also concerned with bringing God's word to the unsaved. As Reverend Kelly points out, gospel programs are often attended by some who have not totally committed their lives to Christ. Performers frequently boast that their singing actually lures people into church who might not come to a Sunday morning worship service. David Steward explains:

I know people who never go to church, and they come to a program to hear singing, and the next thing you know they get involved in the church. I'm talking about addicts, and alcoholics—they started seeking help. The song will lead them into the church, and then they may turn to the minister, and prayer, and they may get stronger and change their whole lifestyle.[39]

The hope is that non-believers who occasionally attend a gospel program for the singing will be moved to realize their own state of sin and in turn will repent and give their lives to Christ. Whether or not a song can actually "save" an individual is unclear. Some feel that the words of a song can bring a person directly to Christ, that an individual can be "saved through singing." Others, however, are reluctant to attribute such powers to singing, arguing that a song may simply awaken an individual and lead him or her back to church to seek salvation. Regardless, all agree that gospel singing is a powerful proselytizing tool for reaching the unconverted.

Many local gospel groups further demonstrate their religious commitment by raising significant amounts of the money for churches and other charitable causes. Ministers or deacons of small churches will often hold gospel programs to raise funds for general church operating costs and to attract new members into their congregations. Sometimes if a small church is financially strapped and in need of physical repairs or new pews, groups will contribute the entire free will offering to a special "building fund." Some groups not only donate their singing services but also contribute money at these programs. With regard to more personal charity, some of the older groups continue to set aside small amounts of money in their treasuries to be used by their members, families, or friends in case of sickness, accident, or death.[40]

Groups occasionally sponsor programs to raise money for secular community causes such as drug rehabilitation programs, homeless shelters, and child care centers. Some will also provide free programs to senior citizen centers, hospitals, prisons, and outdoor neighborhood gatherings. Although direct political involvement is rare, groups may appear at rallies for local candidates, or support worthy causes such as anti-apartheid demonstrations. Most singers view these occasions as opportunities to spread God's word and to demonstrate Christian virtues through their good works.

The discussion in Chapter 3 suggests that local gospel quartet programs closely resemble Sunday morning church services in terms of overall structure and intent. The issues of spirituality examined here reinforce this observation and further reveal the workings of the ritual process. Like the Sunday morning worship service, the gospel program is a consecrated event in which evangelical African-Americans collectively reaffirm the intellectual and emotional aspects of their faith.

In his analysis of religion as a cultural system, Clifford Geertz notes:

As religion on one side anchors the power of our symbolic resources for formulating analytical ideas in an authoritative conception of the overall shape of reality, so on another side it anchors the power of our, also symbolic, resources for expressing emotions—moods, sentiments, passions, affections, feelings—in a similar conception of its pervasive tenor, its inherent tone and temper. For those able to embrace them, and for as long as they are able to embrace them, religious symbols provide a cosmic guarantee not only for their ability to comprehend the world, but also, comprehending it, to give a precision to their feeling, a definition to their emotions which enables them, morosely or joyfully, grimly or cavalierly, to endure it.[41]

It is during these moments of culturally performed ritual, argues Geertz, that the conceptual and emotional dimensions of religious life most noticeably converge:

It is in some sort of ceremonial (ritual) form—even if that form be hardly more than a recitation of a myth, the consultation of an oracle, or the decoration of a grave—that the moods and motivations which sacred symbols induce in men and the general conception of the order of existence which they formulate for men meet and reinforce one another. In a ritual, the world as lived and the world as imagined, fused under the agency of a single set of symbolic forms, turn out to be the same world. . . .[42]

Geertz contends that successful ritual must do more than simply remind participants of the intellectual suppositions that undergird their faith. In addition, the manipulation of meaningful symbolic expressions must render their beliefs emotionally convincing by "invoking deeply felt moral and aesthetic sentiments as experiential evidence for their truth."[43] As religious men and women engage in ritual, they experience some sense of the Almighty as well as comprehend intellectually the sacred formulae of their faith.

Geertz's approach to ritual is especially useful in understanding the mechanics of traditional African-American sacred worship. During a Sunday morning service, the congregation hears again the basic tenets of the evanglical Christian stance—the inherent evil nature of humanity, the possibility of salvation through Christ's death and resurrection, and the need for personal redemption. The universe is clearly defined in terms of good and evil, and all are reminded of the path to salvation. While these themes are touched on in prayer, scriptural reading, testimony, and song, it is during the sermon that God's message is preached in a truly didactic fashion. And yet, as Arthur Paris points out, the process involves more than instruction:

First, in addition to giving flesh to the beliefs and truths that the congregation holds dear, ritual serves to make real the subjects of those beliefs. Specifically, in the context of ritual performance (although not limited to those occasions), there are epiphanies and kairotic moments when the Lord, the Holy Spirit, or the Spirit of God is made present within the community of believers. The "Spirit falls" among the faithful, and they experience His presence. It is not simply that ritual operates to reify the principles of belief and to interpret the day-by-day experience of believers in religious terms; equally importantly, in ritual, "The Word is made manifest and dwells among men."[44]

In a Sunday morning service this transcendent experience of the Holy Spirit is achieved through the chanted sermon, the chanted/sung prayer, testimony, and the various forms of song and music. Faith is not sustained solely through explication of biblical doctrine: the congregation must further be led to feel the power and immediacy of the Almighty among them. Each week the process is repeated as believers are moved to experience and re-experience the reality of

God's Spirit. By doing so, they maintain and renew their Christian faith.

Bearing in mind Geertz's observations concerning the overall nature of religious belief and ritual, and Paris's more specific analysis of African-American worship, the similarities between the Sunday morning worship service and the community-based gospel program come into sharper focus. Both seek to merge the analytical/conceptual and emotional/experiential realms of faith through ritualized performance. During the gospel program, the spoken, chanted, and sung words communicate referential information needed for comprehending the nature of humanity and the universe. But equally important, the highly stylized manner in which the message is delivered stirs the emotional temperament of the worshipers to a point where they actually feel, and possibly experience (if the Spirit descends), the truth of those teachings.

Just as in the Sunday morning worship service, the gospel program's opening devotional service sets a spiritual tone for the event. Songs and prayer praise the Almighty, ask for His guidance, and invite the Holy Spirit to join in the worship. God's teachings are recounted through a scriptural reading, and personal testimony bears witness to His miraculous works. During the song service segment of the gospel program, the spoken introductions, testimonies, and song lyrics further explicate the basic message of Christ's love and redeeming power. The goodness of Christ is constantly opposed by the presence of the Devil, the primary symbol of chaos and evil in the universe. Song introductions are often filled with harsh warnings concerning Satan's treacherous ways, along with admonitions to avoid the temptations of the secular world such as alcohol, drugs, gambling, dancing, and sexual promiscuity. The hardships of daily life—sickness, accidents, unemployment, financial difficulties, and so on—draw lengthy commentary and are often blamed on satanic forces. But the songs themselves are optimistic outpourings of joy and adulation, aiming to convince the listener that Satan and the burdens of the secular world can be transcended through a commitment to Christ. Narrative, testimony, and song serve to bring the deep binary oppositions of good (Christ) and evil (Satan) to the surface, where their confrontation yields ultimate victory for the Almighty and His followers. In short, gospel performance serves to explain and instruct the believer in the basic nature of the cosmos, illuminating the path toward meaning and order in a chaotic universe. The problems are identified, the solution made clear. Believers are comforted and reassured in their faith, while sinners are confronted with the hopelessness of their plight.

While elements of cosmology and spiritual doctrine are conveyed during gospel quartet performance, it is in the realm of feeling and experience that the most profound impact is made. Singers begin to stir emotions through the production of sounds that are recognized as pleasurable in the black church community—expressive and personalized vocal delivery, blending harmonies, innovative song arrangements, and so forth. These sounds and words are rich with connotative associations, often arousing feelings of nostalgia as participants reflect back on old family, friends, and childhood experiences in the South. The singers use appropriate performance strategies—processionals, dramatic narrations, lead switching, etc.—to gain greater audience participation and to heighten the congregation's level of emotional response. When the singers deliver God's message with sufficient emotional intensity, sincerity, and competence, most present will begin to "feel good" as the Spirit stirs within them. Here the performance engages both religious and aesthetic sentiments, as singer Willie Johnson suggests when he comments, "when the singing sounds good, the Spirit just comes alive."

Eventually singers and congregation members may become totally overwhelmed by the feeling of the Spirit, and their innermost beliefs and feelings may be outwardly expressed in demonstrative shouts or an outpouring of tears. Intellect, emotion, and experience converge. As Paris suggests for the Sunday morning worship service, it is at this kairotic moment that God makes His presence known, and the truths of biblical doctrine are reified in mind and heart as "the Word is made manifest and dwells among men." In other words, the participants know God is real, not only through the words of testimonies and song, but because they actually feel His presence within their midst.

While the analytical/conceptual and emotional/experiential dichotomy provides a convenient etic construct for approaching the ritual mechanism, in reality the intellectual and emotional components of faith are inseparable. As Geertz points out, it is during ritual that ideas and emotions merge and reinforce one another in the most profound fashion. From the singer's perspective, one must "know" (intellectually comprehend) "God's Word" (the teachings of the scripture) if one is to experience the Spirit and convey a "spiritual feeling" (emotion) to the audience. On the other hand, the singer who truly knows God's Word can only reach the congregation with this message through impassioned speech and song—for those who sing without "feeling" are assumed to be spiritually "dead." And, in the final judgment, if the audience do not "feel" the message, they probably will not experience the Holy Ghost.

The relationship between spiritual experience and ritual structure is significant. As suggested in Chapter 3, moments of spiritual transcendence at gospel programs tend to occur as participants approach a state of spontaneous communitas—Victor Turner's term for the deep sense of human interconnectedness and social equality experienced during certain phases of ritual. Using Turner's model, several ethnographic studies of southern church communities suggest that folk Protestants experience spontaneous communitas initially and most intensely at the time of personal conversion, a rite of passage when an individual is "born again" and joins a community of believers. These powerful feelings can subsequently be rejuvenated through communal testimony (particularly accounts of personal conversion), prayer, hymn singing, and general religious emotionalism. Through repeated ritual worship, participants may collectively re-experience spontaneous communitas and the rapture of their original conversion experiences.[45] Gospel ritual offers yet another opportunity for this to happen. The structure of the gospel program (as outlined in Chapter 3), the organization of individual group performance strategies (as outlined in Chapter 4), and the aesthetic principles of control and cooperation (as outlined in Chapter 5) foster an egalitarian atmosphere that downplays hierarchy and competition in favor of social equality and group harmony. Ritual structure and aesthetic sensibilities shape performances that encourage a collective, spiritual unity.

Simple observation at gospel programs links the most vivid, spirit-induced behaviors with the onset of communitas. During extended drive sections and processionals, when singers leave the stage to merge with an exuberant audience of worshipers, the frequency of unrestrained shouting, weeping, and holy dance reaches its peak. At such times even the outside observer can feel the totality of group engagement, the intensity of focus, and the flow of collective ecstasy that characterize communitas. But are singers and congregation members actually re-experiencing feelings of their original conversion? During interviews no singers mentioned their conversion when attempting to describe the experience of singing in the Spirit. However, there is ethnographic evidence to support the possibility of such a connection. While singers occasionally mention their conversion during a narration (see Reverend Kelly's sermonette in Chapter 4), they often begin extended drive sections with references to their original calling.[46] Consider again the two drive sections discussed in Chapter 4. Clifford Williams of the Brooklyn Skyways chants:

He brought me up	(He brought me up)	[Sch]
He brought me up	(He brought me up)	
When I was down,	(He brought me up)	
He picked me up,	(He brought me up)	
Turned me all around.	(He brought me up)	
And I remember,	(He brought me up)	
And I remember,	(He brought me up)	
When I was in sin.	(He brought me up)	
Nobody but Jesus,	(He brought me up)	[Ch]
Nobody but Jesus,	(He brought me up)	
Nobody but Jesus,	(He brought me up)	
Nobody but Jesus,	(He brought me up)	
He picked me up,	(He brought me up)	
He turned me around.	(He brought me up)	

Williams recalls his past state of sin and his joyful redemption in hopes of rekindling those emotions in the present, and to induce similar feelings among his listeners. As the drive proceeds Williams invites those who have been "born again" to stand and clap, to become "filled with the Holy Ghost," and be washed with the "holy fire," presumably as they were at the moment of their original conversion. Likewise the second lead singer for the Golden Sons opens his drive by referencing his conversion:

Let me tell you what He done,	(yeah)	[Sch]
Let me tell you what He done,	(yeah)	
Early one Sunday morning,	(early one Sunday morning)	
Early one Sunday morning,	(early one Sunday morning)	
Let me tell you what He done,	(yeah)	
Sanctified my life,	(oh yes He did)	
Sanctified my life,	(oh yes He did)	
Filled me with the Holy Ghost,	(filled me with the Holy Ghost)	
Filled me with the Holy Ghost,	(filled me with the Holy Ghost)	

The singer then breaks into a rhetorical chant about the "Holy Ghost power"—the same power responsible for his original conversion. Believers who share these memories are drawn together into the flow of communitas as they open themselves for possible anointment by the Holy Spirit. Meanwhile, others present who have yet to convert may be inspired to do so.

In spite of their similarities, the gospel quartet program does not accomplish the exact functions as, nor serve as an alternative to, the

Sunday morning worship service. The latter, in fact, forms the center of the ritual life of most southern Protestant African-Americans. For the devoted believer, there is no substitute for hearing God's Word through preaching. While music and song are essential ingredients, the Sunday morning service is built around the sermon which interprets sacred teachings in terms of the earthly experiences of African-Americans. In this sense the Sunday morning worship service places more emphasis on the analytical/conceptual dimensions of the religious experience than does the gospel program. While participants most certainly feel and experience God's presence during the morning service, they are offered a far more in-depth explanation of biblical doctrine than would be possible during a gospel quartet program where singing, rather than preaching, is the primary focus.

A second point of differentiation between the gospel program and the Sunday morning worship service deals with the issue of saving lost souls. All gospel singers see their performing as a way of reaching the sinner with God's message. There remains some question, however, as to whether an individual can actually be saved through singing or whether this can only be accomplished through the preached Word. Further, the gospel program provides no built-in structure for prompting the sinner to come forward and accept Christ, a function carried out through the altar call in a Sunday morning service.[47] Gospel programs aim primarily to confront and challenge sinners in hopes of leading them back to church and eventual conversion.

The local gospel quartet program is best viewed as an extension of the Sunday morning worship ritual—a public occasion where sacred ideation, emotion, and experience become tightly interlocked. Participants come together with expectations of a collective spiritual experience. Yet during the most intense moments of gospel performance other moral and social concerns regularly surface. In addition to reinforcing an evangelical Christian world view, New York City's gospel quartet singers are concerned with preserving a set of values and a way of life associated with another place and time—"back home" in the old rural South.

Notes

1. An excellent review of the subject is found in Gilbert Rouget, *Music and Trance* (Chicago: University of Chicago Press, 1985). The reader interested in glossolalia can begin by consulting Felicitas Goodman, *Speaking in Tongues: A Cross Cultural Study of Glossolalia* (Chicago: University of Chicago Press, 1972), and William Samarin, *Tongues of Men and Angels: The Religious Language of Pentecostalism* (New York: Macmillan, 1972). Possession trance and drumming are explored in Sheila Walker, *Ceremonial Spirit Possession in Africa*

and Afro-America (Leiden: Brill, 1972) and in Erica Bourguignon, *Religion, Altered States of Consciousness, and Social Change* (Columbus: Ohio State University Press, 1973).

2. One of the earliest scholarly accounts of the Holy Ghost and shouting in African-American church worship is Zora Neal Hurston, *The Sanctified Church* (Berkeley, CA: Turtle Island Press, 1981), pp. 91–94. See also Paris, *Black Pentecostalism*, pp. 102–103; Bruce Rosenberg, *Can These Bones Live?: The Art of the American Folk Preacher* (2nd ed., Urbana: University of Illinois Press, 1988), pp. 59, 131; and Albert Raboteau, *Slave Religion* (New York: Oxford University Press, 1978), pp. 236–237.

3. Paris, *Black Pentecostalism*, p. 85.

4. A pioneering work in the experience-centered study of folk belief is Hufford's *Terror that Comes in the Night*. See the discussion of Hufford's method in the Introduction of this work.

5. See for example Titon, *Powerhouse For God*; Elaine Lawless, *Handmaidens of the Lord: Pentecostal Women Preachers and Traditional Religion* (Philadelphia: University of Pennsylvania Press, 1988); Ruel Tyson, James Peacock, and Daniel Patterson, eds., *Diversities of Gifts: Field Studies in Southern Religion* (Urbana: University of Illinois Press, 1988); and Glenn Hinson, "When the Words Roll and the Fire Flows: Spirit, Style, and Experience in African-American Gospel Performance," Ph.D. dissertation, University of Pennsylvania, 1989.

6. Morton Marks, "You Can't Sing Unless You're Saved," and "Uncovering Ritual Structure in Afro-American Music," in Irving Zaretsky and Mark Leone, eds., *Religious Movements in Contemporary America* (Princeton, NJ: Princeton University Press, 1974), pp. 60–134.

7. For more on southern Protestant revivalism see Samuel Hill, *Southern Churches in Crisis* (New York: Holt, Rinehart, and Winston, 1966), pp. 73–118. For more on the development of southern African-American Protestantism, see Paris, *Black Pentecostalism*, pp. 16–30.

8. For more on the problematic nature of discourse concerning the supernatural see David Hufford, "Ambiguity and the Rhetoric of Belief," *Keystone Folklore* 21 (1977):11–24; and Diane Goldstein, "The Language of Religious Experience," *Western Folklore* 17 (1983):105–113.

9. Personal interview with Willie Johnson, March 24, 1986.

10. Personal interview with David Steward, March 16, 1986.

11. Personal interview with Robert Todd, July 7, 1986.

12. Personal interview with the Reverend Floyd King, March 2, 1986.

13. Personal interview with Charlie Storey, March 11, 1986.

14. Personal interview with the Reverend Vernella Kelly, Sept. 10, 1986.

15. Others have reported informants claiming to be "mouthpieces" for the Holy Spirit. See Titon, *Powerhouse for God*, pp. 5–6 and 199; and Brett Sutton, "Speech, Chant, and Song: Patterns of Language and Action in a Southern Church," in Tyson, Peacock, and Patterson, eds., *Diversities of Gifts*, p. 161.

16. Hufford, *The Terror That Comes in the Night*, p. 250.

17. Personal interview with Charlie Storey, August 7, 1985.

18. Personal interview with Willie Johnson, March 24, 1986.

19. Personal interview with Jordan Evans, March 18, 1986.

20. Marks, "You Can't Sing Unless You're Saved," p. 317.

21. Personal interview with Earl Ledbetter, September 6, 1986.

22. Personal interview with Arthur McKoy, February 2, 1986.

23. Personal interview with David Steward, March 16, 1986.

24. Personal interview with Charlie Storey, September 4, 1986.

25. Personal interview with the Reverend Vernella Kelly, Sept. 10, 1986.

26. See Ray Birdwhistell, "Communication," *International Encyclopedia of Social Sciences* 3 (1968): 24–29; and *Kinesics and Context* (Philadelphia: University of Pennsylvania Press, 1970), pp. 65–79.

27. Davis, *I Got the Word in Me*, pp. 26–38.

28. Rouget, *Music and Trance*, pp. 315–326.

29. Personal interview with the Reverend Floyd King, March 2, 1986.

30. Personal interview with Sam Abrahams, April 6, 1986.

31. Personal interview with Jordan Evans, January 20. 1986.

32. Ibid.

33. Personal interview with Bill Dobson, February 11, 1986.

34. Lornell reports similar attitudes among Memphis singers. See Lornell, *"Happy in the Service of the Lord"*, p. 95.

35. Personal interview with the Reverend Vernella Kelly, Jan. 17, 1986.

36. Personal interview with Arthur McKoy, February 2, 1986.

37. Personal interview Jordan Evans, October 29, 1985.

38. Personal interview with Willie Johnson, March 24, 1986.

39. Personal interview with David Steward, March 16, 1986.

40. In this instance the gospel groups serve a similar function to that of the older burial societies which were once popular among African-Americans in the rural South. The practice is evidently not as strong in New York today as it once was.

41. Geertz, *Interpretation of Cultures*, p. 104.

42. Ibid., p. 112.

43. Ibid., p. 90.

44. Paris, *Black Pentecostalism*, p. 144.

45. The relationship between communitas, Protestant conversion, and religious emotionalism was initially mapped out by William Clements in his work with Pentecostals and Baptists in Arkansas. See Clements, "Conversion and Communitas," *Western Folklore* 35 (1976), pp. 35–45. Working with Anglo and African-American folk Protestants in the Blue Ridge Mountains of Virginia and North Carolina, Patrick Mullen interpreted sacred narratives, hymn singing, and other worship practices as attempts to renew and sustain feelings of communitas. See Mullen, "Ritual and Sacred Narratives in the Blue Ridge Mountains," *Papers in Comparative Studies* (Columbus: Ohio State University, 1983), pp. 17–38. See also Titon, *Powerhouse for God*, pp. 404–407.

46. Marks, working from recordings, also contends that gospel singers "relive the call" of their original conversion during "trance-generated" vocalizations. See his analysis of the gospel song "The Way We Used to Have Church" in Marks, "You Can't Sing Unless You're Saved," pp. 311–314.

47. For more on the function of the altar call see Paris, *Black Pentecostalism*, pp. 67–69.

18. The Faithful Harmonizers, Manhattan, 1988 (l to r: Geneva Ray, Clara Macky, William Ray, Wilburt Huntly, Reverend Vernella Kelly). Photo by Jack Vartoogian.

19. A congregation member catching the Spirit, Brooklyn, 1989. Photo by Jack Vartoogian.

Chapter 7
Back Home
Southern Identity in the Urban North

"You see people down here, they know how to have church!" exclaims Jeff Richardson, twenty-five-year-old drummer for the Brooklyn Skyways. "They know how to get down and clap their hands, and shout, and have a good time without any music [instruments]. Up in New York they just mess around, until it's time to hear some music and clap their hands." Richardson narrates as we wind down a two lane country road outside of Sumter, South Carolina on a bright August morning. Willie Johnson, leader of the Skyways, hums an old hymn as he guides the bus toward I-95 and home. The other members of the Skyways and some fifteen friends and relatives sit quietly or doze, still recovering from the busy weekend's activities. Johnson brought the Skyways and company to his home town of Sumter to sing for his nephew's wedding reception on Saturday evening and to perform at two small church programs on Sunday. Though not a profitable tour, the trip was a joyful homecoming for Johnson and his family and a chance for the other Skyways to enjoy a relaxing weekend in the "Southland." But now it's Monday morning and the bus hurtles north on its fourteen-hour journey back to Brooklyn where most will return to work on Tuesday morning.

"People are very sincere about religion down here," Richardson continues, "they know the way, they came up with it. See, this is the place were everything was really created from—the South. They (rural African-Americans) just moved North to expand. But religion was really based right here, in these woods! Before all these big beautiful church buildings were built, you just had dirt roads and wooden churches. See, this is where it all comes from."

Richardson's impassioned homage to the roots of his southern faith is particularly interesting, for unlike the other Skyways, he was not born in the South, but rather in Brooklyn. However, like many second generation migrant African-Americans, he spent childhood summers with his grandmother in South Carolina and continues to visit friends and family on a regular basis. Moreover, he is presently considering relocating in Fayettville, North Carolina. His attitudes are typical of many northern African-Americans, young and old, who maintain strong cultural ties to the South. And for many like him, gospel quartet singing serves as a vital symbolic expression of southern religion and identity.

Although southern migration into New York City has diminished significantly since the 1960s, the great majority of middle-aged and older members of the black church community were born and reared in the rural South. Most originally hail from the southeastern states of North Carolina, South Carolina, Virginia, and Georgia.[1] And most, despite years of residence in New York, continue to identify themselves as "southern people." Further, individuals and entire families frequently travel to the South several times a year for family homecomings, reunions, weddings, and funerals. This allows for family, social, and church networks to remain intact, in spite of the geographical dislocation. A significant number of older urban African-Americans, in fact, consider moving back to the South upon retirement, citing the region's reasonable cost of living, improved race relations (following the lifting of Jim Crow laws), and moderate climate, as well as their desire to be reunited with their extended family and to live in what they perceive as a safer, cleaner environment. The phenomenon of reverse migration is gradually becoming a reality,[2] as Clifford Williams of the Brooklyn Skyways suggests:

People left the South for better living, for better jobs. But the average person still wants to go back home. A lot are doing it, buying houses in the South and moving back. Some retire, some move back for a job, maybe in a different state or town. Houses are cheaper, and you have nice land all around. You can buy two or three houses in the South for what you could in New York. Living is better there, it's not as fast as New York. There's lots of fresh air, and clean, beautiful country. You don't have to worry about the hooligans mugging you. You're not all crowded up.[3]

But what of the younger, second and third generation, New York-born churchgoers? Many like Jeff Richardson appear to retain a strong, self-conscious affiliation with their parents' southern roots, having absorbed a great deal of southern culture first hand during summer vacations and holidays spent with extended family in the

South. They speak with great respect and fondness for the "South-land"—a place, they claim, where people are friendlier and more respectful to one another, families are stronger, crime is less prevalent, the air and water are cleaner, the food is tastier, and life flows at a slower, more sane pace. Most agree that the South is a better place to raise children, citing superior schools and a safer environment than New York City.

In the introduction to the *Encyclopedia of Southern Culture*, co-editors William Ferris and Charles Wilson suggest that the American South "exists as a state of mind both within and beyond its geographic boundaries." They contend that the South, as a cultural mind set, endures among groups of southern migrants, such as African-American Mississippians who settled in south Chicago, or white Appalachians who relocated in Detroit.[4] For southerners residing within or outside of the region, music, religion, and folk custom play an essential role in constructing and maintaining a mythic vision of the old rural South. For example, in folk and popular music dating back to the nineteenth -century minstrel stage, the old South is portrayed as an idyllic, rural paradise. Robert Cantwell aptly notes that early country and bluegrass songs are filled with nostalgic images of the old southern home place, the beautiful hills, the devoted family, and the old-time religion.[5] He argues that these symbols are especially compelling for southern whites who migrated to the urban centers of the North and Midwest:

the Kentuckian, who left home with his family while still a boy but who nevertheless still dreams of going back, weaving his way through the Detroit traffic on a bleary February morning toward his job on the assembly line, listening on the eight-track auto tapedeck he bought with his handsome salary he cannot give up, to Bill Monroe and the Blue Grass Boys, singing "I'm Going Back to Old Kentucky."[6]

While African-American blues songs rarely demonstrate such overt sentimentality, the impulse to recount and romanticize one's southern past plays a vital role in black gospel performance. But the significance of the old rural South is more complex for African-Americans than for their white counterparts. The South as symbol presents African-Americans—particularly those migrants living in urban areas outside the region—with a paradox. Amiri Baraka notes that, while the South represents "the incredible fabric of guilt and servitude identified graphically within the Negro consciousness," it also connotes home: "It was the place that Negroes knew, and given the natural attachment of man to the land, even loved. The North was to be beaten, there was room for attack. No such room had been possible in the South, but it was still what could be called home."[7] Gerald Davis ponders this dilemma and concludes:

At the most fundamental, sensate levels, the South is regarded as "roots," a vaguely perceived but powerful point of reference that secures personality clusters in this geographic region. In a cosmological sense this concept of "roots" also unites African-Americans with a network that has both historical and contemporary significance. Many African-Americans who migrated from the South as long ago as thirty years, as recently as thirty days, regard the region as "backward" and "country," although the South is in many ways more progressive than other areas in the nation. Paradoxically, these same persons, and many thousand others, return annually to the region for high school reunions, church homecomings, family reunions, funerals, and vacations. The South is a secure place of renewal, of contact with humanizing spirits, of communication with the souls of Black Folks.[8]

As Davis and Baraka point out, the nature of this North/South relationship is fraught with ambiguity. On one hand, the rural South signifies a time and place that many African-Americans had to abandon in order to achieve reasonable social and economic status. On the other, it continues to represent a cradle of family, church, social, and historical roots. In spite of its legacy of slavery, racial oppression, and rural poverty, the South still looms large in the psyches of many urban African-Americans as a mysterious spiritual homeland.

The strong influence of evangelical Protestantism, a hallmark of southern culture since the Great Awakenings of the late eighteenth and early nineteenth centuries, has earned black and white southerners the reputation of being particularly religious in temperament. The image of the South as the "Bible Belt," or the heartland of the "old-time religion," is deeply rooted in historical fact and social reality. A strict code of morals tends to be associated with southern religion, as historian Samuel Hill notes:

To be a converted Christian, a saved person, was known to entail appropriate demeanor in gratitude for forgiveness and as worthy of one's new status and identity. Obedience to Christ's teaching was held up as essential. In the context of Southern society, that meant honesty, familial integrity, sociability, and neighborliness on the affirmative side. It also necessitated "abstaining from the appearance of evil," interpreted as cursing, gambling, breaking the sabbath, dancing, and (especially later) drinking. Totalled, the moral impact was toward a disciplined life. One is attentive to what he or she does and does not do, indeed even scrupulous. The instincts of the flesh must be bridled and full run given to the leading of the Spirit. This made for a people who were morally serious about work and secular values as well as about godliness.[9]

Local New York quartet singers constantly express similar attitudes about southern religion and values. They envision the old rural South as a spiritual Mecca where respect for religion, family, hard work, and strict morality form the foundation of social life. These images are contrasted to the evils of contemporary northern urban life, as the following testimonies suggest:

Charlie Storey (All Stars): Down South, the most you usually do is to go to church and to go to work. But you take here in New York, there's always a ball game, a card game, a party going on. People forget about going to church, forget about the good strict life, once they hit New York. And sometimes people come here with religion, and when they leave they done lost it! Some people down south never saw lights burning all night. When they go in the house it's dark. But in New York, the ladies shoe heels hitting the streets all night, these lights burning all night, and some people think it's still daytime. In the Southland, if a person dies, the neighborhood around there, it was silent for a while, very sad for a while. But in New York, before you leave the chapel, people will be laughing and carrying on, just like nothing happened. Here they bury you today, and forget about you before they get you in the ground.

Ralph McLemore (All Stars): People in the South were more serious about Christianity than they are up here. In New York, it's dog eat dog. But in the South, the children were brought up to say "yes sir, no sir" to older people. And if my child sasses you out, and you report it to me, I'm going to whoop him. And in school, the teachers use to whoop the kids. So a few years back, a southern kid had good manners towards any older person. But these kids here in New York, three years old—I wouldn't use the words they say, but they'll tell you plain. See, everything wasn't bad in the South. You look back on those times, we were brought up right, we were taught right. Not that we thought so at the time, but it was a better way of life, an easier way of life, than it is now, here in New York.

David Stewart (Wearyland Singers): I think black people in the southern states, they have more respect for themselves than people up here [in New York] do. People here don't have no consciousness, no respect. The kids have no discipline—they were more disciplined in the South. I can tell you about myself, my mother kept me in church, that's number one. And number two was, I was not out late at night, she knew were I was. And number three, I didn't ever disrespect an elder person, if I did I got a spanking. . . . Sometimes I wonder, if I had been raised in New York, I wouldn't be the same person I am now. Because the environment, all the drugs—you've got to be strong to be raised here, in the ghettos. Kids, fourteen and fifteen years old, killing, robbing and stealing, killing their own parents. That is sad. And there is a difference, you don't hear about these things going on in the southern states.

The urban/North versus rural/South oppositions are particularly vivid in these commentaries. The former is viewed in terms of sin and chaos—crime, drugs, prostitution, broken families, and the general decay of religion and morality. By contrast, the traditional southern way of life is still venerated for its emphasis on religiosity, hard work, self discipline, respect for family and elders, and the practice of strict Christian morality.

Considering the dominant migration patterns it comes as no surprise that most middle-aged and older quartet singers active in New York today were born and reared in the South. Quantitative demographic figures reflecting the exact make-up of quartet audiences are simply not readily available. However, casual observation and informal conversations suggest that the vast majority of black New Yorkers who attend gospel programs were either born in the South or maintain strong family ties to the region. Several examples underscore the validity of this assumption. The emcee presiding at a large Brooklyn church program in the fall of 1988 stalled for time by asking audience members where they were from. By a show of hands, approximately three quarters of the 500 present identified their home states as North Carolina, South Carolina, Georgia, or Virginia. A handful were from Alabama, Mississippi, and Florida. The remainder—less than a quarter of the total, and almost exclusively young—claimed Brooklyn as home. Smaller programs, such as the 1986 anniversary of Reverend Young and the Morning Glories, often take on the ambience of a homecoming or family reunion. All seven groups at the anniversary were either related to Reverend Young or originally from his home community near Columbia, South Carolina. Participants establish and renew social networks with southern friends and family. And it is no coincidence that barbecued chicken, corn bread, collard greens, and other southern style foods are popular dishes at such gatherings.

The conflict between the old, southern religious values and contemporary, northern urban secular life permeates many facets of gospel programs in New York. It is not insignificant that the terms "southern style" and "traditional" still appear on posters advertising gospel quartet programs in Brooklyn, Jamaica, Harlem, and the South Bronx. Such adjectives are used to describe groups who perform in the demonstrative, postwar hard gospel style as opposed to the smoother, contemporary sound that currently dominates the commercial gospel airways and recording industry. Indeed singers and church-goers perceive the hard gospel style as being southern in origin and nature. In their minds black religion and music are rooted in the South, so naturally the best gospel soloists, quartet singers, and church singers came, and continue to come from the region. Most church people would agree enthusiastically with Jeff Richardson's contention that in terms of worship and song, the rural South is "the place where everything (religion and music) was really created."

In pre-program advertising, nearly all groups mention their home borough or community. Thus a flyer for an upcoming program might list groups as follows: "The Spiritual Voices of Brooklyn," "The Wearyland Gospel Singers of Corona," "The Golden Jubilees of Jamaica," "The Haynes Singers of the Bronx," and so forth. However, some New York-based groups continue to use their old southern affiliation on advertising and promotional material. A good example is the Brooklyn-based Gospel Crowns. Because several members are natives of Alabama, the group often bills itself as the "Gospel Crowns of Birmingham, Alabama." A Manhattan group consisting of mostly South Carolinians sometimes advertises itself as "The Gospel Heavyweights of Sumpter, South Carolina," even though the members have lived in New York City for years. Some groups frown on this practice, claiming their competitors are willfully deceiving gospel audiences by pretending to be from out of town. Those who maintain a southern affiliation, however, explain they are proud of their heritage and simply hope to attract additional fans from their southern hometown or state with such advertising.

Recordings or broadcasts of "southern-style," hard gospel quartet singing can implicitly trigger associations with the South among African-American churchgoers. But the music demonstrates its maximum potential as a signifying agent at live performances involving singers and audiences of common southern heritage. Images of southern family, religion, and traditional life are constantly evoked during many gospel programs. Singers will often open their sets by announcing their home state or town, and asking if anyone else in the congregation is from the area. While the lyrics to songs like "Old-Time Religion" and "Meeting Tonight" (see Chapter 2) mention older ways of southern worship, narratives and song commentaries provide the most vivid references. Narratives may remind listeners of their southern roots, evoke sentimental memories of family and childhood experiences, reflect on hardships and burdens, and expound on the need to "get back" to the old southern religion and values that are constantly threatened by the demonic forces of urban secular life. One young singer with the Bronx-based Travelling Sons admonishes his audience not to stray from the old southern-style singing and praying:

You see we've gotten away,   [Re]
    from the old-time religion.

We don't sing like we used to sing,
>we don't pray like we used to pray,
>>back down in North Carolina.
Oh yeah—
Sing with me,
>words that go like this:
>[begins song, "I'll Fly Away"]¹⁰

Singers love to expound upon the hardships they personally faced growing up in the rural South, particularly the lack of basic necessities such as food, clothing, electricity, and adequate shelter. Testimonies lament the difficult times, but always credit God for delivering His people from such conditions. Lee Cloud of the Northernaires introduces a song by reminding his audience that he's just a "country boy" from down south:

I come up the rough side of the mountain,   [Re]
>but look at me tonight church!
Ain't He good y'all?
I used to talk about what a hard time we was having—
Sometimes we would come home from the cotton fields,
>and not know where our next meal was coming from.
But let me tell you if you stay with God,   [Ch]
>He always has a ram in the bush for you.¹¹

Deacon Jones of the Pilgrim Sounds tells a Brooklyn audience:

Y'all should take time out a little while,   [Re]
>and look where the Lord brought you from.
I don't know about you,
>but down in North Carolina,
I had it ha-a-a-rd,
>oh yes I did.
I don't mind letting you know tonight church,
>that I ain't always had this nice suit of clothes to wear,
I want you to know tonight church,
>that I ain't always served God like this.
Things I used to do,
>I'm glad I don't do no more,
Since Jesus,
>came in my life.¹²

Other narratives romanticize the old-time southern ways of worship. Illustrative is Darrell McFadden's opening to the Golden Sons'
rendition of the song "I'm So Glad About It":

I don't know about you tonight,   [Re]
    but God has been good to me.
Has God been good to you tonight?   (yes He has)
    Let me see the hands of those who know that the Lord has been
    good to you.   (yes He has)
There's a song,
    that we used to sing down in South Carolina.
We used to have what you call the old-time revival meetings,
We used to have what they call the amen corner.
People from miles and miles around,
    would come together and worship the Lord's name.
And I remember,
    back in the hills of South Carolina,
There was an old grey-headed man,
    he got up and testified.   (yeah)
And he said:
I thank God,   [Ch]
    for letting me see a day I never seen before,   (well, well, well)
And ah I thank God,   (I thank God)
    for giving me food to eat,   (yeah)   [Re]
        and bread to drink,"   (yeah)
And the old man he got happy,
    and he started to sing a song, said:

It's another day's journey,   [So]
    and I'm glad,   (I'm glad about it)
I'm glad,   (I'm glad about it)
Said I'm glad.   (I'm glad about it)
It's another day's journey,
    church and I'm so glad,   (I'm glad about it)
I'm so glad to be here.[13]

Worth noting is the fact that McFadden, in his early twenties, was
born in Brooklyn, not in South Carolina. But like Jeff Richardson
and many other young singers, he spent his childhood summers with
extended family in the South and was thoroughly immersed in southern rural church practices from an early age. Moreover, those singers
and listeners who are too young or geographically removed from the
South to have personally experienced the "cotton fields" or "old-time

revival meetings" have heard them recounted often in family and church oral history. Images of the old South become deeply ingrained in their own cultural psyches, prompting them, like their elders, to respond to such narrations.

Two distinct though not unrelated pictures of the rural South emerge in these sorts of narratives and song commentaries. One is the South as sacred homeland—a mythic world of gray-haired mothers, hard-working fathers, praying deacons, cotton fields, and old-time revival meetings. Often a specific southern location ("the hills of North Carolina") is cited as the place of the singer's original conversion ("where I first got religion"). Recollections of the sacred homeland are always cloaked in nostalgic, romantic imagery. The other is the South as hardship suffered/transcended. Here the southern experience is depicted in terms of servitude, harsh conditions, and rural poverty. But it is a beast that can be fought and, with God's help, overcome. The social freedoms and material gains achieved by the singers (and their congregations) stand as proof of the church community's victory over hardship and oppression—"We made it out of the cotton fields, ain't God good y'all?" The South as sacred homeland and as hardship suffered/transcended are both evident in the following narrative that Marlene Miller of the Biblettes uses to introduce the song, "Old Time Religion":

I'm reminded of,   [Re]
    Georgia where I came from.
You see, I'm not ashamed,
    to let you know where I came from.
Back then,
    we used to work all day long in the fields,
And Lord back then,
    we used to go to revival meetings ,
        till the dawn . . ? . .
We used to go home,
    wash our clothes,
        had an old tin tub.
We got in an old tub,
    take a bath,
We didn't have no curly kits,   [hair conditioning products]
    like we do today.
So don't be ashamed,
    of where you come from.
I want you to know,
    God is good to me.

We used to go in the kitchen,
     open up the lard can,
          run some lard around our hair.
See we didn't have no curly kits back then,
     like we do today.
I know we're going to have church tonight,
     I know we're going to have church.
The reason I'm telling you this,
     I want you to go back in revival,
I want you to get something out of this, tonight,
     because God is good to you.
See we didn't have plenty of oil and coal,
     like we have today,
We used to gather in the kitchen,
     we had a wood stove,
And back then we had mules and wagons,
     see I'm not too cute to let you know
     what a mule and wagon is.
We'd go to church in that wagon,
     we used to go down an old, dusty road.
And before we got there,
     the young people would jump up off the wagon,
          so their boy friends and girl friends wouldn't see.   [that
          they rode in a wagon]
I know you know what I'm talking about.
I don't care what you got tonight,
     your fancy house,
          your fine car,
You know when you get to church,
     . . ? . .
And when you come in the door,
     you can't hardly say "amen" for Jesus.
If you know what I'm talking about,
     let me see you wave your hands![14]

Miller's narration does more than simply venerate the old-time religion, regular church attendance, hard work, and virtues of rural southern life. Listeners are further instructed not to be ashamed of their southern roots. In fact, the traditional ways of life—working in the fields, washing clothes in an old tin tub, heating with wood, straightening hair with lard, and traveling by mule and wagon—are recalled with a certain degree of pride and respect. Life was difficult in those days, but with God's help the faithful not only persevered but triumphed over adversity. The narrative further serves to remind the congregation that, while they should be happy that God has brought them to a point where they have the conveniences of cars, central heating, curly kits, and comfortable homes, they should never forget the hardships the Lord brought them through. And further, they must never allow themselves to become so sophisticated—so "cute" as Miller says—that they won't say "amen" in church. In short, singers warn their urban congregations not to stray too far from the old-time singing, praying, and religion of their rural ancestors. And if Miller's story and song are delivered with sincere passion, her words may literally take her audience "back in revival" with the invocation of the Spirit and a communal shout.

Narratives are often intended to create reflective moods and subtly ease listeners into nostalgic frames of mind. Ensuing songs, while not necessarily making explicit reference to the South, can touch upon these sentiments. In other words, the correct combination of narrative and song can activate clusters of extra-musical associations, transporting southern listeners back in space and time. Individual listeners might be reminded of their family, church and community back home; of their parents, grandparents, and other loved ones passed on; of the stifling economic and racial barriers they fought (and continue to fight) to overcome; or of their original conversion experience. Spoken and sung texts are layered with these sorts of connotative meanings that are readily apprehended by an audience of southern African-Americans. When Miller quips to her congregation, "I know you know what I'm talking about," and is greeted by an enthusiastic "amen," she confirms that all present have personally experienced the struggle, the hardship, and the triumph of which she speaks. A shared history and identity as southern, black Christians is clearly implied.

The process that generates these cultural and historical associations is clearly demonstrated in the following performance by Earl Ledbetter and the Wearyland Singers:

[chanted introduction]
We're going to leave you,   [Re]
 we're going to leave you now.
I got one song,
 that's been bothering me.
I'm back,
 from the hills of North Carolina.
Had a chance to go there and sing,
 for my mother and father one day.

But there was this,
    old deacon there.
He got up from his seat, ha,
    and he began to walk,
    to the mourning bench.   (yeah)
He said,
    I've been here,
        for seventy-seven long years.
Trying to hold on,
    to God's unchanging hand.
He said, I look at the audience,
    I didn't see nobody say amen.   (yeah)
But he said God's been good to me,
    He been good to me.   (yeah)
Been better to me than I been to my own self.
There's an old song,
    he began to sing,
        when he walked back to his seat.
Some glad morning,   [Ch]
    when this life is all over,
I want two wings to fly away,
    to be at rest.
Give me,   (yeah)
Give me,   (yeah)
Two wings, ha,
To fly away,
To fly away,   (come on son)
    to be at rest.
And it sounds something like this—   [Re]
[instruments start steady beat and chords, singing begins]
Oh some, some glad morning y'all,   [So]
    I'm singing when, when this life is over
I,
    will fly away.
Said I'm going, going to a place,
        joy shall never end,
Oh, I,
    will fly,
        away, fly away.

Just, oh just my Lord,
    just a few more, few more—
        weary days and then,

Lord I, yes I will y'all,
　　will fly away,
Said I'm going—going to a place,
　　Lord I'm going to a place,
　　Lord I'm going to a place,
　　Lord I'm going to a place,
　　Lord I'm going to a place,
　　　　joy shall never end,
Oh, I,
　　will fly,
　　　　away, fly away.[15]

Later, reflecting on his performance of "I'll Fly Away," Ledbetter concluded:

A lot of people out there are southern, and these sorts of things bring back memories. That's why David or I talk about the old man [the deacon]. If he had a song, that's what he would sing. "Some glad morning, when this life is over, I'll fly away." It really makes people think about their lives, and how they came up through the years. Memories of the hard times they had, and their parents and grandparents had. And that song, it goes way back to years ago, and everybody knows it. Everybody knows how they used to sing it, and know we're singing it like this. It's a touching type of thing—it touches them. And by me saying, "I'm back from the hills of North Carolina," somebody in the audience is from North Carolina, and they'll know what I'm singing about. They know how I feel, because we were brought up in slavery, you know. We didn't have what a lot of people have. And that kind of touches the heart, when you find somebody up there singing gospel from North Carolina. Somebody out there says, "Oh, I know what he's singing about."[16]

In his introduction, Ledbetter sets a sentimental tone by reminding his audience that he and his family are from the rural hill country of North Carolina. Ledbetter knows this will gain the attention of North Carolinians and possibly other southerners in his audience. He hopes to set their minds drifting "back home," as his words elicit memories of their parents, church, and community. Next Ledbetter introduces the venerable old deacon, a man whose seventy-seven years of devotion personify the steadfast Christian faith. After a brief testimony the deacon begins to sing an "old song" that foreshadows his death and ascent to Heaven. Ledbetter finally collapses the space and time separating the congregation from the imaginary scene by actually singing the deacon's song, "I'll Fly Away." If he has delivered his words convincingly, they will arouse memories of family and church life in the South. The congregation will be "touched" by the song as present and past are fused in one affecting moment. Interestingly enough, there are no direct references to the South, nor the family, nor any "old-time" ways of life in the lyrics of "I'll Fly Away." They are not necessary. Ledbetter's introduction has already placed the song in the necessary historical context to evoke specific extra-musical associations and a strong emotional response from his southern audience. As he points out, "that song, it goes way back to years ago, and everybody knows it." Thus, a song such as "I'll Fly Away"—already heavily loaded with connotative references and perceived by church audiences as being old and southern—explodes with deep-seated meaning when prefaced by a sentimental narrative concerning the old South, the old deacon, and the old-time religion.

The Wearylands' performance of "I'll Fly Away" offers further evidence that the meaning of a gospel song cannot be fully comprehended through simple verse/chorus lyrical analysis. Isolating the song text—the sung words beginning with "Oh some, some glad morning"—leads to the erroneous conclusion that the song's primary message is future and otherworldly. Listeners are assured that their earthly struggles, those "weary days," will soon pass, for eventually they will "fly away" to their joyful rewards in heaven. But when the chanted song commentary and the larger social context are taken into account, a radically different interpretation emerges. In the setting of a live gospel program with an audience of southern African-Americans, the spoken and sung words communicate referential, extra-musical associations that transcend the denotative lyrical theme of future heavenly reward. Images of the North Carolina hills and the old deacon trigger an emotional response that pulls past into present. The exuberant heavenly joy predicted by the song text may indeed erupt at that moment if the Holy Spirit should choose to descend. In terms of overall meaning, the entire performance is about much more than simply flying away to Heaven. It speaks to the struggles of a shared southern past, the joys of present communal fellowship, and the promise of a glorious future. Listeners, young and old, are reminded of who they are, where they (and their families) originally came from, and how they can achieve victory in this world.

Worth noting is the fact that most of the scenes of southern life and worship portrayed in narratives and song commentaries are set in the past. Many narratives are intensely nostalgic; they express a yearning to transcend time as well as space, to travel back to the old-time ways of past generations. Whether the focus is on the South as sacred homeland or as hardship suffered/transcended, the singer is always looking back in time. She or he longs to recapture the emotional intensity of the old-time religion, the security of the extended family and small town community, and to proclaim victory over past

tribulations. Today's achievements are always contrasted to yester-
day's struggles—"I don't mind letting you know tonight church, that
I ain't always had this nice suit of clothes to wear." By referencing the
old South the musicians seek to evoke a shared history that strengthens the sense of present community. That is, nostalgic narratives
work as one more strategy that singers use to connect with their audience, to reinforce common bonds, and to move the performance
toward communitas. This may explain why narratives about the old-
time South are also used, on occasion, by professional touring quartets and local groups based in the South. For example, the lead singer
of the Pilgrim Jubilee Singers (a well known professional quartet
from Chicago) testifies that he grew up in a three-room shack in Mississippi and that his family "didn't have much back than, but we had
a family altar." Anthony Heilbut suggests the narration serves "to induce camaraderie that quickly draws together a church full of strang-
ers."[17] On a commercial recording, Louis Jordan of the Swan
Silvertones narrates: "Back in the hills of South Carolina where I
come from, they used to have what they called a revival there."[18] The
performance, Morton Marks surmises, aims to "literally revive an old
revival meeting," to "reproduce the South Carolina church when everybody 'got up shouting.' "[19] Glenn Hinson reports that local quartets in North Carolina make reference to childhood hardships and
the old ways of worship in order to establish a sense of "co-identity"
between themselves and their listeners.[20] Daniel Patterson notes that
members of the Golden Echoes, a community-based North Carolina
group, speak often of the brutal poverty their parents struggled to
overcome. But each time group members mount the stage in their
well tailored, matching outfits, they "stand as resplendent embodi-
ments of the material blessings for which the entire community
longs."[21] For city- and town-based southern singers, "back home" may
signify the rural setting and bygone era of one's pre-urban past.[22]

Sentimental narratives set in the old South connote a shared past
and serve to unify gospel singers with fellow listeners who experience
the South as a "state of mind," whether the actual performance takes
place inside or outside the geographic confines of the South. However, for local New York singers, whose daily experience is shaped by
a geographic as well as a temporal separation from their southern
home and heritage, imagery of the old South functions as a particularly powerful symbol of community and roots. The nostalgic por-
trayal of the old rural South by modern gospel quartets, along with
the general popularity of southern-derived gospel quartet singing,
appears to be part of a larger movement to revive and sustain traditional southern beliefs and values in the contemporary urban

North.[23] Such "revitalization movements," anthropologists explain, are "associated with frustrating situations and are primarily attempts to compensate for the frustrations of the society's members. The elements revived become symbols of a period when the society was free, or in retrospect, happy and great. . . . By keeping the past in mind, such elements help to reestablish and maintain the self-respect of the group's members in the face of adverse conditions."[24] The rapid growth of southern-style black religion in the urban North and the subsequent rise of gospel song and gospel quartet singing described in Chapter 1 (and to be further discussed in the following chapter) were certainly responses to adverse social conditions experienced by dislocated rural migrants. Further, these religious and artistic expressions reinforced self-respect and independence for several generations of black city dwellers. However, the images of southern life being revived are hardly symbols of a time (or place) when African-American society was free or great. On the contrary, when gospel singers speak of hardships suffered/transcended, they refer to centuries of slavery, postbellum segregation, Jim Crow laws, and stifling rural poverty. They are certainly not advocating a return to such conditions. Rather, they are seeking to revive and perpetuate a southern, religious world view and core set of values, which, in their view, assisted past generations of African-Americans in their ongoing fight against seemingly insurmountable racial, social, and economic barriers.

This strategy has stong precedent, for historically the southern church has assumed a central role in the struggle for the survival and liberation of African-Americans in the United States. More than any other institution, the church has provided African-Americans with a haven to forge their own sense of cultural identity.[25] The old-time religion, preaching, and singing bolstered black southerners in their resolve to overcome slavery and the institutionalized racism that followed and in their more recent efforts to hurdle the barriers of poverty, inadequate education, and social disparity. In the minds of the southern-born gospel singers, the same religion and values that delivered their forefathers and mothers in the rural South will assist them and their offspring in overcoming the hardships of contemporary urban life. While Satan may manifest himself in new ways in the city— through drugs, rampant crime, prostitution, gambling, and crowded slum housing—the solution to these problems remains the same. Go to church, work hard, respect your family, live a "clean" moral life, and God will see you through. "He always has a ram in the bush for you." The fear, of course, is that younger generations will stray from the church and eventually scorn their southern roots and religious upbringing, opting instead for a secular lifestyle. From the church-goers' perspective, such loss of faith inevitably leads to the decay of moral values and a life fraught with unstable family and love relations, unemployment, crime, drug and alcohol abuse, and so forth.

Images of the old-time rural South serve as metaphors for social, moral, and spiritual salvation within the African-American church community. In New York, and undoubtedly in other urban areas, gospel quartet singers use these symbolic expressions to remind church-goers of the joys and sorrows of their southern heritage and to preserve the old religious values and practices that brought them and their forebears through arduous times. The faithful are left with the fortitude to struggle on against the racial prejudice and economic hardship that urban relocation has failed to eradicate. But the revitalization of southern worship and social values represents only one dimension of the complex role sacred quartet singing has played in the history of African-American urbanization, as a closer examination of the relationship between changing performance styles and urban acculturation will reveal.

Notes

1. This pattern of heaviest migration from Virginia, South Carolina, North Carolina, and Georgia was well established by 1930. See Osofsky, *Harlem*, p. 129.

2. The pattern of north to south "reverse" migration among African-Americans has only recently come to the attention of demographers. The turn-about in the migration pattern evidently began sometime in the mid-1970s, and according to Census Bureau figures nearly 100,000 more blacks have moved into the South than out since 1980. See Kenneth Weiss, "Migration by Blacks from the South Turns Around," *New York Times*, June 11, 1989, p. 36. A forthcoming work by anthropologist Carol Stack promises to shed further insight on the subject.

3. Personal interview with Clifford Williams, August 29, 1987.

4. Charles Wilson and William Ferris, eds., *The Encyclopedia of Southern Culture* (Chapel Hill: University of North Carolina Press, 1989), p. xv. For more on the South as a "region of the mind" see the essays in the "Mythic South" section.

5. Robert Cantwell, *Bluegrass Breakdown* (Urbana: University of Illinois Press, 1984), pp. 226–248.

6. Ibid., p. 245.

7. Baraka, *Blues People*, p. 105.

8. Davis, *I Got the Word in Me*, p. 9.

9. Samuel Hill, ed., *Religion in the Southern United States* (Macon, GA: Mercer University Press, 1983), p. 396. See also Hill, *Southern Churches in Crisis*, pp. 20–39, for more on the unique nature of southern Protestantism.

10. Recorded at the Bethel Baptist Church, Brooklyn, NY, September 28, 1985.

11. Recorded in Hartford, CT, March 17, 1990.

12. Recorded at St. Anthony Baptist Church, Brooklyn, NY, September 24, 1988.

13. Recorded at the Triplex Theatre, NYC, November 11, 1988.

14. Recorded at LaGree Baptist Church, Harlem, NY, September 21, 1985.

15. Recorded at Restoration Plaza, Brooklyn, NY, June 27, 1986.

16. Personal interview with Earl Ledbetter, September 6, 1986.

17. Heilbut, *Gospel Sound*, p. xx.

18. Morton Marks, "You Can't Sing Unless You're Saved," p. 326.

19. Ibid., pp. 328–329.

20. Hinson, "When the Words Roll and the Fire Flows," pp. 331–334.

21. Patterson, "Going Up to Meet Him," p. 99.

22. Brenda McCallum alludes to this point in her work with early Birmingham quartets: "Birmingham's quartet singers kept alive a continuity with the religious traditions of the rural South; their music was a resource of their faith, and helped fulfill their needs for spiritual solace in a time of social stress." See McCallum, "Songs of Work and Songs of Worship," p. 18.

23. Melvin Williams argues that, through southern-derived church worship, the African-American Pentecostals he studied in Pittsburgh were able to "reestablish their lost values and recast their most precious symbols into a system of communication and solidarity." See Williams, *Community in a Black Pentecostal Church*, p. 142. See also Paris, *Black Pentecostalism*, pp. 25–27.

24. Ralph Linton, "Nativistic Movements," *American Anthropologist* 45 (1943): 233. Also see Anthony Wallace, "Revitalization Movements," *American Anthropologist* 58 (1956): 264–281.

25. For more on the role of the black church in the struggle for liberation and social equality see Raboteau, *Slave Religion* pp. 289–318; James Cone, *A Black Theology of Liberation* (New York: Lippincott, 1970); and Gayraud Wilmore, *Black Religion and Black Radicalism* (Maryknoll, NY: Orbis, 1984), pp. 220–241. The use of sacred black music as an agent of social/political change is discussed in James Cone, *The Spirituals and the Blues* (New York: Seabury, 1972), and in Wyatt Tee Walker, *Somebody's Calling My Name: Black Sacred Music and Social Change* (Valley Forge, PA: Judson, 1979).

Chapter 8
"I've Got a Home In That Yonder City"
Urbanization and Sacred Quartet Performance Style

African-American gospel song and quartet singing sprang from the folk music and worship traditions of the rural South. Yet it was amid the turmoil of twentieth century urbanization that the sounds of old-time country church singing and backwoods preaching melded with down-home blues and early jazz to form a distinctly black style of gospel performance. The emergence of gospel music in the 1930s and gospel quartets in the 1940s was in part a response to the rapidly changing social conditions brought about by migration and urbanization. In recent years, there has been a great deal of scholarly interest in the role vernacular music and dance play in the complex process of urban adaptation.[1] The thorny question of acculturation, or cultural modification resulting from close contact between two groups, remains an issue of great concern and continued debate. Urban centers, with their heterogeneous populations and sophisticated systems of mass communication, are ideal sites for observing the cross-cultural exchange of creative ideas and behavioral patterns. Cities are centers for the evolution of syncretic artistic expressions and the development of multi-cultural performance repertoires. But expressive forms such as music do not simply move across cultural boundaries in some independent, superorganic way. The process involves human interaction through intricate social networks, human communication through ever-expanding mass media, and the complex interplay of shifting economic and political forces.

David Coplan's work with African music cultures provides a useful model for the study of music and urban adaptation. Coplan argues that African cities offer increased social opportunities for choice and flexibility that are generally unavailable to rural dwellers. Musicians exploit these possibilities. Through their choice of styles, performance settings, and audiences, city musicians make symbolic statements about "who they are, who they are not, and who they wish to be."[2] Moreover, Coplan contends that popular music and dance events provide African urban migrants with occasions for social interaction and intense communication and thereby supply "a measure of solidarity in an environment characterized by social insecurity, dislocation, and differentiation."[3] The broader relationship of popular music to Third World urbanization is summed up concisely by Peter Manuel:

For many, the changes wrought by urbanization and modernization are accompanied by considerable alienation, exploitation, and impoverishment. As such, the creation of a new social identity assumes a crucial rather than incidental role in survival and adaptation to the new environment. To those immersed in the struggle, popular music may serve as a powerful and meaningful symbol of identity, functioning as an avenue of expression and mediation of conflict.[4]

Musical style and performance have played an equally crucial role in the evolution of modern, African-American urban identity. In his pioneering study of urban blues, Charles Keil observes that "various blues and jazz styles are, at least in their initial phases, symbolic referents of in-group solidarity for the black masses and the more intellectual segments of the black bourgeoisie."[5] Keil identifies two powerful figures within the African-American urban community:

Bluesmen and preachers both provide models and orientations; both give public expression to deeply felt private emotions; both promote catharsis— the bluesman through dance, the preacher through trance; both increase feelings of solidarity, boost morale, strengthen the consensus.[6]

Since today's blues singers no longer perform for exclusively African-American audiences, their role as purveyors of black solidarity is somewhat diminished. But African-American preachers, and their musical counterparts, gospel quartet singers, continue to embody the essence of what Keil refers to as "soul and solidarity,"[7] at least for those African-Americans who remain affiliated with the southern-derived church. Indeed, the stylistic evolution of sacred quartet singing in this century offers great insight into the ongoing process of African-American urban adaptation and identity maintenance. Moreover, that evolution reveals the dynamics of cultural exchange between New York's African-American church community and the broader secular society, as southern church people struggle to construct a meaningful social order in the most urban and profane of environments.

Traditional models of acculturation and assimilation prove grossly inadequate for describing the twentieth-century urbanization experience of southern African-Americans. The transition from rural to urban life was never a simple process involving the adoption of European-American cultural norms followed by eventual assimilation into mainstream life. Deep-seated personal and institutional racism have made such integration impossible for most. Rather, centuries of contact between African and European peoples in the United States led to an extraordinary sharing of ideas and social practices—a two-way exchange resulting in the eventual modification of both cultures. Post-emancipation migration of freed African-Americans into southern cities, the twentieth century Great Migrations into northern and midwestern cities, and the rise of the mass electronic media intensified contact and interchange. The emergence of innovative syncretic musical forms, ranging from minstrel songs and spirituals to blues, jazz, gospel, rhythm and blues, and rock, was the result. For African-Americans, this process involved the constant struggle to embrace and transform select elements of the dominant European-American culture while revitalizing and reinterpreting aspects of their own southern and African heritage. Lawrence Levine notes that the development of vernacular speech, music, ritual, and other symbolic expressions was characterized by:

not merely the emergence of the new but the revitalization of the old. It has been a dual process of creation and re-creation, of affirmation and re-affirmation, of looking both without and within the black community for the means of sustenance and identity and survival.[8]

The evolution of sacred quartet singing in twentieth-century New York City reinforces this paradigm. At various points in the urbanization process, quartet singers have borrowed freely not only from within the expressive repertoires of the African-American church but from outside it as well. New styles emerge as old forms are revitalized. And most importantly, shifting stylistic trends respond to rapidly changing urban social conditions.

The pre-war jubilee/harmonizing quartets described in Chapter 1 reflected the musical tastes and social consciousness of the early twentieth century black populace. Significantly, the jubilee/harmonizing style bore the strong imprint of European-American culture. Despite the constant presence of racial antagonism and systematic social and economic discrimination, the early decades of this century were an exciting and relatively optimistic time for New York's African-Americans. A small but vital middle class, consisting primarily of educators, clergy, businesspeople, and skilled artisans, had established itself prior to the first world war.[9] Black journalists and civil rights groups reflected an increasing awareness of racial pride and a resolve to curtail discrimination. The initial great wave of southern migrants who arrived during the First World War found work in the wartime industries and looked forward to participating in the American dream. For these southerners, New York and the rest of the North represented the new "Promised Land . . . a place where they could begin again, this time, perhaps, on a more human footing."[10] While the migration experience was rough and fraught with uncertainty, the opportunity for a better life was real, as historian Gilbert Osofsky states:

> The average Negro migrant in New York City obviously found life harsh and difficult. For those who came, however, conditions in the North did offer a measure of self-respect and the possibility for future advancement that was generally denied the Negro of the South. "To many of them oppressed within the limitations set up by the South," wrote Ray Stannard Baker [in 1910], "it is indeed the promised land."[11]

By the 1920s Harlem had emerged as the center of African-American cultural and intellectual life, the great black metropolis and home to the burgeoning "jazz age" and the "New Negro Renaissance."[12] Moreover, there was a great deal of musical contact between African- and European-Americans, as thousands of white New Yorkers made their way uptown to Harlem's clubs to hear the new syncopated dance music known as jazz.[13]

The jubilee/harmonizing quartet tradition carried to New York during the initial wave of the Great Migrations was itself a syncretic form derived from the blending of southern African-American church singing with European musical traditions. The early quartet style resulted from the natural transformation of the heterophoric, African-inflected slave singing as it came into contact with European concepts of harmonic structure and vocal articulation. Minstrel troupes, early shape-note teachers, and black college vocal instructors (and their students who later became public school teachers) helped introduce European notions of four-part harmony to large numbers of southern African-Americans. By the second decade of this century, vibrant quartet traditions sprang from densely populated black communities in southern cities like Birmingham, New Orleans, Atlanta, and Norfolk. In short, black quartet singers had been synthesizing European and African musical practices in southern cities well before the first significant waves of northern migration.[14]

In keeping with this pattern, the early New York sacred quartets showed strong influences of mainstream European-American singing as manifested by their use of sophisticated four-part harmony, strict timing and clear vocal diction. Up until the mid-1930s repertoires consisted mostly of slow meter spirituals and folk hymns, delivered in a relatively staid, unemotional manner. Faster songs moved to only lightly syncopated rhythms. The jubilee/harmonizing style was evidently welcomed, or at least tacitly approved of, by members of the older, established church community and those secular oriented African-Americans who aspired to integrate into mainstream European-American urban life. For working class southern migrants, the ability to render tight harmony hymns and spirituals in a "formal" style opened a channel of communication with the European-American and African-American middle classes. Their singing earned them a degree of respectability and prestige, and, in some cases, the potential for financial gain. Indeed, the jubilee/harmonizing style of the Utica Jubilee Singers and the Southernaires had a degree of bi-racial, middle class appeal, as educated black and white listeners enjoyed formal presentations and radio broadcasts of spiritual singing by such polished (and usually college-trained) groups. While the local, untrained groups did most of their singing for African-American church audiences, the best quartets, including the Selah Jubilee Singers and the Golden Crown, won radio spots that allowed them to reach large numbers of white and black middle class listeners.

The glimmers of optimism experienced by black New Yorkers in the 1920s quickly faded with the coming of the Great Depression. Unemployment skyrocketed while extreme overcrowding led to deplorable housing and sanitary conditions.[15] Although the rate of southern in-migration abated somewhat during the 1930s, substantial numbers of rural African-Americans, desperate for any sort of work, continued to arrive. In-migration again increased dramatically with the advent of World War II, placing additional stress on the already severe housing shortage.[16] Morale among urban African-Americans, suggests John Hope Franklin, probably reached an all-time low during the early war years when systematic discrimination blocked them from employment in the lucrative defense factories.[17] In 1943, Harlem residents vented their frustrations in a bloody riot touched off by the shooting of a black serviceman by a white policeman.[18] Still reeling from the economic hardships of the Depression, and disillusioned by the failure of America's triumph over fascism abroad to translate into civil rights reform at home, many black New Yorkers wondered if integration was realistically attainable or, for that matter desirable.[19] Jervis Anderson sums up the fallen spirit of Harlem in the post-war years:

If Black Harlem was once a heaven, or was seen to be one by the migrants and commentators of the nineteen-twenties, it had ceased to be that by the beginning of the nineteen-fifties. When the early optimism had been exhausted, there remained, among the majority of the population, almost all the racial and social hardships that many hoped would be nonexistent in the finest urban community that blacks had ever occupied in the United States.[20]

Anderson's gloomy assessment must be tempered by noting that the later war years and the early postwar period brought unprecedented prosperity for all New Yorkers, including those of African descent. Matters slowly began to improve following President Roosevelt's 1941 executive order banning discrimination in the defense industry.[21] Although black workers lagged behind their white counterparts, unemployment decreased while wages increased significantly throughout the 1940s and well into the 1950s, particularly in the service industries.[22]

For the waves of southern African-Americans who poured into New York during and immediately following World War Two, the contradictions of hope and despair that had characterized the earlier migrations were simply intensified. On the one hand, economic opportunity abounded; on the other, an enduring system of discrimination and segregation forced them into the overcrowded, deteriorating slums of Harlem and Bedford-Stuyvesant. The result was the rapid expansion of the black working class—a group that remained socially and geographically isolated from the greater white populace, but one that possessed the leisure time and capital necessary to support its own popular urban entertainment. For those southern African-Americans who maintained strong ties to the church, the proliferation of semi-professional and professional sacred quartets fulfilled this need. Indeed, it was amid the stress of increased southern in-migration, coupled with the growing economic independence of the black working class, that postwar religious quartet singing burgeoned and made the full stylistic transition from jubilee to gospel.

It should be kept in mind, however, that earlier social developments helped set the stage for this musical transformation. Most importantly, during the period between the two World Wars, growing numbers of southern migrants rendered significant changes in the standard worship patterns of black New Yorkers. As outlined in Chapter 1, the older established black churches that favored more

Europeanized ritual had neither the room nor, in some cases, the desire to absorb their uneducated southern brethren who arrived in alarming numbers. In reaction, many of the migrants established their own smaller churches where they perpetuated the more demonstrative, southern-style evangelical Christianity they grew up with. Unmoved by the staid, European-style hymn singing favored in the middle class churches, the new urbanites turned back to the familiar spirituals, folk hymns and sanctified music of their southern homeland, and eventually to Dorsey's new southern-derived gospel songs. Meanwhile the urban Holiness movement that swept the North during the 1920s and 1930s attracted many southern black Protestants from other denominations. Rebuffed by the larger middle-class Presbyterian, Episcopal, Methodist, and (some) Baptist churches, many recent country arrivals felt more comfortable in the intimacy of the smaller storefront Holiness and Pentecostal establishments and readily changed allegiance. The various Holiness sects, with their emphasis on ecstatic preaching, possession by the Holy Ghost, and driving sanctified music, set an increasingly demonstrative tone for black urban worship.

An analogous situation developed with quartet singing. Evidently the prewar jubilee/harmonizing quartets lacked the more emotive vocal delivery, the heavier rhythmic emphasis, and the intensely spiritual tone that characterized the worship of most southern folk churches and their expanding urban counterparts. Gradually the growing numbers of southern-born churchgoers in New York became dissatisfied with this approach to quartet performance. Audiences were no longer willing simply to sit and listen to good harmony; they wanted emotional involvement, spiritual sincerity, and above all, to "have church" the way they did on Sunday mornings.

The New York quartets were slow to respond to these changing audience tastes and until the mid-1930s continued to concentrate on close harmony, slow meter singing. By the late 1930s, however, a transformation was under way. Following the lead of the Golden Gate Quartet, the local groups began incorporating more syncopated, sanctified-derived rhythms into their arrangements. Lead singers like Thurman Ruth started to walk (but not run) into the audience for dramatic effect, while his Selah Jubilee Singers experimented with gospel-like repetitive choruses and incorporated gospel songs like Dorsey's "Take My Hand Precious Lord" into their repertoire. It was not until well into the 1940s, however, that the hard gospel quartet sound took hold in New York. At this time quartet singers gradually shifted away from the staid jubilee/harmonizing style to the more emphatic hard gospel singing. In contrast to the earlier emphasis on close harmony and total group blend, the new gospel quartets pushed their lead singers to the forefront where they improvised demonstrative testimony and song. Instrumental accompaniment and body percussion contributed a dense rhythmic underpinning to the sound. Presentations became more evangelical in tone, as bringing down the Holy Spirit took precedence over the execution of impeccable harmony. Postwar gospel quartet singing became an exclusively black expression—one that spoke to the beliefs, aspirations, and aesthetic preferences of the working class, southern church community that now formed the majority of New York's African-American population.

New York's early gospel quartet singers drew their inspiration from several sources. Contact with professional gospel singers and quartets was undoubtedly a significant factor. As quartet singing programs became larger and more commercial in the 1940s, professional touring groups like the Kings of Harmony, the Soul Stirrers, and the Dixie Hummingbirds brought their highly stylized, explosive sound to the churches and halls of New York's black neighborhoods. The community-based groups turned out to hear these pioneering hard gospel men preach, testify, shout, dive off stages, and run up and down the aisles. Local singers bought the latter's recordings and incorporated aspects of their music and movement into their own performance repertoires. It was the early touring quartets like the Kings of Harmony, claims Ruth, that introduced the hard gospel style to New York City, which until the mid-1940s had been exclusively, in his words, a "jubilee town."

During the early 1940s, Thomas Dorsey's new gospel music was being ushered into New York churches by two outstanding professional female soloists, Sister Ernestine Washington and Clara "Georgia Peach" Hudmon. Veterans of the southern sanctified church tradition, both eventually settled in New York and became leading proponents of the emotional, Chicago-style gospel that had been pioneered by Sallie Martin, Mahalia Jackson, and Roberta Martin. Unlike their Chicago counterparts, however, Washington and Hudmon occasionally employed male vocal quartets as accompanists for recordings and live performances. William Kelly, who sang with one such quartet, the Harmonaires, recalls that Hudmon often stepped out from the group to walk among the audience, where she sang, shouted, and exhorted all present to feel the Spirit. The demonstrative vocal and theatrical techniques employed by female gospel singers like Washington and Hudmon undoubtedly served as models for male quartets, whose lead singers eventually emulated such performance practices.

While the influence of early touring gospel quartets and professional female soloists was strong in New York, both borrowed freely from the music and worship practices of southern black folk churches. The emotional exuberance that these gospel stars purveyed inevitably owed much to the Holiness movement, as Ralph Moragne of the Sunset Jubilees reflects:

The Holiness people, they actually made what you call gospel singing. We used to go, after we went to our Baptist Church on Sunday night [in Florida], and look through the window—and they were actually singing gospel then! They had piano and tambourine, and they'd make music from that. See, we [quartet singers] rearranged it, but that type of hard gospel singing came out of the Holiness church.[23]

Similarly, gospel quartet singers in New York found readily available models for demonstrative performance in the jubilant music, the emphatic testifying, and the Spirit-induced preaching and holy dancing they heard in the small, evangelical churches of Brooklyn and Harlem. Charlie Storey's experience is no doubt typical of young quartet singers with roots in the Holiness church. Storey was well versed in the ways of sanctified singing and preaching by the time he left his family group and joined the Jubilee Stars in 1942. He recalls that when he came to the group, whose members were older Baptists, they sang flat-footed, without much emotion:

They didn't move much, they had that slow movement. They used to do mostly slow songs, and dragging songs. They weren't excited like I was. But when I went into the group, they changed their temperament of singing and moving. When I got in the group I started moving, walking up and down the aisles, singing to the people, talking to them, just like a preacher—that's what the people liked about me. They were Baptist singers, and they believed in singing nice and easy, not straining their voices too much. But if it's in you, and you have the gift of God in you, and the Spirit, you're going to holler sometimes. You're going to move around, clap your hands, stomp your feet, walk the floor. And when you start it, somebody else will start it. That was it, and people enjoyed it.[24]

Performers like Storey simply drew on their repertoire of Sunday morning worship behaviors as they assumed lead singing roles in the newly emerging gospel quartets.

Just as the rise of the urban Holiness movement and the emergence of Dorsey's gospel song reflected a degree of cultural introversion on the part of the African-American church community, so did the gospelization of sacred quartets in New York and other cities. In response to the trauma of the migration experience and the chaos of the new urban environment—particularly the overcrowded, demoralizing conditions that prevailed during the Depression through the war years and well into the 1950s—black migrants found it necessary to maintain and to revive older southern African-American worship and musical practices. Denied entry into mainstream American life, they retreated to rejuvenate their own distinct African-American culture. Interest in European-American-derived music waned as they looked inward to the folk church for the resources to create powerful new expressions of their southern past.

Although quartets held to the legacy of the heavily European-influenced jubilee/harmonizing style throughout the 1930s, they too were swept into the movement and eventually adopted a more impassioned, spirited approach to their singing. The healthy post-war economy and the demand for more professional, "spiritual entertainment" by working churchgoers provided the necessary socioeconomic foundation for the transition. As increasing numbers of quartets were paid for their services—including the better local performers who sang on weekends but who did not tour full time—singers came under pressure to produce more polished, professional performances that were artistically and spiritually pleasing to their paying clientele. Rather than falling back on older models of professional quartet performance—the jubilee and minstrel quartets whose smooth harmonies pleased white secular as well as black church audiences—the emerging gospel quartets turned to a more southern, church-derived style. This was predictable, considering the quartets were now singing to audiences consisting almost exclusively of rural African-American migrants who had the financial means to support them. Elements of professional showmanship and folk religion were skillfully intertwined by early gospel quartets in the creation of a slick, urban form of popular entertainment that was firmly rooted in rural southern folk music and worship practices.

Through the reintroduction of a consciously demonstrative, improvised vernacular (untrained in European technique) vocal style, stronger rhythms, a basic call and response structure, repetition, and body percussion/movement, the early hard gospel quartets contributed to the revitalization of traditional, southern African-American musical traits. At the broad stylistic level, the music became more "black," as these African elements took precedence over the European traits of complex harmony and smooth vocal phrasing that characterized the older jubilee/harmonizing singing. By forging new expressive forms like gospel quartet singing—forms firmly rooted in older southern black music and worship practices—religious minded urban African-Americans were able to preserve essential aspects of their culture at a time of heightened social stress.

Of course, the new hard gospel style did not immediately supplant jubilee/harmonizing singing. Many groups developed multiple-performance repertoires that allowed maximum flexibility depending on the social make-up of their audiences. Ralph Moragne of the Sunset Jubilees recalls that during the late 1940s and early 1950s many groups carried two lead singers—one who could "preach" and "shout" the gospel songs and one who specialized in the sweeter hymns and lighter jubilee numbers. The "sweet" singer took a more prominent role in performances before larger Methodist and Baptist congregations that favored less demonstrative worship, or on the rare occasion that a group would be called on to sing for a white audience, or during radio broadcasts. The "gospel man" was showcased before smaller Baptist and Sanctified congregations or at larger programs where listeners came ready "to have church." Singers continue this strategy of style and repertoire switching today, selecting between hard or soft, fast or slow, and traditional or contemporary song styles, depending on the particular age, denomination, and social background of their listeners.

The evolution of African-American gospel quartet singing did not end with the closing of World War Two, for, as social conditions change over time, so do a culture's artistic expressions. In recent years another significant stylistic shift appears to be under way. The rise of the contemporary choir sound in the late 1960s, and the success of a new generation of professional artists like Andrae Crouch, Jessy Dixon, the Hawkins Family, Al Green, and the Winans during the 1970s and 1980s, have made a significant impact on some of New York's younger quartets. This softer, contemporary sound, as Horace Boyer points out, is differentiated from the more traditional hard gospel style by the former's emphasis on complex harmonic structure, gentle vocal timbre, highly textured synthesizer/orchestra accompaniments, and less emotional delivery and staid audience response.[25] Although Boyer sees little dissimilarity between the two styles in terms of lyrical content, many contemporary compositions tend to soften the evangelical message, concentrating more on the wonders of God's love than on the need for immediate conversion and communion with the Holy Spirit. Further, impassioned testifying, extended drive sections, and spirit-induced shouting and dancing—hallmarks of traditional hard gospel performance—are conspicuously absent during presentations of contemporary songs. The contemporary gospel sound borrows freely from the vocal and instrumental techniques of black pop music (particularly sweet soul and funk), jazz, and occasionally white rock, pop, and symphonic music.

Younger quartets are responding to the commercial popularity of contemporary gospel by a conscious modification of their own style and repertoire. In New York, groups like the Spiritual Voices, the Golden Sons, and the Ecstatics regularly include a number of softer contemporary songs in most of their performances. These pieces are characterized by sweet, smoothly textured vocals that soar above the swirling accompaniment of minor, diminished, and augmented chords produced on keyboard synthesizers and guitar phase shifters. The tempos range from slow to medium, the rhythms are light, and the delivery is restrained as the singers remain relatively stationary throughout a song. The overall performance is cool and controlled: demonstrative behavior is minimal, and the Holy Ghost rarely descends during a contemporary piece.

The increasing popularity of the contemporary gospel style among younger quartet singers undoubtedly reflects changing attitudes and strategies of urban adaptation. The issue, however, is extremely complex. The relatively short time span during which contemporary gospel has influenced quartet singing, coupled with the difficulties inherent in interpreting recent historical developments, makes definitive conclusions impossible. On one hand, while the civil rights movement and social welfare programs of the 1960s and early 1970s failed to transform urban ghettoes into comfortable, prosperous neighborhoods, limited segments of New York's black community have made substantial economic, educational, and political gains. A highly visible middle class grew in size and influence during the 1960s and 1970s, as increasing numbers of younger African-Americans passed through the educational institutions, assumed professional positions, and eventually acquired economic and political power.[26] Throughout the 1970s, and particularly during the more optimistic early years of the Carter administration, the possibilities for greater economic opportunity and integration into mainstream American life seemed real.[27] On the other hand, as historians Gilbert Osofsky and Harold Connolly point out, in spite of the gains by a few, the majority of New York's African-Americans continue to live under adverse social and economic conditions in the "enduring" and "intensifying" ghettoes of Harlem, central Brooklyn, Jamaica, and the South Bronx.[28] Further, the 1982 recession and the consistent cutbacks in social programs under the Reagan administration took a severe toll on lower and working class inner city blacks, leaving many disillusioned and bitter. Surveying the economic and class conditions of African-Americans in the 1980s, sociologist Bert Landry concluded pessimistically that there has been "slower absolute growth of the black middle class, higher unemployment, especially among the working class, and a growing group of discouraged workers who have dropped out of the labor force, swelling the underclass."[29] Incidents such as the Bernard Goetz subway shooting, the rape and beating of the Central Park jogger, and the mob murders of Michael Griffith (in Howard Beach) and Yusuf Hawkins (in Bensonhurst) reveal the depth of racial animosity that plagued New York City in the 1980s.

Such varying assessments of recent history make it difficult to draw decisive parallels between changing performance styles and attitudes toward acculturation. If we assume an optimistic stance, the following scenario is plausible. During the 1970s, a new generation of New York-born gospel singers came of age. With the benefits of a better education and a slightly higher socioeconomic status than their southern-born parents and grandparents enjoyed, these singers and their audiences exhibited more confidence in terms of their overall social identity and certainly felt more at home in the modern metropolis. Perhaps, at the prompting of this younger generation, the cultural boundaries separating the southern church community from mainstream urban life began to relax. As this process unfolded, the singers were willing to move beyond the confines of the older southern traditions, and borrow more freely from the musical expressions of the secular culture, both black and white. The movement was undoubtedly accelerated by improved educational opportunities, as an increasing number of young singers received more formal training in European classical theory and the fundamentals of jazz music through high school and college programs. An expanding gospel recording and radio industry encouraged the change, sensing the possibility of reaching a larger black secular and white crossover audience with a more modern sound that paralleled developments in black popular music.[30] The result was an overall stylistic shift in gospel music, away from its southern, church-derived roots and toward a more pop-inflected, mainstream sound. Horace Boyer alludes to this transition in commenting:

"New" [contemporary] gospel music signifies a physical and intellectual move from the rural—or what has become to be considered rural—to the urban. In some instances this means a deeper plunge into the mainstream of secular practices, sound, and acceptance.[31]

But just how deeply are local New York quartet singers willing to plunge into mainstream secular sounds and practices? The fact that even the most progressive-sounding young groups are reluctant to abandon the older hard gospel style raises the question of whether the contemporary style is simply a passing fad or will eventually supplant hard gospel as the dominant style of quartet singing. For the moment, the younger groups are attempting to work with both, presenting a carefully planned mix of modern and traditional selections. A young, New York City-born singer with the Ecstatics, explains:

Contemporary is nice, mellow music. It's more laid back, the audience just listens to the words. It's not like a regular gospel shout song where you have to move around and show some showmanship, everybody just lays back and cools out. The contemporary today catches a younger crowd, the music catches them, and then they listen to the words. . . . You have to think about the older people too. They've been in church, and they're the ones who brought us into the world. See, we were brought up on that music, the Word, the message, those older songs. Sometimes you come to a crowd, and there's nothing but old folks in the church. And if you sing contemporary, they aren't going to get into it. If that's all you sing, you're not going to get over. You have to get back to the old-time religion. So we like to stay between hard gospel and contemporary —that way we'll have both crowds.[32]

This statement underscores the importance of moving forward while staying in touch with one's roots, of maintaining a continuum between generations of singers and listeners through the conscious manipulations of style and repertoire. If younger urban singers are more open than their predecessors to the influences of secular life and music, they are by no means ready to forget their traditional upbringing or their parents' southern "old-time" religion. For this younger generation, urban adaptation continues to emphasize the creation of new expressions and the simultaneous affirmation of old traditions.

While shifts in sacred quartet singing from jubilee to gospel to contemporary styles mirror changing social conditions at the macro-cultural level, transitions are marked by significant time lags that suggest a certain conservativeness to the quartet tradition. This is most evident among community-based artists who are under minimal pressure to keep up with rapidly changing commercial tastes. Sanctified music and gospel song were established for a number of years in New York before hard gospel singing became the norm among quartets. In the early 1940s, for example, most local New York quartets were still singing in a style that was distinctly more "Europeanized" than the musical traditions that prevailed in most of the smaller Baptist and Holiness churches. Similarly, while the contemporary gospel style has dominated the commercial industry and the larger choirs for nearly two decades, quartets have begun only recently to seriously embrace the sound. Today, the local quartets reflect one of the most "Africanized" styles of black church music. Considering the evolution of African-American religious song since Emancipation, sacred quartets have not been in the forefront of stylistic change. Rather, the strength of the quartet tradition appears to be in the realm of interpretation and conservation. Throughout the twentieth century quartets have adapted changing styles of church music to the small-group format and served as repositories of those styles after they began to recede in popularity among the greater church community.

The emergence of hard gospel singing in the 1940s is the most significant stylistic development related to social identity. It is not coincidental that the ethnographic information presented in the preceding chapters is drawn primarily from performances by New York's hard gospel quartets. Clearly the postwar gospel quartets crystallized the aesthetic and spiritual aspirations of the masses of southern, working class black Christians during a particularly stressful period of urbanization. They expressed the essence of down-home southern church music and worship through sounds and behaviors that were considered harsh, crude, and even "primitive" by mainstream, middle class white and black urbanites. Their rough, church style stood in stark contrast to the aesthetic norms of acceptable music and worship practice as defined by the dominant European-American culture of the period. In this sense quartet performance served as one of a number of symbolic cultural boundaries that demarcated the black folk church community from the surrounding urban secular world. The distinctive hard gospel performance style and the extra-musical associations triggered by that style, evoked the memories of a shared southern past and the reality of the present struggle to adjust to modern urban life.

Hard gospel quartet performance helped maintain group cohesion while shaping the newly emerging African-American urban identity. Gospel quartet programs, like Sunday morning worship services, provided occasions for southern migrants to come together and celebrate their common cultural heritage through music, worship, and food. To the newly arrived southerner, an afternoon or evening of quartet singing offered an intimate, familiar refuge from the chaos and anonymity of the city. Such events afforded participants the opportunity to re-experience the old-time religion and the old-time values they were reared on. The perils of big city living were communally acknowledged; solutions based upon biblical teachings were proposed. Those who attained moderate socioeconomic success were sternly warned never to forget the struggles of their southern forebears and the goodness of God, who chose to deliver them to a better life. Traditional patterns of song, music, testimony, preaching, prayer, movement and dance were among the many powerful expressions of southern, African-American Christian identity transmitted from one generation to the next. A sense of pride was instilled and social bonds strengthened at a critical time when the forces of the urban secular world threatened to tear the church community apart.

While gospel quartet performances played an important role in the maintenance of southern religion and social life, Sunday morning worship services and week-night prayer meetings fulfilled similar functions on a more regular basis. But quartet performances eased the shock of migration in other ways. Faced with competition from the seemingly limitless choices of secular activities that city life had to offer, the church community responded by developing its own form of popular "spiritual entertainment" via the quartet tradition. For nearly fifty years gospel quartet singers have provided a bridge between the sacred world of the rural southern migrants and the secular reality of their new urban home. Their performances help to assuage the deep oppositions of sacred versus secular, traditional versus modern, rural versus urban, and southern versus northern. In short, while the musical and worship aspects of community-based gospel performance carry strong, rural southern connotations, elements of urban style and professionalism are clearly evident. Even local groups that do not depend on singing for a living dress in carefully matched uniforms, hawk vanity press tapes and records, occasionally travel out of town for special engagements, and often are paid for their services. For artists and audience members, gospel quartet performance provides an occasion for engaging in a form of urban popular culture that is consciously rooted in southern rural traditions. Local gospel singers may play the social role of the successful, well-dressed, semi-professional urban entertainer while remaining true to their rural southern roots and religious beliefs. Their performances strive to mediate the conflict between traditionality and modernity, to shape meaningful order and social identity amidst the chaos of urban transition.

The role of hard gospel quartet singing in easing the tensions of urbanization probably was strongest from the mid-1940s up through the early 1960s—a period characterized by heavy southern in-migration, continued crowding, and the "ghettoization" of African-American neighborhoods. Yet more than two decades after southern migration slowed to a trickle, the hard quartet style continues to predominate at gospel programs. Why? Urbanization is a slow, ongoing, and often incomplete process. People do not forge new social identities overnight, particularly in environments where institutionalized racism continues to pose formidable barriers to assimilation. More-over, many migrants consciously choose to maintain strong social and familial ties to the South and, as noted earlier, are now considering moving "back home" upon retirement. For older members of the church community, traditional gospel quartet singing provides a di-rect link to their earlier life experiences. Younger, New York-born quartet singers may appear more urbanized than their parents, but they, too, must struggle to negotiate their dual identities as southern blacks and urban Americans. Their symbolic performances mirror this struggle: the adaptation of elements of mainstream American culture must be accompanied by reaffirmation of southern African-American roots. They cautiously introduce contemporary songs and sounds without abandoning the old gospel favorites or the hard style of singing. As a result the postwar gospel quartet style still flourishes among young and old community-based singers. As we enter the final decade of this century, local gospel quartets continue to perform al-most exclusively for African-American audiences of southern lin-eage. This situation reflects the continued social segregation of the black church community and a resolve by its members to maintain their distinct southern heritage.

No legitimate discussion of African-American urban acculturation and music can ignore the question of cultural appropriation by the European-American controlled popular media. The larger issue con-cerning the politics of popular music and the mass media is one of intense debate.[33] Adherents of the Marxist Frankfurt school, partic-ularly Theodor Adorno, argue that mass production automatically reduces music to commodity, thus robbing it of its vitality and poten-tial for social criticism.[34] More recent Western-Marxist writers have challenged this paradigm, contending that popular culture and mass media are sites of cultural struggle between the dialectic forces of ac-ceptance of and resistance to the ruling class hegemony.[35] Raymond Williams, while stressing the power of hegemonic forces to incorpo-rate and control expressions of resistance, suggests that residual (tra-ditional) and emergent (new) cultural products occasionally manifest themselves as alternatives or in opposition to the dominant social or-der.[36] Postwar gospel quartet singing appears to be one such emer-gent product, for it did indeed stand in opposition to, and resisted appropriation by, the dominant European-American culture.

Amiri Baraka argues convincingly that African-American music has been particularly susceptible to appropriation and financial ex-ploitation by the white-controlled American media industry. As blues, jazz, and related black music moved away from the African-American masses, they were diluted by the media for popular consumption by middle class audiences. Baraka reasons that genres like popular ragtime, Dixieland, swing (and later fusion and disco) were not valid expressions of black working class culture, and by implication could not stand as markers of African-American identity. Rather, the commercial prostitution of authentic black styles spurred musicians to reinvigorate their art through the creation of more Africanized (or at least non-Western sounding) expressions like "shouting" rhythm and blues and be-bop.[37] The former is particularly interesting, for it emerged as a popular form in midwestern cities during the late 1930s and early 1940s, precisely at the time when hard gospel quartet singing was taking hold. This rough, downhome style of early urban blues, notes Baraka, featured "shouting" singers, "screaming" saxophones, and "blasting" rhythm sections—a far cry from the smoother, more sedate swing music and jump blues that enjoyed national popularity during this period. The audience for such music was predictable, as Baraka states:

Rhythm & blues was still an exclusive music. It was performed almost exclusively for, and had to satisfy, a Negro audience. For this reason, it could not suffer the ultimate sterility that would have resulted from the total immersion in the mainstream American culture. It too was a music that was hated by the middle-class Negro and not even understood by the white man.[38]

The parallels between such early urban blues and hard gospel quartet singing are striking. Like the blues shouters, the postwar gospel quartets were stylistically and culturally too far removed from mainstream American life to be noticed and appropriated by the national media. Their sound was too raw and unrefined. The rhythms were too heavy, the vocal delivery too rough, and the overall presentation too demonstrative and religious. White listeners who fancied the tight harmonies and lilting rhythms of the jubilee quartets heard too much shouting, screaming, and blasting. The hard quartets were just too "black" sounding for European-American audiences of the day to comprehend and appreciate. Further, the intensely evangelical tone of the music undoubtedly turned off most white secular listeners, and caused many middle class African-Americans to dismiss quartet singers as primitive holy-rollers. As a result, the hard gospel quartets found their audience limited to working class, southern African-American Protestants. Although their music was recorded by small independent labels and broadcast on radio, it functioned as popular/mass mediated music in a restricted sense, as it was consumed almost exclusively by a small, clearly circumscribed segment of the American population. Because hard gospel quartet singing remained relatively obscure within the confines of the black church, it was never directly appropriated nor diluted for popular consumption by a non-African-American audience. It survived, and continues to survive today, as a repository of southern African-American aesthetic style and spirituality.

This is not to suggest that gospel quartet singing had no effect on American popular music. Indeed, as Anthony Heilbut argues throughout *The Gospel Sound*, gospel singing provided a firm foundation for much postwar secular pop music, including rock and roll.[39] The influence, however, was indirect, primarily through ex-quartet and ex-gospel singers who crossed over to perform early rock and roll, vocal rhythm and blues, and soul music. Contemporary popular music owes much to the likes of Little Richard Penniman, James Brown, Wilson Pickett, Lou Rawls, Sam Cooke, Clyde McPhatter, Aretha Franklin, Dionne Warwick, Cissy Houston, and the Staple Singers—all of whom began as quartet or gospel singers. The chances are great that these stellar performers might never have been heard by larger non-black audiences, nor have made their immense impact on the music world, if they had remained isolated within the church community. These crossover stars, not quartet or gospel singers themselves, ushered the sounds of the black church into mainstream postwar American popular music. The former were simply not heard by white Americans; they remained nearly invisible to the national recording industry and the larger public.[40] The vocal R&B and soul singers were primarily responsible for translating gospel singing into secular terms that were palatable to European-American and non-church African-American audiences. Their success is well documented, and their soulful vocal techniques inspired countless white imitators. But their three minute, carefully produced commercial "hits" rarely captured the raw energy, and certainly not the spiritual power, of a live gospel performance. Meanwhile, quartet singers stayed at home and continued to please church audiences, unhampered by pressures to "whiten" their sound for commercial gain and potential exploitation.

The issue of appropriation takes on new dimensions with the rise of contemporary gospel music in the 1970s and 1980s. The crossover success of a handful of contemporary singers like the Hawkins Family, Al Green, and Andrea Crouch raises serious questions concerning the integrity of the new gospel sound. As they smooth the rough edges and mute the evangelical fervor of traditional gospel to reach a wider secular audience, will their music continue to express the power and beauty of traditional black church singing? Or will it, as

Viv Broughton implies, run the risk of becoming "bland and super-ficial" pop?[41] Can input from secular popular music reinvigorate black church singing? Or will crossover dreams inevitably lead to the diluting homogenization described by Nelson George in his recent work, *The Death of Rhythm and Blues*? As younger singers move away from the harder southern style, will their performances continue to serve as markers of black pride and identity? Or will the "crass commercialism" that Horace Boyer warns of result in rendering the music culturally impotent?[42] Further, will white gospel singers, particularly proponents of the rapidly expanding "contemporary Christian" music industry, capitalize on the black contemporary style and reap the financial benefits? Obviously more time must elapse before these questions can be answered, but community-based quartets may play an important role in the eventual outcome. If quartet singers—especially younger ones—persist as custodians of the older, southern-derived gospel styles, they will undoubtedly exert a somewhat conservative influence on the overall field of gospel singing. As a result, the music may remain more firmly grounded within the black church, where it is less susceptible to appropriation and subsequent dilution by the commercial music industry. On the other hand, if the younger quartets, following the lead of the modern gospel choirs and soloists, eventually gravitate toward the contemporary style, they will open additional avenues for musical exchange with the dominant secular culture as well as the possibility for commercial exploitation.

The model and interpretations offered in this chapter suffer from a degree of reductionism that seems inevitable when interpreting the meaning of multiple performance styles spawned under conditions of rapid social change and cross-cultural contact. Neither the stylistic parameters nor the chronological periods that purportedly demarcate harmonizing, jubilee, hard gospel, or contemporary quartet singing are as concise as one would wish. Exactly where and when one style begins and the other leaves off is often unclear. Nor, in reality, do a monolithic African-American church community, a black secular community, or a dominant European-American culture exist independently of one another. Equally problematic is the notion of "group identity" as a construct firmly rooted in the consciousness of all African-Americans, or in the consciousnesses of all members of any ethnic group, for that matter. While the European-American majority has chosen to segregate Americans of African descent into a racially defined category, the social forces of class, gender, age, religion, and occupation all have an impact on the way individual

African-Americans identify themselves. Further, there is no magical instant when an immigrant or migrant group can be said to be totally urbanized, acculturated, or assimilated. Adjusting to urban life is an ongoing process that mirrors the dynamic nature of cities themselves. And finally there is a fine line between cross-cultural musical exchange and cultural appropriation, particularly in an era when the electronic media revolution has made *everyone's* music accessible to *everyone* for purposes that range from appreciation and celebration to appropriation and commercial exploitation.

Social experience and the transformation of expressive styles are phenomena too elusive to fit neatly into prescribed cultural models. Yet it is undeniable that African-American sacred quartet singing has gone through a series of significant stylistic shifts throughout this century and that such shifts can be roughly correlated to changing social conditions brought on by the migration of southern black people to the cities of America. Musical style and symbolic performance reveal important clues to the nature of cultures in transition, as Nelson George implies when he says: "You can tell where black people are at any given time in history by our music."[43] But whether sacred quartet singing will continue to serve as a barometer of African-American urban adaptation depends on its continued survival and popularity within the church community. This question inevitably leads us back to the relationship between the community-based singers and their professional counterparts and raises additional issues concerning the sacred and secular dimensions of the tradition.

Notes

1. See for example Bruno Nettl, ed., *Eight Urban Music Cultures* (Urbana: University of Illinois Press, 1978); Coplan, *In Township Tonight!*; Peter Manuel, *Popular Music of the Non-Western World* (New York: Oxford Universtiy Press, 1988), pp. 1–23; Americo Paredes and Ellen Stekert, eds., *The Urban Experience and Folk Traditions* (Austin: University of Texas Press, 1971); Barbara Kirshenblatt-Gimblett, "The Future of Folklore Studies in America: The Urban Frontier" *Folklore Forum* 16 (1983): 175–234.

2. Coplan, *In Township Tonight!*, p. 233.

3. David Coplan, "The Urbanization of African Music: Some Theoretical Observations." *Popular Music* 2 (1982): 113–130.

4. Manuel, *Popular Music of the Non-Western World*, p. 16.

5. Keil, *Urban Blues*, p. 43.

6. Ibid., p. 164.

7. For a detailed discussion of the concept of "soul" as a basic ideological component of the African-American urban experience, see Keil, *Urban Blues*, pp. 164–190.

8. Levine, *Black Culture and Black Consciousness*, p. 189.

9. Osofsky, *Harlem*, pp. 17–34.

10. Baraka, *Blues People*, pp. 95–96.

11. Osofsky, *Harlem*, p. 34.

12. See Anderson, *This Was Harlem*, pp. 137–231. Gilbert Osofsky argues that the images of Harlem as a high-spirited, exotic "Great Playground" that were perpetuated in the press and literature of the 1920's were something of a distortion, for in reality most African-Americans during this period lived in impoverished conditions. See Osofsky, *Harlem*, pp. 179–187. While this is probably true, the fact remains that this period was marked by a great deal of black/white contact, particularly in the area of music.

13. See Anderson, *This Was Harlem*, pp. 139–144 and 168–180.

14. For more on the relationship of southern urbanization and early African-American quartet singing, see Seroff, "On the Battlefield," pp. 34–36, and Lornell, *"Happy in the Service of the Lord"*, pp. 19–20.

15. Nathan Glazer and Daniel Moynihan, *Beyond the Melting Pot* (2nd ed.; Cambridge, MA: MIT Press, 1970), pp. 28–29. Osofsky argues that Harlem's housing could not handle the deluge of southern migrants arriving during the 1920s. High rents necessitated the subdivision of apartments, and overcrowding eventually transformed the once prosperous neighborhood into a slum. See Osofsky, *Harlem*, pp. 135–141. Continued migration during the 1930s and stepped-up migration during the 1940s simply exacerbated the problem.

16. Between 1930 and 1940 New York's black population rose from 327,706 to 458,444—an increase of approximately 40 percent. Between 1940 and 1950 the population jumped from 458,444 to 727,977—an increase of nearly 60 percent. Figures from *New York State Census, 1930, 1940, 1950*.

17. John Hope Franklin, *From Slavery to Freedom: A History of Negro Americans* (6th ed.; New York: Alfred Knopf, 1988), p. 403.

18. Anderson, *This Was Harlem*, pp. 295–298.

19. Although civil rights reforms began in the late 1940s under the Truman administration, government intervention failed to yield significant economic, housing, educational, or political gains for the vast majority of African-Americans during the 1950s and early 1960s. See Franklin, *From Slavery to Freedom*, pp. 411–435.

20. Anderson, *This Was Harlem*, p. 347.

21. Franklin, *From Slavery to Freedom*, pp. 387–389.

22. Glazer and Moynihan, *Beyond the Melting Pot*, pp. 29–30.

23. Personal interview with Ralph Moragne, May 1, 1986.

24. Personal interview with Charlie Storey, April 18, 1986.

25. Boyer, "A Comparative Analysis of Traditional and Contemporary Gospel Music," pp. 127–145.

26. See Bart Landry, *The New Black Middle Class* (Berkeley: University of California Press, 1987), pp. 67–93; and Franklin, *From Slavery to Freedom*, pp. 493–497.

27. This shift is somewhat muddled by the fact that "mainstream" American urban culture of the 1970s and 1980s was itself much more African-American influenced—particularly in terms of vernacular music, dance, dress, and speech—than was pre-1950s American life.

28. See Osofsky, *Harlem*, pp. 189–201; and Harold Connolly, *A Ghetto Grows in Brooklyn* (New York: New York University Press, 1977), pp. 226–234.

29. Landry, *The New Black Middle Class*, p. 224.

30. For more on the crossover phenomenon in popular secular music see Nelson George, *The Death of Rhythm and Blues* (New York: Pantheon, 1988), pp. 141–197.

31. Boyer, "A Comparative Analysis of Traditional and Contemporary Gospel Music," p. 128.

32. Personal interview conducted by Ray Allen, June 6, 1986. Examples of the contemporary ("Just a Prayer") and hard gospel styles ("He Consulates Me") can be heard on the Ecstatics LP, "Just a Prayer Away" (G.T.S. Records #1079, 1984).

33. For an informative summary of this debate see Manuel, 1988, *Popular Music of the Non-Western World*, pp. 7–15.

34. Theodor Adorno, *Introduction to the Sociology of Music* (New York: Continuum, 1976), pp. 21–38.

35. See for example Stuart Hall, "Notes of Deconstructing the Popular" in R. Samuelson, ed., *People's History and Social Theory* (London: Rutledge, 1981), pp. 227–240, and Simon Frith, *Sound Effects* (New York: Pantheon, 1981).

36. Raymond Williams, *Marxism and Literature* (New York: Oxford University Press, 1977), pp. 121–127.

37. See Baraka, *Blues People*, pp. 166–222, and "Black Music: Its Roots, Its Popularity, and Its Commercial Prostitution," in William Ferris and Mary Hart, eds., *Folk Music and Modern Sound* (Jackson: University of Mississippi Press, 1982), pp. 177–193.

38. Baraka, *Blues People*, p. 169. Unlike their hard shouting church counterparts, some of the early shouting rhythm and blues artists including McKinley "Muddy Waters" Morganfield and Chester "Howlin' Wolf" Burnett were eventually "discovered" by a new generation of British and white American rock musicians. See Robert Palmer, *Deep Blues* (New York: Penguin, 1981), pp. 255–264.

39. Heilbut, *Gospel Sound*, pp. ix–xxxv.

40. A notable exception to this generalization is Mahalia Jackson, who managed to reached a wide national audience with her spectacular gospel singing during the 1950s and 1960s. See Laurraine Goreau, *Just Mahalia, Baby* (Gretna: Pelican, 1984).

41. Broughton, *Black Gospel*, p. 117.

42. Boyer, "A Comparative Analysis of Traditional and Contemporary Gospel Music," p. 144.

43. George, *Death of Rhythm and Blues*, p. xvi.

Chapter 9
Spiritual Entertainment
Sacred Folk Music and Popular Culture

A rainbow-colored poster hanging in the window of Phil's Barber Shop loudly announces a "1988 Fall Gospel Festival" to be held on September 24 at St. Anthony Baptist Church, 425 Utica Avenue, Brooklyn. Sponsored by the church's Willing Workers Club, the event headlines the popular Jackson Southernaires of Jackson, Mississippi, and features a number of well-known Brooklyn singers. Tickets are $18 at the door, or $15 if purchased in advance at "Birdell's Records, Phil's Barber Shop and the Usual Places."

The advertising works well, for on the evening of the 24th a crowd of over five hundred packs St. Anthony's. Following a brief devotional service consisting of hymns and prayer, emcee "Evangelist" Minnie Johnson brings on Brooklyn's Deacon Jones and the Pilgrim Sounds. The group provides a rousing fifteen minute set, culminating in a moving processional. They are followed in quick succession by the St. Anthony Men's Choir, soloist Mary Ross, and another Brooklyn quartet, the Golden Harmonizers. The crowd grows restless as the Spiritual Voices are called forward, but responds enthusiastically to the young Brooklynites' sweet harmonies. Lead singer Keith Johnson delivers an impassioned testimony about the group's recent car accident and miraculous survival (see Chapter 4) before launching into an exuberant version of "Can't Nobody Do Me Like Jesus." Ten minutes later the Voices leave the floor amid congregational shouts and tears. They are followed by the Wandering Souls, a semi-professional quartet originally from Shelby, North Carolina, that currently work out of Brooklyn. Harold Williams leads the group in a tight twenty minute set, but the congregation, still recovering from the Spiritual Voices' electrifying set, is only mildly receptive.

Around 11p.m. Minnie Johnson finally calls the Jackson Souther-naires. The group runs through a number of medium-tempo, con-temporary pieces, before moving into a rocking gospel number featuring the searing double-leads of Frank Williams and Luther Jen-nings. Pandemonium ensues, as the audience erupts with unabashed shouting and holy dance. The Southernaires cool things down with a soulful hymn, only to re-ignite the congregation with a hard driving finale. When Minnie Johnson delivers the final benediction shortly after midnight, everyone seems exhausted but satiated. The local singers head home to rest and ready themselves for Sunday morning church, while the Jackson Southernaires move on down the gospel highway to their next show.

This incident illustrates two central themes of this book. First, gos-pel quartet singing is clearly alive and well in New York. And second, the tradition flourishes, simultaneously, as popular (commercial) en-tertainment and as sacred (noncommercial) folk music. Of course the modern, multi-million dollar gospel recording and radio industries overshadow the vigorous but relatively inconspicuous grassroots scene, and commercial quartets have been relegated to secondary status behind contemporary choirs and soloists. As a result, only a handful of today's quartets can boast respectable record sales and sig-nificant radio attention. But in spite of rapidly changing popular tastes in the commercial marketplace, community-based quartet sing-ing in New York has sustained itself for more than sixty years.

Surveying quartet activity in New York it is tempting to make strict distinctions between the commercial, "popular" quartets and their community-based, "folk" counterparts. The commercial quartets are professionals who tour and sing for a living. They communicate their art primarily through the mass electronic media (records, audio and video cassettes, and radio) and large-scale live performances. Out of financial necessity, the professionals must place priority on showman-ship and entertainment. By contrast, the community-based groups depend on non-singing day jobs for their living. Most of their singing is at local churches, where they reach smaller audiences directly through live, unmediated performances. In such settings, religious conviction generally takes priority over monetary gain, a fact that ul-timately pushes local performances away from popular entertain-ment into the realm of sacred ritual.

Constructing rigid dichotomies between mass-produced/commer-cial and community-based/non-commercial music is in keeping with a scholarly tradition that views so-called "popular" and "folk" arts as separate and often antithetical entities. But recent scholarship, stress-ing the common roots and interactional nature of cultural practices, calls into question the usefulness of such mutually exclusive categories.[1] John Blacking, for example, points out that overemphasis on labeling and classification often obscures the reality of the music making process.[2] In the case of sacred quartet singing, to reduce musical styles, performers, and performances to the duel categories of popular/commercial and folk/noncommercial is a gross oversimplification. Such a reduction ignores the shared goals and complex interrelationship of the professional and local groups. Ultimately, both aspire to provide "spiritual entertainment." The local groups may lean slightly in the direction of the spiritual, while the professionals emphasize entertainment, but the differences are by no means clear cut. For some time New York's local and professional quartets have experienced a tense but interdependent relationship. The nature of this relationship reveals the complex interplay of commercial, aesthetic, and spiritual concerns that lie at the heart of sacred quartet singing.

The professional quartets and their local counterparts spring from the same cultural source. At the most fundamental level, they share a working class, Protestant, African-American heritage that includes musical practices deeply rooted in southern folk tradition. Be they professionals or amateurs, all African-American quartet singers learned the rudiments of sacred singing from family and community churchgoers, as outlined in Chapter 2. Further, all the professionals began as community singers, gaining their initial group experience in noncommercial family or church quartets. Even the best "came up the hard way," singing in small churches within local networks.

Just as they share common cultural and musical roots, so do the professional and local groups share the same audience. Unlike the better known college-trained and professional pre-war jubilee groups who, on occasion, performed for white and black middle class listeners, postwar gospel quartets have sung almost exclusively for black, working class church audiences. The professional singers may reach larger numbers of listeners through their recordings and touring appearances, but in terms of cultural background, class, and religious persuasion their following is essentially identical to that of the local groups.

Based on this common cultural heritage and decades of intensive interaction, it is not surprising that the professional and local groups demonstrate a remarkable consistency of performance styles. This is most evident in live performance, where both rely on a mixed repertoire of older hymns and church songs, well-known gospel songs from the 1940s, 1950s, and 1960s, and a handful of contemporary compositions. Hard singing still predominates. Professional and local groups make use of the performance strategies described in Chapter 4, and both adhere to the aesthetic concerns for originality, personalization, and control discussed in Chapter 5. While live performances and recordings of professional quartets serve as important sources of style and repertoire for the local singers, the exchange works both ways. Over the years the professionals have occasionally appropriated songs and arrangements from the local groups with whom they have appeared on live programs. Moreover, as outlined in the previous chapter, performances by professional groups consist primarily of stylized interpretations of traditional church music and worship practices. Here one might be enticed to fall back on standard categories and reduce the situation to an instance of "folk" culture (the local quartets) imitating "popular" culture (the commercial quartets) originally derived from the "folk" culture (traditional church practices). But such an equation is too superficial, since it ignores the reciprocal exchange between the commercial and local singers. In reality a community of singers—a few professional and many amateur—is constantly interpreting and reinterpreting African-American sacred music and worship practices within a framework that is ritualistic and theatrical in nature.

Local groups, however, seldom match the high levels of artistic quality exhibited by the professional quartets. No one in the church community would deny that the professionals are consistently the best performers. Groups like the Dixie Hummingbirds, the Jackson Southernaries, and the Mighty Clouds of Joy are held in the highest esteem by the local singers and audiences. Their lead singers simply stun audiences with finely honed vocal techniques and astounding power. Their harmonies are always flawless. Their overall presentations are tightly executed. In terms of showmanship, they are rarely outdone. However, it is not uncommon for a group of talented young locals to put on an exceptional performance and steal the show from the headliners. The best local groups, particularly those who tour on weekends, develop their own unique stage techniques that sometimes rival those of the professionals. They will not hesitate to preach, testify, walk the aisles, or cut a few dance steps in order to "get over" with their audiences. Although the professional groups are generally acknowledged as the most sophisticated showmen, it is difficult to draw sharp distinctions between them and their local counterparts based solely on levels of theatrical stylization.

Regardless of talent, the primary criteria used by the church community to distinguish the "majors" from the "home groups" are recordings and full-time touring schedules. Any quartet that wishes to tour professionally today must first reach a mass audience through the electronic media. It needs a recording that receives national distribution and regular airplay on the major urban gospel radio stations such as New York's WWRL. Only a handful of legendary masters who never left the road, like the Dixie Hummingbirds and the Soul Stirrers, can depend on reputation alone to draw large audiences. This situation makes it extremely difficult for younger groups to break into the field, since the commercial gospel recording and radio industries are currently dominated by soloists and choirs. Only a few independent labels with significant national distribution continue to record quartets with any regularity. Among the most active of these are Maleco, Sure Fine, Nashboro, Atlantic International, and Light. Still, quartet recordings by the Jackson Southernaires, the Gospel Keynotes, the Violinaires, the Pilgrim Jubilees, the Williams Brothers, the Swanee Quintet, the Highway QC's, Slim and the Supreme Angels, Willie Banks and the Messengers, and the Mighty Clouds of Joy are nationally distributed and receive substantial radio airplay. Such exposure builds and maintains a broad enough audience to support full-time touring. Many of the community-based and semi-professional groups also have recordings. For as little as a thousand dollars, a group can produce a vanity record album or cassette. These recordings, however, have no distribution and are sold primarily by the groups themselves at programs where they sing. Rarely do they receive commercial airplay, nor are they regularly carried in New York's two major gospel record shops—Birdell's Records in Brooklyn and Rainbow Music in Manhattan. Because they are unable to crack the tightly controlled commercial recording and radio industries, vanity recordings are of limited value in developing an audience beyond the local New York scene. As expected, recordings made by the professional quartets are of significantly higher quality than the vanity albums and cassettes produced by the locals. Professionals often use extra musicians or overdub additional synthesizer, string, and percussion accompaniments to produce slick, pop-inflected arrangements. Local groups must simply use their own personnel, or perhaps a few pick-up musicians of limited ability. The results are often sloppy. Vanity records and cassettes are notorious for being haphazardly recorded, poorly mixed, and packaged with inferior photographs and graphics.

There is an interesting discrepancy between what groups record and what they play at live performances. In terms of repertoire, professional and local groups include a generous number of slower, modern compositions on their recordings. The smooth harmonies and synthesizer accompaniments on these selections often sound closer to the Motown style of the Temptations and Stevie Wonder than to southern church music. The adaptation of this more commercially viable style is, at least for the professional groups, probably a response to recording industry pressures and the success of crossover secular singers. The hard gospel and up-tempo songs that find their way onto disc or tape are boisterous, but generally pale by comparison to a live performance. Prefacing songs with extensive testimonies or stretching numbers out with lengthy drive sections is the exception, not the rule, for modern recordings, unless a live performance is featured. Rather, most pieces run between four and five minutes in length, probably to conform to the standards of radio. The musical arrangements on professional recordings have become quite sophisticated, incorporating complex harmonic structures and instrumental techniques borrowed from black popular music. Further, it is not ununsual for a traditional, hard lead vocal to be paired with a dense instrumental backing of contemporary sounding guitars, synthesizers, strings, and horns.

But in live concert, before a church audience, a totally different picture emerges. Here, the professionals and local groups appear with stripped-down bands consisting of only guitar, bass, drums, and sometimes keyboard. Both fall back on the older hymns and traditional gospel pieces. A group may begin its set with several short, contemporary sounding numbers, especially if it is pushing a current hit. But eventually the singers will roll out their more traditional repertoire of hard gospel song, testimony and dance. A finale piece commonly lasts for fifteen minutes or more, as groups strive to invoke the Spirit and shout the church. The fervent energy of such live performances is rarely captured on recordings.[3]

Even with today's booming gospel industry, sales of black gospel quartet recordings are relatively small. To go professional, a group must also depend on a steady touring schedule. The full-time professionals sing every weekend following circuits set up by local black promoters in medium-sized and larger cities throughout the South, the Midwest, the Northeast, and the West Coast. The vast majority of these engagements are at larger churches, auditoriums, and schools located in black urban neighborhoods. But the local and semi-professional New York groups also take advantage of these and other networks. Groups like the Golden Sons, the Spiritual Voices, the Ecstatics, the Brooklyn Skyways, the Wearyland Singers, and the Biblettes travel outside the New York City area at least once a month. They are often invited as special guests at the anniversary of another semi-professional group or as honori at the hometown church of one of their members (usually in the South). In an evening they can venture out to various towns on Long Island or in New Jersey or Westchester County or to Philadelphia, Baltimore, Hartford, Albany, or Boston. On a long weekend they will travel south to numerous cities in Virginia, the Carolinas and Georgia, or west to Buffalo, Columbus, Detroit, or Cleveland. Once a year, group members may coordinate vacation schedules to allow for a full week to travel through the South or Midwest. Weekend and vacation touring allows them to keep their steady day jobs in New York while occasionally appearing out of town as featured acts. Although a group like the Brooklyn Skyways cannot command the high fees of a commercial star, for a night in Sumter, South Carolina, the group is elevated in status from local amateur to professional headliner. In such instances the distinction between the commercial and non-commercial performers is unquestionably blurred.

At a critical point in their early careers, talented local groups like the Brooklyn Skyways and Mighty Gospel Giants made a conscious decision not to give up their day jobs to pursue full-time singing careers. This pattern is typical. The hardships and financial uncertainties of life on the road, coupled with family commitments, led most to abandon professional aspirations in favor of a more settled and secure life style where singing was an avocation.[4] Willie Johnson of the Brooklyn Skyways recalls:

In about 1963 or '64 we tried going on the road. We went out for twenty or thirty days but things didn't work out. See I didn't want to go out and lose everything I had. We were on this package with the Dixie Hummingbirds, the Clouds of Joy, and the Swanee Quintet. But if you're not the big stars like them, you get the last pennies. And when you have eight guys and don't make no money—I mean guys with families back home, who have to pay the rent and buy food—if you don't make good money you don't have a group. If you don't have a family you might get by, but once you have a family, you just can't survive off that. So today all the fellows have their families and they have good jobs. One's an accountant, a couple work for the Post Office, and I have this bus company. Hey, we go out of town [to sing] on weekends whenever we want. And everybody has been on their jobs long enough that we can take off time together to travel, sometimes we go for a week or ten days. We've been overseas to Bermuda three times.[5]

Large, commercial gospel programs, such as the one described in the introduction to this chapter, provide a common meeting ground for professional and local quartets. Here the interaction is direct and intense. Commercial programs in the 1980s are not on the grand scale of those of the 1950s or early 1960s, when Thurman Ruth, Fred Barr, and Doc Wheeler brought packaged shows to large venues like the Apollo Theatre (seating capacity 1,500), and Lawson's Auditorium (seating capacity 1,500) or big churches such as Harlem's Salem Methodist (seating capacity 2,900), and Brooklyn's Washington Temple (seating capacity 2,500). Such gospel extravaganzas featured up to half a dozen big-name male quartets like the Dixie Hummingbirds, the Swan Silvertones, the Soul Stirrers, and the Harmonizing Four; stellar female and mixed ensembles like the Ward Singers and the Caravans; and several outstanding semi-professional local groups like the Brooklyn All Stars or the Mighty Gospel Giants. But today's commercial programs are nevertheless impressive. Large churches and public school auditoriums with seating capacities of five hundred to a thousand are common sites. In contrast to the big gospel shows of the 1950s, contemporary programs headline only one or two big-name quartets. Several out-of-town, semi-professional groups may appear along with five or six local groups. The local groups are expected to sell tickets and bring in their own following.

There are critical differences between today's large gospel extravaganzas and the smaller local programs and anniversaries. The commercial shows with out-of-town stars tend to include more groups and draw larger audiences who pay higher ticket prices. All groups, including the locals, receive some financial remuneration, and many sell records, tapes, and pictures. Profits go to the promoter who organized the show. By contrast the local programs generally include fewer groups and draw smaller crowds. Money is raised through a free will offering, and most groups sing for free or for minimal compensation. Profits are split with the sponsoring church or, in the case of an Anniversary, go to the honored group.

The structures of the local and commercial gospel programs are roughly identical, although the devotional service is often longer in smaller settings, where congregation members are more willing to engage in lengthy periods of testimony. The atmosphere is, unquestionably, more intimate at the local programs, particularly when the audience numbers fewer than a hundred. Many people know each other personally, and it is common practice for singers to acknowledge family and friends directly from the stage as they introduce songs. For example, one evening in a small Harlem church the Reverend Vernella Kelly of the Faithful Harmonizers prefaced a song by asking several elderly friends in the congregation to stand while she thanked God for giving them the strength to come out to the program. Singers will compliment previous performances and poke fun at competitors. The nature of the communication is intensely interpersonal. Groups sit in the audience as participants rather than isolating themselves in dressing rooms. Moreover, there is a great deal of spontaneity and openness, allowing individuals or groups not originally scheduled to participate to perform. During the course of a program, young (pre-teen) church members or an elderly deacon may be called on to contribute a song. All groups are allotted roughly the same amount of performance time, but if the "Spirit comes" they are allowed to sing longer. The communal, egalitarian structures described in Chapter 3 are most prominent in these smaller events. The social dynamic feels close and tight-knit, like a small church service.

At the larger commercial programs, where tighter scheduling is a priority, devotional services tend to be shorter. The local groups are ushered on and off as quickly as possible, while the headliners are allocated the last and longest performance slots—often half an hour or longer. Singers often congregate in dressing rooms and enter through special backstage areas that separate them spatially from their audiences. In larger performance contexts, social roles are strictly defined and a more hierarchical pattern of organization prevails.

From these observations one might conclude that the larger gospel extravaganzas have taken on the trappings of secular, commercial shows, while the smaller community programs remain firmly rooted in community ritual. Kip Lornell makes such an assumption, arguing that postwar gospel quartet singing in Memphis strayed from its community-based church roots toward secular entertainment. He further draws strict distinctions between the settings in which local and professional groups sing, suggesting that the former perform primarily "for a community of relatives, peers, and neighbors in a local church," while commerical singers appear "in a larger, more spacious setting for an audience with whom they have had little, if any, contact."[6] But dividing gospel events and audiences into such mutually exclusive categories proves problematic. Though differences exist, they are relative, not absolute. Even the largest gospel programs in New York—those attracting an audience of one thousand or more—are not of the magnitude or conventional structure of a mainstream secular rock or pop concert. In terms of informality and social interaction, they are much closer to small church-based programs than to pop music events held in large clubs or concert halls. Seats are not reserved. House lights are never turned out (or even dimmed) to create a gulf between artist and audience. Groups move instruments and equipment on and off the stage while others are singing or being announced. Audience members and singers constantly walk about during performances, congregate in the back to chat, or run downstairs to grab dinner. Even the featured out-of-town artists sometimes sit in the back or just outside the main hall to sell records and socialize.

Dressing rooms—usually shared by the headliners and the locals— are basically open to the public, and are often packed with friends and family.

Ironically, today's commercial gospel shows in New York City actually share more in common with the pre-1950 programs than with the huge gospel extravaganzas of the 1950s and the early 1960s. As was the norm prior to 1950, current amateur groups sing alongside the most successful professional stars. Indeed, locals often take up as much as three quarters of the time at an average program. Although they are under stringent time constraints, they usually find a way to recognize friends, family or local clergy. When Phil Johnson of the Spiritual Voices pauses between songs to acknowledge the minister of his neighborhood church, there is a deep sense of social communion, even in a hall filled with nearly a thousand people. Local groups often bring their own fans who serve as "cheerleaders" when they take the floor. The audience may be large, but for the local performers it is hardly anonymous. The singers' direct, personal interaction with their listeners fosters an atmosphere of intimacy and informality, even in large, seemingly impersonal settings. Moreover, while the local singers relate to their audience with a degree of familiarity, the professionals too have built significant followings of loyal devotees within the New York church community. Touring groups establish their own local social networks through promoters and the local groups with whom they perform. More often than not they are personally acquainted with at least some of their listeners. And even when professionals sing before a relatively anonymous African-American congregation, shared cultural and spiritual bonds allow for an immediacy of rapport, paving the way for more direct, personal communication. When the Dixie Hummingbirds, a group that has been performing in New York for years, come to town for Big Dan's Anniversary at Bright Light Baptist Church, they will not be singing in an impersonal environment to a totally anonymous audience. Rather, they are drawn into the complex web of social and cultural relations, emerging as ancillary members of New York's African-American church community.

Most importantly, nearly all participants view the higher-priced ticket shows primarily as sacred church events and secondarily as entertainment. The promoter and headlining act are, to be sure, concerned with producing a spectacular show that will attract a large crowd and turn a profit. And audience members willing to spend fifteen dollars or more for a ticket certainly expect exceptional singing executed in a professional manner. Yet the vast majority in attendance, including most of the local groups, are first and foremost out to "have a good time in the name of the Lord." Hence the emcee and singers are constantly reminding everyone that they are gathered to "have church" and not simply "to see a show." If a group gets in the Spirit and runs over its allotted performance time, tensions may arise with the promoter, who is trying to keep the program on schedule. The headliners are kept waiting and some audience members complain the stars will appear too late or will be cut short. But everyone understands that the Holy Spirit does not comply with human clocks, and the program goes on, even if the promotor has to pay additional rent to keep the church or hall open for an extra hour.

The real proof that the spiritual dimensions of the larger quartet programs are not eclipsed by commercial concerns lies in the fact that people do indeed "have church." Even in the late 1950s, when huge gospel programs were being held in secular spaces like the Apollo Theatre, the events never lost their "churchy" feel. Thurman Ruth claims that women would regularly "get happy" and throw their pocketbooks, even in the larger theaters and auditoriums. Groups would inevitably shout the house, dissolving a carefully scheduled show into timeless sacred ritual. Apollo manager Bobby Schiffman recalls that "the gospel shows had a way of throwing the schedules out of whack because when the Holy Spirit arrived, the theater would go into pandemonium and time went by the wayside. It was something you could not control."[7] Today the frequency of ecstatic worship and Spirit possession by groups and audience members at large shows is roughly equivalent to that in smaller programs. The expanse of space is rarely an inhibiting factor, unless the event is sparsely attended and audience members sit widely dispersed. A packed hall of 500 gospel enthusiasts will yield as much shouting and holy dance as an intimate gathering of fifty in a storefront church.

Rigid dichotomies like commercial versus noncommercial, professional versus local, popular versus folk, and secular entertainment versus sacred ritual are overly reductive and ultimately misleading when applied to the classification of gospel quartets or the events in which they sing. Rather the situation is best viewed in terms of a continuum in which age, commercial aspirations, artistic concerns, level of performance stylization, degree of interpersonal communication, perceived sincerity of spiritual commitment, and audience size, nature, and location serve as the primary variables. At one end of the continuum fall groups like the Heavenly Tones, the Faithful Harmonizers, the Golden Jubilees, and Charlie Storey and the All Stars. Their members tend to be older, all with day jobs or retired. Their singing is confined almost exclusively to small New York programs and anniversaries where their audience consists primarily of friends, family, fellow singers and churchgoers. On rare occasions they are invited to perform on larger programs with professional quartets. They are always ready to sing for little or no money and regularly raise funds for needy churches. Several have poorly recorded vanity label albums with limited distribution. They sing in a powerful but relatively unstylized fashion: they frown on flamboyant showmanship, but often "get happy" during performances. While they enjoy the social camaraderie of rehearsals and singing for acquaintances, spiritual mission takes precedence. Their audiences know that their religious commitment is beyond question, that they truly "live the life." Such groups usually succeed in conveying a spiritual feeling to the congregation, even if one of their members is absent, a guitar is slightly out of tune, or a difficult turn in the harmony is not perfectly executed.

Moving along the continuum, we come to groups like the Brooklyn Skyways, the Wearyland Singers, the Biblettes, and the Mighty Gospel Giants. They consist of middle-aged individuals who work full-time day jobs or manage small businesses. At some point in their careers they flirted with the notion of going professional, but for financial and familial reasons decided against the move. They are satisfied with the status of semi-professional locals. Most of their singing is confined to the New York area, but occasionally they travel out of town to appear on programs and anniversaries of groups they have worked with over the years. In New York they sing at small church programs and often appear on larger ticket shows with the professionals. Sometimes they know their audiences on a personal, intimate level and at other times they do not. They are usually paid something for singing, although most of their fees go toward travel, uniform, and equipment expenses. Singing gratis for local anniversaries and worthy causes is not uncommon. They too have vanity press albums that move only through self distribution. Stylistically they are rooted in the postwar hard gospel sound, though they are capable of rendering an occasional smooth contemporary number.[8] Their performances are relatively stylized, characterized by lengthy testimonies, semi-choreographed dance steps, and processionals. Their spiritual commitment is considered sound by most, although some older community members occasionally accuse them of excessive showmanship.

Next come groups like the Ecstatistics, the Spiritual Voices, and the Golden Sons. They are young, ambitious, poised on the brink of going professional. They still have day jobs, but sing every weekend, splitting their time between the larger New York programs and out-of-town engagements. They expect to be paid for their services. They have more professionally produced recordings and tapes that get no national distribution, but occasionally air on New York's WWRL. With the right break and a recording on a nationally distributed label they would probably move to full-time touring. In keeping with the trends of the commercial industry these younger groups have successfully adopted the contemporary choir sound to a quartet format, mixing smoother modern compositions with more traditional hard gospel numbers. Their presentations are highly stylized, making generous use of theatrical devices including choreographed dance steps, acting out song lyrics, tearing off jackets, jumping off stages, and running up and down the aisles. They are in the precarious position of impressing local audiences with their spiritual sincerity while polishing their show in order to command healthy performance fees, particularly when they venture out of town. Some listeners are convinced of their religious commitment, while others dismiss their antics as the "showboating" of spiritual charlatans.

At the far end of the continuum is the small group of professional quartets that sing for a living. They reach a relatively large, anonymous black audience through recordings and radio. They tour full time, singing approximately four nights a week in different cities, mainly for black churchgoers who attend large ticket programs. In terms of interpersonal communication, they are farthest removed from their audience, although the gulf by no means approaches the level of anonymity experienced by secular pop stars. The middle-aged and older groups rely almost exclusively on a traditional gospel repertoire, while some of the younger singers introduce more contemporary sounds and compositions. Performances must be tight, highly stylized, and of impeccable quality to justify their hefty fees. They are all great showmen, but the best dispense with the most pretentious theatrics, relying rather on their vocal virtuosity, their subtle use of movement and dance, and their repertoire of greatest hits to get over with audiences. They do get happy, or at least appear to get happy, when they perform. More often than not they live up to their title of "house wreckers" by bringing down the Spirit. Many of the more conservative churchgoers, however, question their spiritual sincerity, arguing that they are singing for the almighty dollar rather than Almighty God.

Quartets slide along this continuum at different points in their careers. All begin as local church singers. The most talented advance to the ranks of semi-professionals and a few move on to become full time singers. During the late 1950s, the Brooklyn All Stars and the Skylight Singers made the jump. The Skylights eventually came off the road and returned to their earlier status as semi-professional local singers.[9] The Brooklyn Skyways, the Mighty Gospel Giants, and the

Singingaires were on the brink of professional careers in the late 1950s and early 1960s, but eventually cut back and settled for singing part-time. Whether the Golden Sons or Spiritual Voices will move a notch closer to professionalism remains to be seen. Most New York singers appear to be satisfied with their status as local singers. They enjoy out-of-town work when the occasion arises, but remain primarily committed to their local following.

Although the most spiritual amateur quartets and the most ambitious professional quartets lie at opposite ends of the continuum, their careers are inextricably intertwined. The majors serve as models of artistic excellence for the local singers. The former's commercial success and high social status within the black church community attract younger singers into the fold and serve to bolster the self-esteem of older performers. Appearing with the professionals on large ticket programs allows the best local singers a chance to be heard by large audiences and provides hungry young groups with a potential springboard for vaulting into a more commercial realm. For their part, the local groups serve as valuable training grounds for younger singers who may someday move into the ranks of professionalism. Further, the locals maintain a strong community interest in quartet singing, and thereby nurture the substantial audience necessary to support the professional singers. Without the locals' promotional assistance and their enthusiastic followers, it would be difficult to turn out sizable crowds for live shows. But perhaps most importantly, the home groups are a constant reminder that gospel programs are sacred events. In this capacity they keep the professional groups spiritually honest. The locals' presence serves to hold in check the commercial and entertainment concerns that might otherwise overwhelm a presentation that consisted exclusively of professional singers.

The question of spiritual commitment versus financial gain continues to spark fierce debate between those quartet singers with professional aspirations and those who consciously choose to stay at home. If "salvation is free," as most contend, how can groups justify charging money for services that are theoretically part of their spiritual mission? On the other hand, if God gives an individual the "gift of song," should not the church financially support his or her calling to "sing the Word"? There are no clear answers. Many of the older, community singers like James Fitzpatrick of the Heavenly Tones view spiritual and financial concerns as contradictory:

Now if you ask a famous group—like the Dixie Hummingbirds—to come to your church, and they tell you we'll be there for so many thousand dollars, you know they are just coming for the money. And they're going to give the audience a good show, but there ain't no God in there. They just come and give a good show for the greenback. Or you ask a local group to come to your anniversary, and they say, "Well look brother, we'll come for a hundred dollars." But you see, they done killed the Spirit right there. They're just doing it for the dollar![10]

On the other hand, aspiring young quartet singers like Darrell McFadden of the Golden Sons see no serious conflict in singing God's praises for money:

I count it [getting paid to sing] as a blessing. He [God] awards us for doing good work, it's one of the rewards we receive. Now you don't always have to be blessed in a financial way, you can be blessed in a spiritual way. I mean plenty of times we do programs where I just felt good about singing, we didn't have to get anything [pay]. Around here in Brooklyn, this is our home, this is where we started. We don't mind doing charities and benefits, we can't neglect our local churches. But if it's a money making program, we see to it that we get ours. If the promoter benefits from it, we are getting paid too. If we're drawing in people for him [the promoter], it's no more than right that we get ours. . . . People accept us for what we are. That's why we're one of leading male quartets in the New York area. See God has blessed the Golden Sons, we have a strong spiritual contract. We are ambassadors for Christ! And with God, all things are possible. We can make good money, thousands of dollars apiece, and I'm claiming it. We're going to make it.[11]

Money aside, all New York quartet singers must pay heed to religious and artistic concerns if they are to produce acceptable "spiritual entertainment." Those who remain community based must emphasize their spiritual integrity if they are to survive, while those who gravitate toward professionalism must place priority on creating presentations that are artistically innovative and entertaining to an audience of paying customers. In either case they occupy an intriguing zone where art, commercialism, and religion overlap.

The debate over spirituality and commercial success among quartet singers is simply one manifestation of a larger issue concerning the relationship between sacred and secular African-American artistic expressions. Since the days of slavery, the music of the black folk church has existed in a dialectical tension with whatever secular music was popular at the time.[12] As Albert Murray astutely puts it, the "blue devils" and the "holy ghost" have long wrestled for the souls of black folks during their respective Saturday night and Sunday morning rituals.[13] The struggle continued in spite of the widely acknowledged irony that African-American sacred and secular musical traditions sprang from a common source and have fed each other for centuries. The situation intensified with the advent of commercial radio and recordings in the 1920s. Mass media greatly facilitated the exchange of musical ideas between church and "worldly" singers, while tempting the former to package their religion for commercial consumption, and in some cases to abandon their faith altogether for more lucrative careers as secular performers. These developments led to the assumption that gospel music, including quartet singing, was drifting in a steadily secular direction, a movement accelerated by the postwar recording boom and the burgeoning popularity of gospel-derived soul music in the early 1960s. Kip Lornell takes this stance in arguing that the trend toward secularization of gospel quartets in the 1950s contributed to their eventual decline in popularity:

The spiritual folks slowly became dissatisfied with the increasing secularization of gospel music by quartets. They saw gospel quartets being treated like popular music stars, riding in large, expensive automobiles, wearing fine clothes, and making generous salaries. Many church members felt that some quartets had moved too far from the spirit and ideals of the Lord's teachings, causing them to look with disfavor upon the more commercial, ostentatious groups.[14]

Lornell claims that Memphis quartets lost their community base when promoters began pushing large gospel extravaganzas in secular settings such as halls and auditoriums. In such settings, he contends, showmanship and popular secular tastes prevailed.[15] There is certainly some truth to this argument, and it is often repeated by older singers who cannot reconcile singing for the Lord and singing for financial gain. Further, it is undeniable that the number of professional quartets increased dramatically in the postwar years. Yet the presumption of a movement toward secularization ignores certain fundamental changes in quartet performance style that suggests another interpretation.

The transition from jubilee- to gospel-style quartet singing in the immediate postwar years coincided with the emergence of a decisively more spiritual, evangelical atmosphere at live performances. The prewar jubilee/harmonizing quartets stood flat-footed and concentrated on producing beautiful harmony. Further, some of the best known New York groups, including the college-trained Utica Jubilee Singers and the Southernaires, as well as the Norfolk Jubilee Singers and the Golden Gates, recorded and broadcast folk, jazz, and blues numbers as well as their sacred repertoire. The latter two occasionally appeared at secular clubs like the Cafe Society Downtown where they enjoyed a middle class, predominantly non-black following. But the situation changed radically with the rise of hard gospel quartet singing, as groups incorporated various aspects of demonstrative southern worship into their performances. Granted, the testifying, preaching, and holy dancing were often codified into semichoreographed formats and sometimes lacked the spontaneity of bona fide church practices, but the results were no less impressive. The audiences did shout, they did fall out, they did indeed "have church." Paradoxically, while the music gained in commercial appeal, the performances became more religious in tone. Gatherings at large auditoriums were ritualistically transformed into church-like events. Groups who sang or recorded secular material jeopardized their standing with church audiences.

While the number of professional gospel quartets proliferated during the 1950s, overall developments in the singing tradition could hardly be characterized as a move toward secularization. In terms of performance style the process moved rather in the opposite direction, toward "sacredization." But why this turn of events? Surely it was due in part to the changing nature of quartet audiences. As outlined in the previous chapter, by the postwar years local and professional quartets were singing almost exclusively to working-class, evangelical southern African-Americans, who were willing and financially able to support popular entertainment that was deeply rooted in southern religion. Perhaps the renewed emphasis on spirituality served further as a subconscious safeguard for singers and their followers, who realized the potential hazards posed by the increasing commercial potential of gospel quartet music. They rightfully feared that the temptation of financial gain might lure singers and fans away from church and into the clutches of the corrupt secular world. If they were going to indulge in popular entertainment, the show had to be so firmly anchored in sacred behavior that the participants would not accidentally backslide into worldly mirth. They could not allow Saturday night to encroach on Sunday morning. To ensure against such transgressions gospel quartet singers had to do more than produce the beautiful harmonies of their jubilee/harmonizing predecessors. They had to sing, preach, and testify God's word until He sent the Holy Ghost into their midst. The strategy was good but not perfect. Many fine quartet singers, including Sam Cooke, Lou Rawls, and Wilson Pickett, defected to the world of pop and soul music. But most stayed, and as a result gospel quartet singing remained firmly grounded in the African-American church experience. A quintessential expression of black sacred culture, the quartet tradition stood firm against the onslaught of the European-American controlled secular marketplace. Though it did not escape unscathed, its integrity was unquestionably preserved, and today quartet singing is one of the last repositories of traditional southern-style singing in the commercial gospel field.

In recent years traditional gospel quartet singing has again come under siege, but this time the threat stems from within its own ranks. The rise in popularity of the contemporary choir sound is now posing a serious challenge to the older, southern-style gospel soloists and quartet singers. While most New York church audiences still favor the down-home gospel sound, the commercial recording and radio industries have embraced contemporary gospel in earnest. In response the younger New York quartets are gradually, and with a degree of previously described caution, adapting the smoother modern style to the small harmony group format. On one hand, this signals a serious break from older church traditions, for contemporary gospel compositions lack the stridently evangelical message of the older hard gospel songs, and they are rendered in a relatively restrained manner that rarely leads church people to shout. Yet most contemporary quartet singing remains spiritual in essence. Modern songs and performance styles are introduced in the context of sacred ritual, usually sandwiched around more traditional hymns and hard gospel songs. The emergence of contemporary-style quartets should not be misinterpreted as simply another move toward secularization that will lead to the inevitable demise of the tradition. On the contrary, this latest stylistic innovation underscores the flexibility and tenacity of sacred quartets, as a new generation of African-American church singers strives to transform small group harmony singing in response to the changing tastes and experiences of their younger audiences. From this perspective we can be guardedly optimistic about the future of sacred quartet singing within the African-American church.

Notes

1. By the 1960s folklorists were grappling with models that suggested interrelationships between folk, popular (mass), and elite (academic) art forms. Yet they continued to draw sharp distinctions between such forms, defining "folk" as traditional, conservative, self-conscious, and reflexive. See Henry Glassie, *Pattern in the Material Folk Culture of the Eastern United States* (Philadelphia: University of Pennsylvania Press, 1968), pp. 1–33; and Roger Abrahams and George Foss, *Anglo-American Folksong Style* (Englewood Cliffs, NJ: Prentice Hall, 1968), pp. 4–11. In his later writings Abrahams proposes a continuum between folk, popular, and high art based on the level of personal interaction between performer and audience. This latter approach informs the analysis presented here. See Roger Abrahams, "The Complex Relations of Simple Forms," in Dan Ben-Amos, ed., *Folklore Genres* (Austin: University of Texas Press, 1976), pp. 193–214.

For a critical review of the folk/popular dichotomy in folksong scholarship see Richard Middleton, "Editor's Introduction to Volume 1" in Richard Middleton and David Horn, eds., *Popular Music* Vol.1 (Cambridge: Cambridge University Press, 1981), pp. 3–7, and Philip Bohlman, *The Study of Folk Music in the Modern World* (Bloomington: Indiana University Press, 1988), pp. xiii–xx.

2. John Blacking, "Making Artistic Popular Music: The Goal of the True Folk," in Middleton and Horn, eds., *Popular Music*, pp. 9–13.

3. Charles Keil argues that blues and polka recordings tend to reflect an Apollonian sense of dreamlike perfection that is dialectically opposed to the Dionysian-like collective intoxication of live performance. The model works well for gospel quartet recordings and performance. See Charles Keil, "People's Music Comparatively: Style and Stereotype, Class and Hegemony," *Dialectical Anthropology* 10 (1985): 119–130.

4. For a sobering description of the hazards of life on the road as a professional gospel singer, see Heilbut, *Gospel Sound*, pp. 255–263.

5. Personal interview with Willie Johnson, March 24, 1986.

6. Lornell, *"Happy in the Service of the Lord"*, pp. 94–95.

7. Ted Fox, *Showtime at the Apollo* (New York: Holt, Rinehart and Winston, 1983), p.231. For an intriguing account of gospel music at the Apollo during the 1950s see pp. 214–238.

8. Middle-aged groups like the Skyways and Wearyland Singers often use younger musicians, who introduce more contemporary stylistic elements into the groups' sound.

9. Lornell notes a similar phenomenon among Memphis groups such as the Spirit of Memphis, who enjoyed a successful touring and recording career during the 1950s before coming off the road and resuming status as semi-professional singers in the early 1960s. See Lornell, *"Happy in the Service of the Lord"*, p. 60.

10. Interview with James Fitzpatrick, March 18, 1986.

11. Interviews with Darrell McFadden, August 18, 1987, and June 25, 1989.

12. For further information on the relationship between sacred and secular music during slavery see Dena Epstein, *Sinful Tunes and Spirituals* (Urbana: University of Illinois Press, 1977), pp. 207–216.

13. Albert Murray, *Stomping the Blues* (New York: Random House, 1976), pp. 21–42.

14. Lornell, *"Happy in the Service of the Lord"*, p. 32.

15. Ibid., p. 100. See also p. 59.

Chapter 10
By and By
The Future of Sacred Quartet Singing

Most observers contend that sacred African-American quartet singing reached its zenith between the mid-1940s and the late 1950s. Following this fifteen year period, when quartets dominated the
commercial gospel field, the tradition supposedly suffered an irre-
versible decline in popularity, as Doug Seroff laments:

The golden age of gospel quartet ended more than twenty-five years ago
[roughly 1960]. The intervening period has witnessed the transformation of
traditional quartet singing into precipitate anachronism. What was univer-
sally understood a generation ago has become obscure in the present. Black
vocal quartets play no significant role in "contemporary" gospel music.[1]

By "traditional quartet singing" Seroff is evidently referring to the
older jubilee and early gospel quartets that emphasized tight harmony singing with little or no instrumental accompaniment. His assessment is relatively accurate with regard to the commercial arena,
although it ignores the fact that a dozen or more big-name quartets
continue to tour and receive ample radio play, while significant numbers of younger groups are experimenting with contemporary gospel. But Seroff and others whose musical tastes tend toward the
antiquated miss the point that, while singing styles change, the basic
small group harmony unit survives. On today's quartet recordings,
lead singers often overshadow the background, bass singers have all
but vanished, and instruments tend to clutter the sound at the expense of the singing. But in live performance, groups like the Blind
Boys of Alabama, the Gospel Keynotes, or the Jackson Southernaires
still produce exhilarating vocal harmonies with a down-home flavor
that ignite church audiences.

Fortunately Seroff tempers his gloomy forecast by noting the existence of a strong community-based quartet tradition in Birmingham, a phenomenon that endures in spite of the whims of the gospel industry.[2] Kip Lornell notes a similar trend in Memphis, stating:

> With quartet singing all but out of the free-wheeling commercial market, the future of this type of music seems to lie with community quartets. Despite a timorous revival of interest in quartet singing since 1980, there are no sure signs that this music will ever again enjoy a strong base of commercial support. Small group harmony singing has been such a basic, important form of black religious music, though, that its impact will no doubt be felt for many years.[3]

Whether professional groups like the Winans or Take Six will successfully adapt group harmony singing to the trends of the contemporary gospel industry and thus rejuvenate the commercial potential of quartet singing remains to be seen. But at present, the strength of quartet singing does indeed appear to lie in community-based performance. Between 1985 and 1989 I personally observed at least a hundred local quartets in New York City, Long Island, and northern New Jersey. But the scene is so immense that this sampling may represent only the tip of the iceberg. New groups are always appearing at programs, and older ones carry on unnoticed outside the confines of their small church networks. Definitive statistics are simply unavailable, but it is not unreasonable to surmise that hundreds of African-American quartets are active in New York City. While the older a cappella singing that Seroff venerates is certainly a rarity today, the notion that small group harmony singing represents an anachronistic survival is unfounded. Lornell correctly asserts that the small harmony group—whether labeled quartet or gospel group—will continue to exert a significant impact on black religious song for some time to come.

Two further observations bode well for the future vitality of quartet singing in New York. First, in keeping with a long-standing tradition, middle-aged and older groups continue to incorporate younger singers into their ranks. For example, groups such as the Brooklyn Skyways, the Mighty Gospel Giants, the Wearyland Singers, the Sunset Jubilee Singers, and the No Name Gospel Singers have cross-generational personnel. This arrangement assures a degree of continuity in tradition as elements of style and repertoire are passed from older to younger singers. An even more promising sign is the significant number of high quality young groups that are presently active in and around New York. In addition to the Spiritual Voices, Ecstatics, and Golden Sons there are fresh talents like the Soul

Convertors of the Bronx, the Brown Family of Hempstead (Long Island), and the House Wrecking Bibleways of Brooklyn.

The persistence of the small harmony group in New York and elsewhere as a basic social and performance unit is remarkable. Evidently there is something deep and fundamental about the resonance of one-on-a-part vocal harmony that larger choral ensembles or choirs fail to capture. Granted, the parts themselves have changed over the years with the loss of the bass and the addition of the high tenor and/or background lead, but the basic structure of four or five human voices chording together remains intact and appealing. Further, the small vocal group is quite practical in terms of organization and transportation. Even with the addition of non-singing musicians, a group of eight or nine is considerably easier to rehearse and move around than a choir of forty or fifty voices. The former can fit in two cars or a van, the latter demands a bus or a fleet of automobiles. In terms of social dynamics the small vocal group offers the opportunity for intimate camaraderie that larger choirs do not. Although tensions always arise, years of rehearsing and singing together often lead to life-long friendships among group members. The group may become the center of social life as well as the primary outlet for creative expression.

In contemplating the possibility of a revival of interest in quartet singing during the 1980s, Kip Lornell proposes a cyclic model, suggesting that "at least in Memphis, black gospel quartet singing has moved full circle from the folk tradition to popular culture and back again. Perhaps this cycle will begin once more."[4] This theory is useful in describing the careers of certain individual groups such as the Spirit of Memphis or New York's Skylight Singers, but it falls short as a broader paradigm. Quartet singing has been a popular folk tradition in New York and other urban areas since at least the 1920s. Certain groups did receive significant media attention and moved into the realm of popular entertainment during certain periods—the Utica Jubilee Singers during the late 1920s, the Southernaires and Golden Gate Quartet during the 1930s and 1940s, the Selah Jubilee Singers during the 1940s, and the Skylights and the Brooklyn All Stars during the 1950s and 1960s. But the community folk scene has continued throughout. Indeed, local activity unquestionably increased dramatically during the postwar years, but the degree to which it has subsided is difficult to calculate. Charlie Storey claims there were more quartets in New York during the 1950s and early 1960s than there are today. The Reverend Edward Cook of the Mighty Gospel Giants surmises local activity peaked during the early 1970s, while promoter "Big Dan" McCallum believes there are as many or more groups active today as there were thirty-five years ago. Because the community groups have been so poorly documented, an accurate assessment is probably impossible. The trends of the commercial industry may be somewhat cyclical, but community support for quartet singing in New York has been ongoing and shows no immediate signs of abating.

The final problem confronting the researcher working with a specific community is the application of local interpretations to the broader field of study. To what extent is New York's African-American local quartet scene representative of black religious music cultures in other parts of the United States? Are there networks of local quartet singers in other northern, western, and southern cities? If so, do they sing at ritualized programs and anniversaries similar to those in New York City? Are their performances organized and evaluated in the same manner as the ones described in this inquiry? Does gospel quartet performance hold the same deep meanings in terms of southern religion and identity maintenance for singers outside the New York City community, say in Chicago, in Atlanta, or even in rural Mississippi? While it is impossible to offer conclusive answers to all these questions, there is ample evidence that similar community-based quartet scenes do exist in many regions of the United States. Surveying the development of the tradition, Kip Lornell cites Birmingham, Norfolk, Atlanta, Jacksonville, Chicago, Detroit, and Cleveland as early "strongholds" of community quartet singing.[5] Doug Seroff mentions Birmingham (and the adjacent cities of Fairfield and Bessemer, Alabama), Dallas, Houston, New Orleans, and Chicago.[6] A 1987 survey, conducted by folklorist Michael Licht for the District of Columbia Commission on the Arts and Humanities, identified more than 150 gospel groups and quartets in the Washington, DC area. Licht's description of the local scene is familiar:

The Nation's Capitol is home to a vital tradition of Afro-American sacred music. The District's 500 Black congregations support well over 1000 choirs and ensembles . . . The sounds of praise do not cease at the end of Sunday's church services. Each week our neighborhoods reverberate with two or three gospel programs featuring dozens of Washington's active groups and quartets. The eloquent and joyous testimony of these artists links the deep heritage of spiritual, jubilee, and gospel traditions with contemporary musical styles, making an underlying message of faith accessible to today's listeners.[7]

A valuable series of regional anthologies produced by the British-based Heritage label documents the popularity of sacred black quartet singing in a number of United States cities. To date, volumes devoted to reissued recordings of New Orleans (HT 306), Detroit (HT 311), Atlanta (HT 312), San Francisco (HT 314), Cleveland (HT 316) and Newark (HT 324) quartets have been released, with compilations featuring Chicago, St. Louis, Cincinnati, and Charlotte singers in production. While these anthologies focus on the more professional groups that recorded during the 1930s, 1940s, and 1950s, liner notes attest to the existence and influence of non-professional groups who sang primarily in local churches. For example, in his assessment of the San Francisco Bay area, researcher Ray Funk concludes:

Community based a cappella religious quartets became popular by the late thirties. Although there were probably such groups much earlier, it is in the late thirties with the influx of new residents from Arkansas, Louisiana and Texas searching for work in the shipyards and on the docks that these groups seem to have become popular. This population explosion brought to the Bay Area a large number of young men who had grown up singing in southern churches, sometimes in choirs, sometimes in family groups and often in quartets. Within a few years, they caused an upsurge in local quartets.[8]

Recent ethnographic studies that include information on local quartet singing are promising. From the works of Kip Lornell (in Memphis), Doug Seroff (in Birmingham), Lynn Abbot (in New Orleans), Daniel Patterson (in the Raleigh/Durham area of North Carolina), Burt Feintuch (in rural Kentucky), and David Evans (in rural Mississippi),[9] along with my own observations in Philadelphia and Newark,[10] we can conjecture that the general quartet performance patterns observed in New York are typical of those practiced by African-American gospel groups in other towns and cities. The evolution and cultural significance of sacred quartet performance described in this work is by no means restricted to New York City. It is unquestionably a story that has been repeated, albeit with important local variations, in African-American church communities across the United States. On any spring or fall Sunday afternoon, in any major city with a significant African-American population, it is safe to assume that a gospel quartet is singing. From New York to Chicago to Atlanta to Los Angeles, groups take to the floors of small churches to testify, preach, sing, and shout the gospel message in a cathartic spiritual outpouring meant to transcend, at least momentarily, the hardships of earthly struggle. Quartets weave together performance strategies according to traditional aesthetic norms, creating spiritual entertainment meant to please the ear and strengthen the soul. Their ritualized performances celebrate a rich southern African-American heritage, soothe the stormy transition to modern urban life, and help bind together a community of believers.

The need for further research and comparative analysis of African-American sacred community quartet singing remains a pressing concern. The knotty relationship of performance style, belief, and urbanization demands additional interpretation. In particular the urban/rural, north/south identity question may exhibit significant regional variations that will only be fully understood when additional comparative data are available. The impact of contemporary gospel music on small group harmony singing is yet another area that will demand more extensive consideration. The shift from traditional hard gospel to the smoother contemporary sound may indeed have profound implications for younger singers in terms of their self-identification, their religious world view, and their overall relationship to the dominant secular culture.

In addition to quartet singing, there are other areas of African-American religious music that urgently need investigation. The community-based choirs, like those studied by Mellonee Burnim in Indianapolis, have become increasingly popular among younger African-American singers over the past twenty-five years.[11] Intriguing questions come to mind. Why are many younger people choosing to join choirs rather than smaller quartets or groups? How does the training, performance, and evaluation of choirs compare with that of quartets? Do choirs cater to a different audience, and, if so, what is the make-up and character of that audience? Why are more women attracted to choirs than to quartets, and what can their experiences reveal concerning the gender issues of gospel performance?

And finally, there is an appalling lack of information on sanctified music and song, as well as other forms of twentieth century African-American church-related singing. This is particularly surprising in light of the widely acknowledged fact that sanctified music and worship practices form the foundation of much post-1930 gospel music. Only with better historical and ethnographic-based descriptions of sanctified worship and expressive performance—song, music, dance, testimony, prayer, and preaching—will the evolution of gospel song and gospel quartets come into clearer focus.

In closing I offer a final plea for the continued and expanded ethnographic study of community-based American vernacular musics. Compiling the biographies of the major figures and constructing the commercial history of any popular music expression—be it black gospel, rhythm and blues, jazz, soul, country western, rockabilly, rock and roll, salsa, soca, or zydeco—is certainly a worthy undertaking.

But listening to recordings, viewing videos, and critiquing performances by a handful of commercial stars does not produce the necessary data for understanding the deeper meanings that these musical
expressions hold for artists and the members of their communities.
The manner in which these styles function in local, non-commercial
settings must also be investigated, using the techniques of ethnographic observation, participation, and interviewing. We must become intimately familiar with artists, audiences, and the
organizational patterns of local performances before we move towards better interpretation of community-based music cultures. Only
then can we begin to understand how musical expressions shape and
reflect social values, mediate deep-seated conflicts, and serve as markers of ethnic identity, group solidarity, and regional pride. The
breadth of community-based musical activity in this country is nothing short of astounding, and offers those culturally oriented students
of American music a rich and challenging field of study.

Notes

1. Seroff, "On the Battlefield," p. 45.
2. Ibid., pp. 45–51. Seroff ends his essay on an optimistic note, suggesting
that due to the "timeless" nature of harmony singing, the "re-emergence of
a cappella quartet singing seems almost inevitable."
3. Lornell, *"Happy in the Service of the Lord"*, p. 33.
4. Ibid., p. 33.
5. Lornell, *"Happy in the Service of the Lord"*, pp. 19–20.
6. Seroff, "On the Battlefield," pp. 34–45.
7. Michael Licht, "DC Gospel Groups 1987," from a survey by the Folk
Arts Program of the DC Commission on the Arts and Humanities, 1987.
8. Ray Funk, liner notes to "San Francisco Bay Gospel," Heritage HT 314,
LP Record, 1987.
9. Lornell, *"Happy in the Service of the Lord"*; Seroff, "On the Battlefield";
Lynn Abbott, "The Soproco Singers: A New Orleans Quartet Family Tree"
(New Orleans: National Park Service, 1983); Patterson, "Going Up to Meet
Him"; Feintuch, "A Non-Commercial Black Gospel Group in Context";
Evans, "Roots of Afro-American Gospel Music."
10. In addition to my work in the New York City community, I have also
done extensive field work with local gospel groups in Philadelphia (1983–
1984), Memphis (1980–1982), and Newark (1985).
11. Mellonee Burnim, "The Black Gospel Music Tradition: Symbol of
Ethnicity," Ph.D. dissertation, Indiana University, 1980.

Listening and Viewing

The written word can never completely communicate musical experience. The reader must become listener and viewer if she or he is to appreciate fully the sacred quartet performances described in this book. The No Name Gospel Singers, Charlie Storey and the All Stars, the Golden Jubilees, the Heavenly Tones, and the Faithful Harmonizers can be heard on an album/cassette series entitled "New York Grassroots Gospel: The Sacred Black Quartet Tradition" (Global Village Music GVM-206). The series, which includes a booklet with extensive notes and song annotations, is available through Global Village Music, Box 2051 Cathedral Station, New York, NY, 10025. The No Name Gospel Singers have produced their own live concert tape that can be acquired by writing to: T.N.N.G.S., C/O Aaron Chestnut, Box 64 Brownsville Station, Brooklyn, NY 11212.

The other local gospel quartets mentioned in this study appear on small vanity labels with limited distributions. The Ecstatistics recordings are available from Gospel Talent Sounds Inc., 176 Herkimer St., Brooklyn, NY 11216. Cassettes of the Golden Sons can be obtained from Robert Campbell, 308 Chauncey St., Brooklyn, NY 11233. The Biblettes has its own label: Biblettes Records, P.O. Box 8380, Newark, NJ, 07108. Recordings of Wonder Boy and the Spiritual Voices can be purchased directly from Phil's Barber Shop on Ralph Avenue in Brooklyn. The Brooklyn Skyways and the Mighty Gospel Giants have recorded for Savoy Records, which is now owned by Maleco Records, 3023 W. Northside Drive, Jackson, MS 39213. Maleco is currently a leading producer and distributer of modern gospel quartet music; hopefully the company will begin reissuing its Savoy gospel material in the near future.

Recent reissues of jubilee and early gospel quartet recordings include performances by early New York quartets mentioned in this work. "From Jubilee to Gospel: A Selection of Commercially Recorded Black Religious Music, 1921-1953," (John Edwards Memorial Foundation JEMF-108), compiled by William Tallmadge, features selections by the Utica Jubilee Singers, the Golden Gate Quartet, the Norfolk Jazz Quartet, the Alphabetical Four, and the Selah Jubilee Singers. Anthony Heilbut's "All of My Appointed Time, Forty Years of A Cappella Gospel" (Stash Records ST-114) includes selections by the Golden Gate Quartet, Georgia Peach and the Harmonaires, the Soul Stirrers, and the Kings of Harmony. The classic recordings of the Norfolk Jubilee Singers can be heard on "Norfolk Jubilee Quartet," (Heritage HT 310), compiled by Ray Funk (the entire Heritage jubilee/gospel quartet series is outstanding). "I Hear Music in the Air/ A Treasury of Gospel Music" (RCA CD 2099-2-R) includes three superb sides by the Golden Gate Quartet, as well as selections by the Newark-based Southern Sons. Two other reissue compilations provide excellent introductions to the early southern gospel quartet tradition. Doug Seroff's "Birmingham Quartet Anthology: Jefferson County, Alabama (1926-1953)" (Clanka Lanka CL-144.001), features the Birmingham Jubilee Singers, the Famous Blue Jay Singers, the Heavenly Gospel Singers and others. Anthony Heilbut's "Fathers and Sons" (Spirit Feel SF-1001) includes the original Soul Stirrers, the Five Blind Boys of Mississippi, and the Sensational Nightingales. These and other reissue recordings can be ordered through Down Home Music, 1031 San Pablo Ave., El Cerrito, CA 94530, or through Rounder Records, One Camp Street, Cambridge, MA 02140. An extensive discography of in print gospel recordings is found in the 1985 edition of Anthony Heilbut's *The Gospel Sound.*

To date there are two outstanding documentary films that focus on community-based gospel quartets (plans for a New York documentary film are presently under consideration). "A Singing Stream: A Black Family Chronicle," produced by Daniel Patterson and Tom Davenport, offers a fascinating glimpse into the music and family life of members of the North Carolina-based Golden Echoes. The film is available through Davenport Films, Rt. 1 Box 527, Delaplane, VA 22025. "On the Battlefield," produced by Geoffrey Hayden and Dennis Marks, with assistance from Doug Seroff, examines the history of Birmingham's rich jubilee and gospel quartet tradition. It is available through Home Vision, 5547 North Ravenswood Avenue, Chicago, IL 60640.

Of course the best way to experience gospel quartet singing is at a live performance. Weekend gospel programs occur regularly in

African-American communities throughout the country. Local record shops and radio stations are good sources of information about upcoming programs. In New York listen to WWRL (AM 1600) and check with Birdel's Records on Nostrand Avenue in Brooklyn and Rainbow Music on 125th Street in Manhattan.

Bibliography

Abbott, Lyn. *The Soproco Singers: A New Orleans Quartet Family Tree*. New Orleans: National Park Service, 1983.

Abrahams, Roger. "Introductory Remarks to a Rhetorical Theory of Folklore." *Journal of American Folklore* 81 (1968): 143–157.

———. *Deep Down in the Jungle: Negro Narrative Folklore from the Streets of Philadelphia*. 1st rev. ed. Chicago: Aldine, 1970.

———. "The Complex Relations of Simple Forms." In Dan Ben-Amos, ed., *Folklore Genres*. Austin: University of Texas Press, 1976, pp. 193–214.

———. *The Man of Words in the West Indies: Performance and the Emergence of Creole Culture*. Baltimore: Johns Hopkins University Press, 1983.

Abrahams, Roger, and Richard Bauman, eds. *"And Other Neighborly Names": Social Process and Cultural Image in Texas Folklore*. Austin: University of Texas Press, 1981.

Abrahams, Roger, and John Szwed, eds. *Afro-American Folk Culture: An Annotated Bibliography of Materials from North, Central, and South America and the West Indies*. Philadelphia: Institute for the Study of Human Issues, 1978.

Adorno, Theodore. *Introduction to the Sociology of Music*. New York: Continuum, 1976.

Allen, Barbara, and William Lynwood Montell. *From Memory to History: Using Orla Sources in Local Historical Research*. Nashville, TN: American Association for State and Local History, 1981.

Allen, Ray. "Singing in the Spirit: An Ethnography of Gospel Performance in New York City's African-American Church Community." Ph.D. dissertation, University of Pennsylvania, 1987.

———. "Gospel Quartet Performance and Ritual in New York City's African-American Church Community." *Urban Resources* 4 (Spring 1987): 13–18.

———. "African-American Sacred Quartet Singing in New York City." *New York Folklore* XIV (1988): 7–22.

Allen, William Francis, Charles Pickard Ware, Lucy McKim Garrison. *Slave Songs of the United States*. New York: A. Simpson Company, 1867.

Anderson, Jervis. *This Was Harlem: A Cultural Portrait 1900–1950*. New York: Farrar, Straus & Giroux, 1981.

Armstrong, Robert Plant. *The Affecting Presence: An Essay in Humanistic Anthropology*. Urbana: University of Illinois Press, 1971.

———. *The Powers of Presence: Consciousness, Myth, and Affecting Presence*. Philadelphia: University of Pennsylvania Press, 1981.

Baer, Hans, and Noel Polk, eds. "Special Issue: Black Church Ritual and Aesthetics." *Southern Quarterly* 23 (Spring 1985).

Baldwin, James. *Go Tell It on the Mountain*. New York: Dial, 1953.

———. *Notes of a Native Son*. Boston: Beacon, 1955.

———. *Just Above My Head*. New York: Dial, 1979.

Baraka, Amiri (LeRoi Jones). *Blues People*. New York: Morrow, 1963.

———. "Black Music: Its Roots, Its Popularity, and Its Commercial Prostitution." In William Ferris and Mary Hart, eds., *Folk Music in Modern Sound*. Jackson: University of Mississippi Press, 1982, pp. 177–193.

Barth, Fredrik. *Ethnic Groups and Boundaries*. Boston: Little and Brown, 1969.

Bauman, Richard. *Verbal Art as Performance*. Prospect Heights, IL: Waveland Press, 1977.

Bauman, Richard, and Joel Sherzer, eds. *Explorations in the Ethnography of Speaking*. New York: Cambridge University Press, 1974.

Bauman, Richard, and Americo Paredes, eds. *Toward New Perspectives in Folklore*. Austin: University of Texas Press, 1972.

Bell, Colin, and H. Newby. *Community Studies: An Introduction to the Study of the Local Community*. London: Allen and Unwin, 1971.

Ben-Amos, Dan. "Towards a Definition of Folklore in Context." *Journal of American Folklore* 84 (January/March 1971): 3–15.

———. "Analytical Categories and Ethnic Genres." In Dan Ben-Amos, ed., *Folklore Genres*. Austin: University of Texas Press, 1976.

Ben-Amos, Dan, and Kenneth Goldstein, eds. *Folklore Performance and Communication*. The Hague: Mouton and Company, 1975.

Berger, Peter, and Thomas Luckmann. *The Social Construction of Reality*. Garden City, NY: Doubleday, 1966.

Birdwhistell, Ray. *Kinesics and Context*. Philadelphia: University of Pennsylvania Press, 1970.

Blacking, John. *How Musical Is Man?* Seattle: University of Washington Press, 1973.

———. "The Problem of Ethnic Perceptions in the Semiotics of Music." In Wendy Steiner, ed., *The Sign in Music and Literature*, pp. 184–194. Austin: University of Texas Press, 1981.

———. "Making Artistic Popular Music: The Goal of the True Folk." In Richard Middleton and David Horn, eds., *Popular Music*, Volume 1. Cambridge: Cambridge University Press, 1981, pp. 9–13.

Bohlman, Philip. *The Study of Folk Music in the Modern World*. Bloomington: Indiana University Press, 1988.

Boyer, Horace. "A Comparative Analysis of Traditional and Contemporary Gospel Music." In Irene Jackson, ed., *More Than Dancing: Essays on Afro-American Music and Musicians*. Westport, CT: Greenwood Press, 1985, pp. 127–146.

———. "Contemporary Gospel Music." *Black Perspective in Music* 7 (Spring 1979): 5–11, 22–58.

———. "Gospel." *Music Educators Journal* 64 (May 1978): 34–43.

———. "Gospel Music Comes of Age." *Black World* 20 (1973): 42–48, 68–79.

Broughton, Viv. *Black Gospel*. Dorset, England: Blanford Press, 1985.

Burnim, Mellonee. "The Black Gospel Music Tradition: Symbol of Ethnicity." Ph.D. dissertation, Indiana University, 1980.

———. "The Black Gospel Music Tradition: A Complex of Ideology, Aesthetic, and Behavior." In Irene Jackson, ed., *More Than Dancing: Essays on*

Afro-American Music and Musicians, pp. 147–167. Westport: Greenwood Press, 1985, pp. 147–167.

———. "Cultural Bearer and Tradition Bearer: An Ethnomusicologist's Research on Gospel Music." *Ethnomusicology* 29 (Fall 1985): 432–447.

Chernoff, John. *African Rhythm and African Sensibility*. Chicago: University of Chicago Press, 1979.

Cone, James. *A Black Theology of Liberation*. New York: Lippincott, 1970.

———. *The Spirituals and the Blues*. New York: Seabury Press, 1972.

———. "Sanctification, Liberation, and Black Worship." *Theology Today* 53 (July, 1978): 139–152.

———. *Speaking the Truth: Ecumenism, Liberation, and Black Theology*. Grand Rapids, MI: Wm. Eerdmans, 1986.

Connolly, Harold. *A Ghetto Grows in Brooklyn*. New York: New York University Press, 1977.

Coplan, David. *In Township Tonight!: South Africa's Black City Music and Theatre*. New York: Longman, 1985.

Courlander, Harold. *Negro Folk Music USA*. New York: Columbia University Press, 1963.

Davis, George, and Fred Donald. *Blacks in the United States: A Geographic Perspective*. Boston: Houghton, Mifflin, and Company, 1975.

Davis, Gerald. *I Got the Word in Me and I Can Sing It, You Know: A Study of the Performed African-American Sermon*. Philadelphia: University of Pennsylvania Press, 1985.

DeLerma, Dominique-Rene. *Bibliography of Black Music*. Westport, CT: Greenwood Press, 1981.

DjeDje, Jacqueline Cogdell. "Change and Differentiation: The Adoption of Black American Gospel Music in the Catholic Church." *Ethnomusicology* 30 (Spring/Summer 1986): 223–252.

———. "Gospel Music in the Los Angeles Black Community: A Historical Overview." *Black Music Research Journal* 9,1 (Spring 1989): 35–79.

Du Bois, W. E. B. *The Souls of Black Folk*. Chicago, 1903.

Dundes, Alan. *Mother Wit from the Laughing Barrel: Readings in the Interpretation of Afro-American Folklore*. Englewood Cliffs, NJ: Prentice Hall, 1973.

Dunn, Ginette. *The Fellowship of Song*. London: Croom Helm, 1980.

Epstein, Dena. *Sinful Tunes and Spirituals*. Urbana: University of Illinois Press, 1977.

Evans, David. "Record Reviews: Black Religious Music." *Journal of American Folklore* 84 (1971): 472–480, and 86 (1973): 82–86.

———. "The Roots of Afro-American Gospel Music." *Jazzforschung* 8 (1976): 119–135.

———. *Big Road Blues*. Berkeley: University of California Press, 1982.

Fauset, Arthur. *Black Gods of the Metropolis*. Philadelphia: University of Pennsylvania Press, 1944.

Feintuch, Burt. "A Non-Commercial Black Gospel Group in Context: We Live the Life We Sing About." *Black Music Research Journal* 1 (1980): 37–50.

Feld, Steven. "Flow like a Waterfall: The Metaphors of Kaluli Musical Theory. "*Yearbook For Traditional Music*" 13 (1981): 22–47.

———. *Sound and Sentiment: Birds, Weeping, Poetics, and Song in Kaluli Expression*. Philadelphia: University of Pennsylvania Press, 1982, 2nd edition 1990.

Feld, Steven. "Sound Structure as Social Structure." *Ethnomusicology* 28, 3 (1984): 383–409.

Ferris, William. *Blues from the Delta*. Garden City, NY: Anchor, 1979.

Ferris, William, and Mary Hart, eds. *Folk Music and Modern Sound*. Jackson: University of Mississippi Press, 1982.

Ferris, William, and Charles Wilson, eds. *The Encyclopedia of Southern Culture*. Chapel Hill: University of North Carolina Press, 1989.

Finnegan, Ruth. *Oral Poetry*. New York: Cambridge University Press, 1977.

Fletcher, Tom. *One Hundred Years of the Negro in Show Business*. New York: Burdge, 1954.

Foster, George. "What Is Folk Culture?" *American Anthropologist* 55 (1953): 159–173.

Fox, Ted. *Showtime at the Apollo*. New York: Holt, Rinehart and Winston, 1983.

Franklin, John Hope. *From Slavery to Freedom: A History of Negro Americans*. 6th ed. New York: Alfred Knopf, 1988.

Frazier, E. Franklin. *The Negro Church in America*. New York: Schocken Books, 1964.

Frith, Simon. *Sound Effects*. New York: Pantheon, 1981.

Funk, Ray. Liner notes to "Norfolk Jubilee Quartet, 1927–1938." Heritage HT 310, LP record, 1985.

———. Liner notes to "San Francisco Bay Gospel." Heritage HT 314, LP record, 1987.

Funk, Ray, and Peter Grendysa. "The Southernaires." *Goldmine* (June 21, 1985): 16, 24.

Gardner, Judith, and Richard McMann. *Culture, Community, and Identity*. Detroit: Wayne State University Press, 1976.

Geertz, Clifford. *The Interpretation of Cultures*. New York: Basic Books, 1973.

George, Nelson. *The Death of Rhythm and Blues*. New York: Pantheon, 1988.

Georges, Robert, and Michael Jones. *People Studying People*. Berkeley: University of California Press, 1980.

Glassie, Henry. *Pattern in the Material Folk Culture of the Eastern United States*. Philadelphia: University of Pennsylvania Press, 1968.

———. *Passing The Time in Ballymenone: Culture and History of an Irish Community*. Philadelphia: University of Pennsylvania Press, 1982.

Glassie, Henry, John Szwed, and Edward Ives. *Folksongs and Their Makers*. Bowling Green, KY: Bowling Green Popular Press, 1971.

Glazer, Nathan, and Daniel Moynihan. *Beyond the Melting Pot*. 2nd ed. Cambridge, MA: MIT Press, 1970.

Godrich, John, and Robert Dixon. *Blues and Gospel Records: 1902–1942*. Essex, England: Storyville, 1982.

Goldstein, Kenneth. *A Guide for Fieldworkers in Folklore*. Hatboro, PA: Folklore Associates, 1964.

———. "On the Application of the Concepts of Active and Inactive Traditions to the Study of Repertory." In Richard Bauman and Americo Paredes, eds., *Toward New Perspectives in Folklore*. Austin: University of Texas Press, 1972, pp. 62–67.

Goreau, Laurraine. *Just Mahalia, Baby*. Gretna: Pelican Company, 1984.

Gurevitch, Michael, Tony Bennett, James Curran, and Janet Woollacott, eds. *Culture, Society, and the Media*. London: Methuen, 1982.

Hall, Edward. *The Hidden Dimension*. New York: Anchor Books, 1969.

Hall, Stuart. "Notes on Deconstructing the Popular." In R. Samuelson, ed., *People's History and Social Theory*, pp. 227–240. London: Routledge, 1981.

Hayes, Cedric. *A Discography of Gospel Records: 1937–1971*. Copenhagen, Denmark: Knudsen, 1973.

Hebdige, Dick. *Subculture*. London: Methuen, 1979.

Heilbut, Anthony. "The Secularization of Black Gospel Music." In William Ferris and Mary Hart, eds., *Folk Music and Modern Sound*. Jackson: University of Mississippi Press, 1982, pp. 101–118.

———. *The Gospel Sound*. 2nd ed. New York: Anchor, 1985.

Herskovits, Melville. *The Myth of the Negro Past*. Boston: Beacon Press, 1941.

Hill, Samuel. *Southern Churches in Crisis*. New York: Holt, Rinehart, and Winston, 1966.

———, ed. *Religion in the Southern United States*. Macon, GA: Mercer University Press, 1983.

Hinson, Glenn. When the Words Roll and the Fire Flows: Spirit, Style, and Experience in African-American Gospel Performance. Ph.D. dissertation, University of Pennsylvania, 1989.

Hufford, David. *The Terror That Comes in the Night*. Philadelphia: University of Pennsylvania Press, 1982.

Hurston, Zora Neal. *The Sanctified Church*. Berkeley, CA: Turtle Island Press, 1981.

Hymes, Dell. "The Ethnography of Speaking." In T. Gladwin and W. Sturtevant, eds. *Anthropology and Human Behaviors*. Washington, DC: Anthropological Society of Washington, 1962, pp. 15–53.

———. *Foundations in Sociolinguistics*. Philadelphia: University of Pennsylvania Press, 1974.

———. *In Vain I Tried to Tell You: Essays in Native American Ethnopoetics*. Philadelphia: University of Pennsylvania Press, 1981.

Jackson, Irene. *Afro-American Religious Music: A Bibliography and a Catalogue of Gospel Music*. Westport, CT: Greenwood Press, 1979.

Jackson, Mahalia. *Movin' On Up*. New York: Hawthorn Books, 1966.

Johnson, James Weldon. *The Book of American Negro Spirituals*. New York: Viking Press, 1925.

Keil, Charles. *Urban Blues*. Chicago: University of Chicago Press, 1966.

———. *Tiv Song*. Chicago: University of Chicago Press, 1979.

———. "People's Music Comparatively: Style and Stereotype, Class and Hegemony." *Dialectic Anthropology* 10 (1985): 119–130.

Kirshenblatt-Gimblett, Barbara. "The Future of Folklore Studies in America: The Urban Frontier." *Folklore Forum* 16 (1983): 175–234.

Landry, Bart. *The New Black Middle Class*. Berkeley: University of California Press, 1987.

Lawless, Elaine. *Handmaidens of the Lord: Pentecostal Women Preachers and Traditional Religion*. Philadelphia: University of Pennsylvania Press, 1988.

Levine, Lawrence. *Black Culture and Black Consciousness*. New York: Oxford University Press, 1977.

Lévi-Strauss, Claude. *Structural Anthropology*. New York: Basic Books, 1973.

Limon, Jose. "Western Marxism and Folklore: A Critical Introduction." *Journal of American Folklore* 96 (1983): 34–52.

Linton, Ralph. "Nativistic Movements." *American Anthropologist* 45 (1943): 230–241.

Lomax, Alan. *Folk Song Style and Culture*. New Brunswick, NJ: Transaction, 1968.

Lornell, Kip. "Afro-American Gospel Quartets: An Annotated Bibliography." *John Edwards Memorial Foundation Quarterly* 17 (Spring 1981): 19–23.

———. *"Happy in the Service of the Lord": Afro-American Gospel Quartets in Memphis*. Urbana: University of Illinois Press, 1988.

Lovell, John. *Black Song: The Forge and the Flame*. New York: Macmillan, 1972.

Manuel, Peter. *Popular Music of the Non-Western World*. New York: Oxford University Press, 1988.

Marks, Morton. "Uncovering Ritual Structure in Afro-American Music." In Irving Zaretsky and Mark Leone, eds., *Religious Movements in Contemporary America*, pp. 60–134. Princeton, NJ: Princeton University Press, 1974.

———. "You Can't Sing Unless You're Saved: Reliving the Call in Gospel Music." In Simon Ottenberg, ed., *African Religious Groups and Beliefs*, pp. 305–331. Cupertino: Folklore Institute, 1982.

Marsh, J. B. T. *The Story of the Jubilee Singers*. Boston: Houghton, Osgood and Company, 1880.

Maultsby, Portia. "Afro-American Religious Music: A Study in Musical Diversity." Springfield, MA: Hymn Society of America, n.d.

Mays, Benjamin, and Joseph Nicholson. *The Negro's Church*. New York: Institute of Social and Religious Research, 1933.

McCallum, Brenda. "Songs of Work and Songs of Worship: Sanctified Black Unionism in the Southern City of Steel." *New York Folklore* 14 (1988).

McGowan, James. *Here Today! Here to Stay! A Personal History of Rhythm and Blues*. St. Petersburg, FL: Sixth House, 1983.

McManus, Edgar. *A History of Negro Slavery in New York State*. Syracuse, NY: Syracuse University Press, 1966.

Merriam, Alan. *The Anthropology of Music*. Evanston, IL; Northwestern University Press, 1964.

Murray, Albert. *The Omni-Americans*. New York: Vintage, 1970.

———. *Stomping the Blues*. New York: Random House, 1976.

Nettl, Bruno, ed. *Eight Urban Music Cultures*. Urbana: University of Illinois Press, 1978.

Oliver, Paul. "Gospel Music." *New Groves Encyclopedia of Music* (1980): 549–559.

———. *Songsters and Saints*. London: Cambridge University Press, 1984.

Osofsky, Gilbert. *Harlem: The Making of a Ghetto*. New York: Harper and Row, 1971.

Ovington, Mary White. *Half a Man*. New York: Hill and Wang, 1911.

Palmer, Robert. *Deep Blues*. New York: Penguin, 1981.

Paredes, Americo, and Ellen Stekert, eds. *The Urban Experience and Folk Traditions*. Austin: University of Texas Press, 1971.

Paris, Arthur. *Black Pentecostalism: Southern Religion in an Urban World*. Amherst: University of Massachusetts Press, 1982.

Patterson, Daniel. " 'Going Up to Meet Him': Songs and Ceremonies of a Black Family's Ascent." In Ruel Tyson Jr., James Peacock, and Daniel Patterson, eds. *Diversities of Gifts: Field Studies in Southern Religion*, pp. 91–102. Urbana: University of Illinois Press, 1988.

Pena, Manuel. *The Texas-Mexican Conjunto*. Austin: University of Texas Press, 1985.

Raboteau, Albert. *Slave Religion*. New York: Oxford University Press, 1978.

Raichelson, Richard. "Black Religious Folk Song: A Study in Generic and Social Change." Ph.D. dissertation, University of Pennsylvania, 1974.

Redfield, Robert. *The Little Community and Peasant Society and Culture.* Chicago: University of Chicago Press, 1960.

Ricks, George. *Some Aspects of the Religious Music of the United States Negro.* New York, Arno Press, 1970.

Roberts, John Storm. *Black Music of Two Worlds.* New York: Morrow 1972.

Rosenberg, Bruce. *Can These Bones Live?: The Art of the American Folk Preacher.* 2nd ed. Urbana: University of Illinois Press, 1988.

Rouget, Gilbert. *Music and Trance.* Chicago: University of Chicago Press, 1985.

Rubman, Kerill. "From 'Jubilee' to 'Gospel' in Black Male Quartet Singing." M.A. thesis, University of North Carolina, 1980.

Seroff, Doug. Liner notes to "Birmingham Quartet Anthology: Jefferson County, Alabama (1926–1953)."Clanka Lanka CL 144.001, LP record, 1980.

———. "The Whole Truth About T. Ruth." *Whiskey, Women, and* 9 (July 1982) and 10 (November 1982).

———. "Polk Miller and the Old South Quartet." *John Edwards Memorial Foundation Quarterly* 18 (1982): 147.

———. "On the Battlefield: Gospel Quartets in Jefferson County, Alabama." In Geoffery Haydon and Dennis Marks, eds., *Repercussions: A Celebration of African-American Music,* pp. 30–53. London: Century, 1985, pp. 30–53.

Simond, Ike. *Old Slack's Reminiscences and Pocket History of the Colored Profession from 1865–1891.* Chicago, by the author, 1891.

Southern, Eileen. *The Music of Black Americans: A History.* 2nd ed. New York: Norton, 1983.

Spencer, Jon Michael. *Protest and Praise: Sacred Music of Black Religion.* Minneapolis: Fortress Press, 1990.

Stern, Stephen. "Ethnic Folklore and the Folklore of Ethnicity." *Western Folklore* 36 (1977): 188–206.

Stewart, Ruth Ann. *Black Churches in Brooklyn.* New York: Long Island Historical Society, 1984.

Stone, Ruth. "Toward a Kpelle Conceptualization of Musical Performance." *Journal of American Folklore* 94 (1981): 188–206.

Sutton, Constance, and Elsa Chaney, eds. *Caribbean Life in New York City.* New York: Center for Migration Studies in New York, 1987.

Szwed, John. "Musical Adaptation Among Afro-Americans." *Journal of American Folklore* 82 (1969): 112–121.

———. "An American Anthropological Dilemma: The Politics of Afro-American Culture." In Dell Hymes, ed., *Reinventing Anthropology.* New York: Random House, 1969.

Szwed, John, and Norman Whitten, eds. *Afro-American Anthropology.* New York: Free Press, 1970.

Tallmadge, William. Booklet accompanying "Jubilee to Gospel: A Selection of Commercially Recorded Black Religious Music, 1921–1953." John Edwards Memorial Foundation JEMF-108, LP record, 1980.

Tedlock, Dennis. "On the Translation of Style in Oral Narrative." In Richard Bauman and Americo Paredes, eds., *Toward New Perspectives in Folklore.* Austin: University of Texas Press, 1972, pp. 114–133.

Thompson, Robert Ferris. "An Aesthetic of the Cool." *African Arts* 7(1973): 1–43, 64–67, 89–92.

――――. *African Art in Motion.* Berkeley: University of California Press, 1974.

――――. *Flash of the Spirit.* New York: Random House, 1983.

Titon, Jeff. *Early Downhome Blues.* Urbana: University of Illinois Press, 1977.

――――. "African-American Religious Music, Record Reviews." *Journal of American Folklore* 96 (1983): 111–113.

――――, general editor. *Worlds of Music.* New York: Schrimer Books, 1984.

――――. *Powerhouse for God.* Austin: University of Texas Press, 1988.

Toelken, Barre. *The Dynamics of Folklore.* Boston: Houghton Mifflin Company, 1979.

Toll, Robert. *Blacking Up: The Minstrel Show in Nineteenth-Century America.* New York: Oxford University Press, 1974.

Turner, Victor. *The Ritual Process.* Ithaca, NY: Cornell University Press, 1969.

――――. *From Ritual to Theatre.* New York: Performing Arts Journal Press, 1982.

Turner, Victor, and Edward Bruner, eds. *The Anthropology of Experience.* Urbana: University of Illinois Press, 1986.

Tyler, Stephen. *Cognitive Anthropology.* New York: Holt, Rinehart, and Winston, 1969.

Tyson, Ruel Jr., James Peacock, and Daniel Patterson, eds. *Diversities of Gifts: Field Studies in Southern Religion.* Urbana: University of Illinois Press, 1988.

Vlach, John. *The Afro-American Tradition in the Decorative Arts.* Cleveland: Cleveland Museum of Art, 1978.

Walker, Wayatt Tee. *Somebody's Calling My Name: Black Sacred Music and Social Change.* Valley Forge, PA: Judson Press, 1979.

Wallace, Anthony. "Revitalization Movements." *American Anthropologist* 58 (1956): 264–281.

――――. *Religion: An Anthropological View.* New York: Random House, 1966.

Waterman, Richard. "Gospel Hymns of a Negro Church in Chicago." *International Folk Music Council* 3 (1951): 87–93.

Williams, Melvin. *Community in a Black Pentecostal Church: An Anthropological Study.* Pittsburgh: University of Pittsburgh Press, 1974.

Williams, Raymond. *Marxism and Literature.* New York: Oxford University Press, 1977.

Williams-Jones, Pearl. "Afro-American Gospel Music." In Vaden Butcher, ed., *Development of Materials for a One Year Course in African Music for the General Undergraduate.* Washington, DC: U.S. Department of Health, Education, and Welfare, 1970, pp. 199–219.

――――. "Afro-American Gospel Music: A Crystallization of the Black Aesthetic." *Ethnomusicology* 19 (1975): 373–385.

Wilmore, Gayraud. *Black Religion and Black Radicalism.* Maryknoll, NY: Orbis Books, 1984.

Index

This book was set in Baskerville and Eras typefaces. Baskerville was designed by John Baskerville at his private press in Birmingham, England, in the eighteenth century. The first typeface to depart from oldstyle typeface design, Baskerville has more variation between thick and thin strokes. In an effort to insure that the thick and thin strokes of his typeface reproduced well on paper, John Baskerville developed the first wove paper, the surface of which was much smoother than the laid paper of the time. The development of wove paper was partly responsible for the introduction of typefaces classified as modern, which have even more contrast between thick and thin strokes.

Eras was designed in 1969 by Studio Hollenstein in Paris for the Wagner Typefoundry. A contemporary script-like version of a sans-serif typeface, the letters of Eras have a monotone stroke and are slightly inclined.

Printed on acid-free paper.